Praise for *Women of Means*

"If you've ever wished you had all the money in the world, read Women of Means by Marlene Wagman-Geller. Written in her usual witty prose, these enthralling but petrifying mini-biographies show that when a woman is too wealthy, it can be a curse rather than a blessing."

—Jill G. Hall, author of *The Black Velvet Coat*

"Does money facilitate happiness, fulfillment, the good life? How much time do we all spend wishing we had more of it? These questions and more bubble up from Marlene Wagman-Geller's crisp, exacting prose in her powerful compilation of stories about the richest women in history. Wagman-Geller's stories made me gasp and lodged my chin firmly on my chest as she chronicled the lives of women without a financial care in the world, whose appetites led so often to disaster. And, no, Patrizia, I would rather gleefully ride the bicycle!"

—R. D. Kardon, author of *Flygirl*

"The best women's history books are deeply researched and, therefore, filled with personal details that provide an intimate portrait. Marlene Wagman-Geller's Women of Means *does not disappoint. It is wild and witty, gossipy, and glamourous. A sheer delight. I could not get enough of reading about heiress Barbara Hutton's outrageous lifestyle, Jackie O as a stepmom, Patty Hearst's many adventures, Peggy Guggehein's collection of art (and men) and Almira Carnarvon, the real-life counterpart to Lady Cora of Downton Abbey. Simply splendid."*

—Becca Anderson, author of *Badass Women Give the Best Advice*

Women of Means

Also by Marlene Wagman-Geller

Great Second Acts: In Praise of Older Women

Women Who Launch: Women Who Shattered Glass Ceilings

Still I Rise: The Persistence of Phenomenal Women

Behind Every Great Man: The Forgotten Women Behind the World's Famous and Infamous

And the Rest Is History: The Famous (and Infamous) First Meetings of the World's Most Passionate Couples

Eureka! The Surprising Stories Behind the Ideas That Shaped the World

Once Again to Zelda: The Stories Behind Literature's Most Intriguing Dedications

Women of Means

Fascinating Biographies of Royals, Heiresses, Eccentrics, and Other Poor Little Rich Girls

Marlene Wagman-Geller

CORAL GABLES

For permission requests, please contact the publisher at:
Mango Publishing Group
2850 S Douglas Road, 2nd Floor
Coral Gables, FL 33134 USA
info@mango.bz

For special orders, quantity sales, course adoptions and corporate sales, please
email the publisher at sales@mango.bz. For trade and wholesale sales, please
contact Ingram Publisher Services at customer.service@ingramcontent.com or
+1.800.509.4887.

Women of Means: Fascinating Biographies of Royals, Heiresses, Eccentrics,
and Other Poor Little Rich Girls

Library of Congress Cataloging-in-Publication number: 2019935672
ISBN: (p) 978-1-64250-017-2 (e) 978-1-64250-018-9
BISAC category code: BIO013000 BIOGRAPHY & AUTOBIOGRAPHY
/ Rich & Famous

Printed in the United States of America

*To my women of spiritual means—in memory of my mother,
Gilda Wagman, and my daughter, Jordanna Shyloh Geller.*

"I hate almost all rich people, but I think I'd be darling at it."

—Dorothy Parker (1893–1967)

Table of Contents

∼Foreword∼

Okay, let's get this part out of the way first: If I had been born into an enormous fortune, I would have been generous, as well as cautious about marriage and other personal entanglements. My purchases would not have been ostentatious, and I would not have been arrogant. And, of course, that is exactly how *you* would act. In short, we would not behave as did the twenty-eight subjects of Wagman's collection. What connects them are the excesses and eccentricities that result when enormous wealth meets immaturity.

In *A Delicate Balance*, Edward Albee's Pulitzer Prize winning play of 1967, Agnes laments that as men age, they are eventually obsessed with money and death—"making ends meet until they meet the end."[1] The women in these pages could not escape death—many died young, and most died in abject conditions—but for most of their lives, they did not have to be concerned with making ends meet. But if people of wealth are to be content, they have to have ends to be served by their means, and they must be as deliberate as those who are slowed and matured by financial concerns. The actions of the women you are going to meet in *Women of Means* were flagrant, and eventually desperate, but never deliberate.

Will Rogers said about people playing the ukulele, "Not even a trained musician can tell if [they're] playing on it or just monkeying with it."[2] Most of the Women of Means monkeyed with life, filling it, as Wagman says, with "champagne and bile." It's a bitter mix, and these women were, for the most part, a

---

1   Albee, Edward. *A Delicate Balance: A Play.* New York: Athenaeum, 1966.

2   Gragert, Steven K. and M. Jane Johansson. *The Papers of Will Rogers, Volume IV: From the Broadway Stage to the National Stage. Norman:* University of Oklahoma Press, 2005.

bitter lot. After all, they were victims. Having much often makes one want more, so they were victims of their own greed. Most of them grew up sheltered from the vagaries of life and the teaching power of poverty, so they were victimized by the greed of others. They were victims of their bad decisions, the majority of which seemed to center around their spectacularly destructive choices of sexual partners and husbands, as well as some catastrophic parenting. Money makes plain people attractive, and attractive people irresistible, and there were plenty of people willing to cheat, threaten, or seduce them into opening their hearts, their bank accounts, and the doors to their boudoirs.

As Wagman's stories gives us a look inside their hearts and wealth (and their boudoirs), we experience *schadenfreude*—the pleasure of vicariously experiencing the misfortune of others— but that is not the only gift Wagman and her women bestow. All of us have the same size hearts as they did, even those living paycheck to paycheck. We are all—even men (or perhaps *especially* men)—quite capable of falling victim to hubris. The mysterious lover Cressida in Shakespeare's tragedy lays the blame on women's lust:

> Ah, poor our sex! This fault in us I find,
>
> The error of our eye doth direct our mind:
>
> What error leads must err. O, then conclude
>
> Minds swayed by eyes are full of turpitude.[3]

---

3 Shakespeare, William. *Troilus and Cressida*, V:2, lines 131–134.

In response, the wise slave Thersites translates her speech as, "My mind is now turn'd whore."[4]

And perhaps it is there—at the intersection of privilege and pain—that we should meet the *Women of Means*.

BEN CASSEL

Yucca Valley, California

March 2019

---

4   Ibid, line 136.

Prologue

A Rocky Ride

"Let me tell you about the rich. They are different from you and me."

—F. Scott Fitzgerald

The oxymoron "poor little rich girl" strikes a discordant note; how could the possessors of wealth be designated by an adjective denoting pity? An abundance of green allows one to purchase pleasure dome domiciles, cars with exotic logos, jewels that seduce. Equally magical, money provides freedom to spend one's days pursuing a passion rather than a paycheck. The possessors of deep pockets are not reduced to taking their change to Coinstar while salivating for payday. The Dollar Store is not the only place they can purchase whatever catches their eye; a daily ritual is not borrowing from Peter to give to Paul.

The contemporary crop of heiresses—those whose lives are a magical mystery tour—provide fodder for the paparazzi; the public's hunger is insatiable for those removed from the plane of "the rest of us." One leader of the pack is Paris Hilton, whose great-grandfather's empire of eponymous hotels—and marriage to Zsa Zsa Gabor—garnered the family fortune and fame. Her sizzling sex tape, *A Night in Paris*, thrust her into the limelight, followed by the hit series *The Simple Life*—a reality version of *Green Acres*. The series transplanted the child of privilege from Beverly Hills to Arkansas. Since then, she has been the subject of public sightings tooling around Los Angeles in her custom Barbie-pink Bentley with a pink-clad pooch, performed court-mandated community service shod in Louboutin heels, narcissistically dated a Greek shipping magnate similarly named Paris, and posed on a magazine cover wearing nothing but her Calvin Klein briefs.

Hilton's rivals in the media glare are the British Ecclestone sisters, Tamara and Petra. Apparently, when the weaving sisters sit at their loom, they do not follow the pattern "all men are created equal." The girls are the recipient of a genetic lottery as they favor their Amazonian mother, Croatian model Slavica, and are the heiresses of their billionaire father, Formula One's Bernie. The leggy girls can leave any Tinsel Town star in the economic dust. On the opposite end of the spectrum from Eliza Doolittle who sang, "All I want is a room somewhere / Far away from the cold night air..." Petra is the owner of the former Spelling Los Angeles mansion, the Manor, which bore a price tag of eighty-five million dollars. As it would not do to adorn its walls with velvet art, she purchased one of Britain's cultural treasures, a seventeenth-century, twenty-million-dollar Van Dyke. Tamara's well-heeled London neighbors are Prince William and Duchess Catherine of Cambridge. And while the Bond novel is entitled *From Russia with Love,* hailing from the former Communist heartland is Ekaterina Rybolovleva, whose daddy gifted her a slice of real estate that would make even a Gossip Girl gasp: an eighty-eight-million-dollar Manhattan penthouse as her crash pad while attending an American university. After all, dorm life is not for everyone. Another heiress who eschewed living in residence halls is Liesel Pritzker of the Hyatt Hotel dynasty, best known for her feature role in the 1995 film *The Little Princess.* Her memorable quotation as Sara Crewe went, "I am a princess. All girls are. Even if they live in tiny old attics. Even if they dress in rags, even if they aren't pretty, or smart, or young. They're still princesses, all of us." The $560 million award she garnered in settlement from suing her father allowed her to purchase a $2.25 million condo near her Columbia University campus. She explained to *The New York Times,* "I figured that it would make more sense to buy." Obviously, princesses don't rent. How far afield from these Xanadus are the homes that come replete with license plates. Billionaires dwell in a galaxy far, far away from those who conscientiously clip coupons, who are Boxing Day veterans, who are artful bill-collector dodgers. The rich cannot fathom standing with nose pressed against glass vistas, eying Tantalus' grapes. To once more borrow the words of the Cockney flower-girl regarding the set-for-life folk, "Wouldn't it be loverly?"

If it is true that we are shaped by our favorite childhood protagonists, perhaps one can, albeit tongue in cheek, point the finger of blame for heiresses' narcissism on *Eloise*, circa 1949, the original fictional poor little rich girl. The Plaza Hotel born and bred child had a fabulously wealthy mother, one not keen on maternal proximity, who happened to be friends with Coco Chanel. Eloise was under the care of an infinitely patient British nanny to whom her AWOL parent furnished useful lines of credit. "Charge it, please!" may have been Eloise's first words. She spends her days wreaking havoc in the august Plaza; her mantra, "Getting bored is not allowed." When her mother's lawyer comes to call, she feeds him rubber turtles for which he rewards her with an indulgent smile. No matter how poorly she acts, in her *tsoris*-free childhood, there is always room service. Eloise's enduring appeal is she is based on the fantasies of children: endless money, freedom from parents, adults as servants, not masters. The classic book must have served as the blueprint of bottomless entitlement for daughters of privilege and created unrealistic notions for those hailing from small-town, middle-class stations. A far more authentic rendition is the classic children's book character Madeline, who lives in a Catholic boarding school in Paris with eleven roommates and only becomes distinguishable when she succumbs to an attack of acute appendicitis.

The Wizard of Omaha and modern alchemist Warren Buffet coined the phrase, "the lucky sperm club" to denote the well-heeled who either by birth or by marriage brandish open-sesame-gold credit cards. One would assume that belonging to a club with the word "lucky" in its name would be something about which to brag; however, this situation does not always prove true. Buffet understands the danger of wealth—fortunes made from the sweat of another's brow—and vowed his children would not be the sole recipients of his fortune. He stated the perfect amount to leave one's heirs is "enough money so that they would feel they could do anything, but not so much that they could do nothing." Excess can be a motivation buster and leave one with a sense of psychological impotence. Buffet, the financial Solomon, is the possessor of insight to which other fabulously wealthy fathers should have been privy. Inherited fortunes are not always loverly.

One well-intentioned papa was Frank W. Woolworth, who made his billions on an empire founded on nickel-and-dime store chains. He worked almost every day of his sixty-six years; his granddaughter, Barbara, never troubled herself with gainful employment. She lived by the mindset of "if you got it, flaunt it," and flaunt it she did: on mansions and men. As it transpired, the richest woman in the world was one of the unhappiest, and as a result, she self-medicated with the Band-Aids of alcohol and drugs. Part of the problem for heiresses is the biblical injunction, "To whom much has been given, from him much is expected," a heavy mantle for anyone to shoulder, especially those born in a silken swath of entitlement.

The aphorism "necessity is the mother of invention" naturally gives rise to the corollary that too much wealth is a breeding ground for non-productivity. Unemployment—whether it entails

standing in a welfare line or rattling around in a palazzo—is
the anti-salve for the soul. The devil's work for these idle hands
is often alcohol and drugs—crutches for banishing ennui. As
Fitzgerald, the balladeer of Jazz Age indulgence, and no flincher
from the glass himself, wrote, "In the morning after you were
never violently sorry—you made no resolutions, but if you had
overdone it and your heart was slightly out of order, you went
on the wagon for a few days without saying anything about it,
and waited until an accumulation of boredom projected you
into another party." Inheritors, especially members of third
generation fortunes, become the ideal Petri dish for nourishing
addiction. Mountains of money is the bait that encourages
nibbles from the unsavory—the sycophants happy to muscle in
on those with multi-digit bank accounts. Obsequious gigolos
and foraging gold-diggers are not averse to riding shotgun in
a Ferrari.

Just as Helen of Troy's beauty launched a thousand ships, those
to the manor born—or wed—launch an avalanche of paparazzi
lenses. What drives the powerful attraction between the ultrarich and media scrutiny is the public hunger to peer through
any chinks in the castle—to glimpse lives founded on the Bank
of Mom and Dad or moneybag spouse. To satiate people's desire
to look into the lives of the rich, Robin Leach hosted *Lifestyles
of the Rich and Famous* where he led drooling viewers on
tours of gaudy and grand estates. Pre-*Cribs*, the show captured
the public's obsession with the world of the one percent,
often nomadic jet-setters. Leach ended each episode with his
trademark, "Champagne wishes and caviar dreams." Post-teasing
sign-off audiences were left with mouths agape—the night filled
with gasps of can-such-things-be. Viewers, many of whose lives
could be a reality show entitled *Lifestyles of the Poor and the
Desperate*, were left not with a champagne aftertaste but one

more akin to bile as they envisioned their morrows' commute in crowded subways, noonday repasts served on trays, their only retirement death. Trying to keep one's head above the water, to borrow from the last line of *The Great Gatsby*, "So we beat on, boats against the current..."

A reality series for those who did not make a New Year's resolution to watch television designed to exercise one's intellectual IQ is The Real Housewives series, which showcases designer-dressed domestic divas in gated communities who have model-worthy bodies and whose faces attest to the prowess of plastic surgeons. They have traveled far from *Roseanne*, a far more familiar figure to those who borrow from Peter to give to Paul. *Rich Kids of Beverly Hills* is another show that affords a peephole through which to ogle the trust fund tribe. The program's camera followed five of these twenty-somethings as they offered insightful nuggets such as the truly rich do not only sip Dom Perignon, but wash their hair in the bubbly. Who knew? Watching them frolic through their responsibility-free lives makes one nod in agreement with the comedienne Sophie Tucker who shared the autobiographical tidbit, "I've been rich, and I've been poor. Rich is better."

However, a nod to the collateral damage of surplus funds was found in the case of Ethan Couch whose crime coined the term "affluenza." The Fort Worth Texas teen's favorite boast was there was nothing his rich parents couldn't get him out of. After stealing two cases of beer from Walmart and driving with a blood alcohol level three times the legal limit, he plowed down four bystanders and left one of his passengers with a brain injury. The judge determined Ethan was a victim—of "affluenza," an upbringing of extreme indulgence that left him minus a sense of moral boundaries. In lieu of jail, he left for a $450,000-a-year

California rehab. He proved correct in his belief his parents could get him out of everything; he also showed there was no "equal protection under the law." If a teen from the working-class city of Watts in Los Angeles had committed the same crime, there would have been no country club punishment waiting in the wings. In the words of Dennis the Menace's Mr. Wilson, "Good grief." When reading about Ethan, I was reminded of Fitzgerald's golden couple in *The Great Gatsby*, "They were careless people, Tom and Daisy—they smashed up things and creatures and then retreated back to their money or their vast carelessness, or whatever it was that kept them together and let other people clean up the mess they had made..."

While the Couch case ignited outrage against a judicial system whose scale of justice was weighted toward the rich, what truly garners the spotlight is when millionaires spiral south. *Schadenfreude*—a word derived from the German—expresses the concept of joy in the misfortunes of others. Although this concept points to the negative in human nature, it is nevertheless a universal archetype. A British expression with a similar meaning is "Roman holiday," a metaphor from a poem by Lord Byron where a gladiator opines he is about to be "butchered to make a Roman holiday:" the spectators would derive pleasure from his agony. The ancient game had ties to the Greek tragedy of Christina Onassis, one endlessly played out in the international press; it detailed her birth as the only daughter of a shipping tycoon and chronicled her addictions to men, food, and barbiturates. She was privy to all the pain money could buy. The public appeal was that her story was a nonfictional morality play; it provided a comforting clamor when the mighty fall from the heights. In the Greek mythological tale of Midas, the king paid dearly for his golden touch. Wealth and breeding offer little defense against human frailty. The histories of the Gettys, the

Rothschilds, the Kennedys—dynasties dogged by misfortune— suggest the democracy of pain. The fact their lives played out in an atmosphere of media glee over the suffering of their houses has made their crosses far heavier to bear.

The idea of the inherent dangers of bowing to Mammon is deeply ingrained in Western culture; from ancient Syria hails the tale of *The Sword of Damocles*. King Dionysius of Syracuse, aware of Damocles' envy, decided as they shared a strong physical resemblance, offered to exchange places with him for a night. Damocles was enjoying his meal served on gold plates, the strains from the musicians, the gyrations of the dancers until he spied a sword suspended over his head. Afterwards, he no longer felt pleasure in wearing the crown. The tale of Dionysius conveyed the sense of the constant fear in which the wealthy and powerful exist. From ancient Rome comes the story of *Cornelia's Jewels*. A rich woman brought along a huge chest of gems when she went to visit Cornelia, a poor widow. After she had presented her treasures, she turned to Cornelia and asked how it felt to have none of her own. Cornelia put her arms around her two sons and replied, "Here are Cornelia's jewels." The Bible, the blueprint for Western society, was similarly instrumental in ingraining us against the pursuit of Mammon. It admonished, "the love of money is the root of all evil;" that it is "Easier for a camel to pass through the eye of a needle than a rich man to enter the kingdom of heaven," and that "the meek shall inherit the Earth."

Nevertheless, the quest for money is the grease that oils society, and those who have attained it sit in a sanctified sphere. Yet the eye of disapproval is reserved for the heirs of largesse when their birthright fails to deliver the pearl of contentment. The fact that wealth is not the *open sesame* to Nirvana is a hard nugget to swallow for those whose credit card bills have as many digits as their phone numbers, for those who feel they have known want since their prenatal days. Although there are numerous stories pointing to the pain that results when falling from a great height, we empathize with the *Fiddler on the Roof's* Tevye, who ruefully sang, "Would it spoil some vast eternal plan / If I were a wealthy man?"

The idea for *Women of Means* came to me as I was driving to meet my friend for lunch at my favorite seaside restaurant, Georges on the Cove, (which, by the way, serves Nazi-worthy soup of Seinfeldian fame) in the desirable zip code of La Jolla, Spanish for the jewel. As I took the winding road into this enclave, I marveled at its magnificent cliffside homes overlooking the Pacific; its storefronts showcased everything label-lovers could covet. How diametrically different from where I teach at a high school in National City in proximity to the Tijuana border, where many walls display gang writing and graffiti. The neighborhood stores advertise bail bonds and cash advances; the homeless hold up woebegone placards. (The most memorable signs: Will Work for Weed; To Ugly to Prostitute.) As with the people on the pavement in Edwin Arlington Robinson's poem "Richard Cory," I wondered what it would be like to be the possessor of sky-high wealth: how it would feel to sleep under who-knows-what-thread-count sheets rather than threadbare, to drive a car assembled in the current decade, or to jet to exotic locales rather than frequenting RV campgrounds. It entailed a flight of fancy to envision a scenario where the high of consumerism was not followed by a flood of guilt. Thus, was the genesis of my investigation into the lives of those like Richard Cory, who "glittered when he walked." From my voyeurism, I learned the truth of Fitzgerald's observation, "The rich are different from you and me." What I also discovered was the truth of an old poem that posed the issue: If two vases were on a shelf—one made of priceless porcelain and one made of common clay—and they fell, which would break? A multi-splendored bank account does not guarantee a suit of armor: John Jacob Astor, Isador and Ida Strauss, Benjamin Guggenheim, all passengers on the *Titanic*, perished in the icy waters of the Atlantic; the same fate as those in steerage.

Some wealthy women who are not included in *Women of Means* are those who proved equal to the golden fairy dust the fates sprinkled on them. Although they could have fallen into the stereotype of the bonbon-popping princess syndrome that makes a cult of idleness, they sidestepped that path. Ivanka Trump had an upbringing different than the girl next door. Her childhood home was a gilded penthouse on Manhattan's Fifth Avenue; her local store was Tiffany. Her father is the blunt gazillionaire, now the Chief Executive; her mother the former Czech ski champion Ivana. When the Donald strayed for a younger trophy wife, his first wife famously made the pronouncement, "Don't get mad—get everything." The logical assumption is their only daughter would sit on her last name—minus the "T." Au contraire: she graduated summa cum laude with a degree in economics from the University of Pennsylvania and became an apprentice to the Trump empire.

Another heiress who did not recline in the hammock of her ancestry is Julia Louis-Dreyfus. As Elaine Benes in *Seinfeld*, she had to put up with a neurotic roommate to afford rent and wrote drivel for the J. Peterman catalog. Her role was far from any parallel to her off-screen life: she is the daughter of French billionaire Gerard Louis-Dreyfus, "not that there is anything wrong with that." Although she never had to work a day to dwell in luxury's lap, she went on to television immortality as our generation's funny girl and earned tens of millions of dollars.

While these two very well-heeled ladies are leaving footprints in business and comedy, the daughter of Beatle billionaire Sir Paul has become a fashion force. As the progeny of rock royalty, she could spend her days resting on designer laurels; instead, she creates her own. Her eponymous label has graced the wardrobes of A-listers, garnering international acclaim on high fashion catwalks. Heiresses of their ilk are not included in *Women of Means* because they do not fit the oxymoron of "poor little rich girls;" they have successfully navigated the gauntlet of inherited wealth. Their stories do not provide the book's requisite schadenfreude; they merely provoke an envious grrrrrrrrr... Happy lives make uninteresting stories. As Ella Wheeler Wilcox wrote, "It's the sadness of the singer that makes the sweetness of the strain..."

In contrast to these having-it-all heiresses are the girls whose emotional angst surpasses their billion-dollar inheritances. Paris Jackson's childhood, high up on the eccentric scale—face masks in public, brother Blanket dangling from a German hotel balcony, growing up in *Neverland*—nevertheless proved happy. Unfortunately, after the death of her father, she spiraled out of control, culminating in a suicide attempt. One can only hope her parallels to Michael—growing up mired in notoriety, huge sums of money, feuding family members—do not end in a similar unhappy-ever-after.

The heir to the Doris Duke tobacco fortune, Georgia Inman, had an upbringing as eccentric as Paris's; however, hers was hellacious, a horror story of Dickensian abuse. As children, she and her twin brother inhaled freebase fumes and sadistic nannies delighted in traumatizing their charges. On the surface, they were the recipients of unimagined privilege; in lieu of anything as mundane as a puppy, they had a pet lion and brought diamonds for show-and-tell. However, the other untold show-and-tell was getting locked in a filthy, rat-infested basement and forced to eat vomit and feces. Perhaps, they can still escape the grasp of the long fingers of the past. Georgia's twin told Dr. Phil, "I don't want to be a victim. I want to be a victor."

The murder of Gianni Versace, the favored designer of Princess Diana and the man responsible for creating the safety-pin dress that made Elizabeth Hurley's career, left niece Allegra Versace a sizable slice of his fantastic fortune. She developed anorexia and said of her eating disorder, "I call this my period of absence. Above all, I wanted one thing—to be no one, to not be recognized, not be hunted down." Time will tell if the three young heiresses can rise above their golden chains.

At the Plaza, the hotel offers Eloise-themed birthday extravaganzas for parents who eschew more mundane venues, and a painting of Eloise depicts the fictional heroine with her trademark smirk. A little girl observing the portrait was overheard asking, "Mommy, do we like Eloise?" The answer to her question can be contemplated at the close of *Women of Means*.

Investigating the lives of those to the manor born, or wed to the lord of the manor, allowed me to be a voyeur into the lives of the upper crust as I have never been a recipient of a trust fund, from a maiden aunt or otherwise. The lives of the wealthy made me realize the veracity of the old adage, "All that glitters is not gold." I hope you enjoy reading about these larger-than-life heiresses whose biographies leave the lingering question of whether the American Dream actually segues into the American nightmare.

Afterwards, you may either be glad to have escaped the mantle of entitlement or still shell out for lottery tickets.

(I hate when I place my lottery tickets in the machine, and it flashes back the insult/injury message: Sorry Not a Winner.)
In either contingency, in the words of Bette Davis, "Fasten your seatbelts, it's going to be a bumpy night"—one chauffeured by the members of the "lucky sperm club."

Chapter 1

Did I Make the Most of Loving You? (1876)

No episode of *Downton Abbey* rivals the caustic cauldron of intrigue that riddled the Abbey's nonfictional counterpart, Highclere Castle, home of the elite of Edwardian England. Even Lady Cora Crawley, the tempest-tossed titled main character, did not have a life as dramatic as Highclere Castle's ancestral heroine whose life was a bouillabaisse of adultery, abortion, and illegitimacy with the added twist of a mummy's curse.

In the Victorian era, marrying socially ambitious heiresses was almost de rigueur for the titled and entitled rich but pound-poor English lords whose taste for chorus girls, yachts, and horses had depleted the ancestral coffers. Resourceful blue bloods offered an exchange of their pedigrees for the wealth of husband-hunting heiresses. A marriage of convenience followed: cash for cachet.

George Edward Stanhope Molyneux Herbert, the fifth Earl of Carnarvon, enjoyed a hedonistic lifestyle of travel and collecting rare artifacts. The fly in this privileged ointment was though the aristocrat was long on lineage, he was short on money, a situation that led to a quest for a golden goose. A rich wife could rescue him and prevent his three-hundred-room monster-mansion, Highclere, from changing hands—something it had not done since 1679. The property's history dates back 1,300 years; the Bishops of Winchester were its first owners (hence the television name Abbey). Sir Charles Barry, the architect of the Palace of Westminster put in charge of a nineteenth-century remodel, provided a prescient warning, "It is pregnant with the most alarming danger to your Lordship's pocketbook." Lord Carnarvon was on the verge of bidding it a non-cheery cheerio when, like the arrival of the cavalry in a Western, all was saved.

Almina Victoria Marie Alexandra was, at least officially, the daughter of the British army officer Captain Frederick Charles Wombell and his French wife, Marie Boyer. The birth certificate would not have borne too much scrutiny as paternity actually belonged to Marie's lover, Baron Alfred de Rothschild, scion to the fabulously wealthy banking family. Rothschild was the director of the Bank of England, the first Jew to attain that position, and in a bid to avoid scandal he never admitted paternity, especially as the result of adultery. In compensation, the baron acted as Almina's godfather, and when he let it be known he was willing to lavish a king's ransom on her dowry, the suitors circled. The banker's hope was a member of the nobility would give his daughter the social standing she had been denied when he had not bestowed on her the Rothschild name.

Lord Carnarvon, an aristocrat in quest of wealth drawn by the lure of the multimillion-pound catnip, was willing to overlook Almina's illegitimacy and Jewish father. The wedding took place in 1895 at St. Margaret's Church, Westminster Abbey. Both bride and groom were thrilled; Lord Carnarvon could keep Highclere, and Almina became the chatelaine of a giant dollhouse. As the new Lady Carnarvon said of her palatial estate, "I suppose if you know how many rooms you've got, you haven't got a very big house." Almina's playhouse came replete with footmen and uniformed maids, and Van Dyke and Gainsborough portraits graced its walls. There was also a corner desk upon which Napoleon had planned his battle strategies. Evelyn Waugh, the lady's nephew through marriage, used the expression, "very Highclere" to mean "the best of everything." With her newfound position and the Rothschild bottomless pocket, Almina spent on a scale that would even cause contemporary hedge-fund darlings to gasp. Rothschild networked for his darling daughter and orchestrated a visit from the Prince of Wales. Almina threw herself into preparations that included spending 360,000 pounds for the lavish weekend.

Unfortunately, the marriage came with an Achilles' heel; namely, a lack of sexual chemistry between Almina, nicknamed the pocket-sized Venus, due to her diminutive stature, exquisite beauty, and her decade-older spouse. The lack of lust was partially because, besides Alfred's passion for antiquities, he was fixated on photographs of scantily clad girls, and at the height of his voyeurism, he commissioned three thousand nudes. Into this marital mix came Prince Victor Duleep Singh, a godson of Queen Victoria, the son of the last Maharajah of Lahore, who had been a close friend of Carnarvon since their student days at Eton. On a youthful vacation to Egypt, Victor had fixed up the peer with a prostitute in order to lose his virginity; however, Carnarvon had also picked up a sexually transmitted disease that almost proved fatal. Although he recovered, the lord was traumatized, hence his preference for visual gratification. While Carnarvon was not erotically interested in Lady Almina, Victor was more than happy to pick up the slack. He practically lived at Highclere providing his host with a friend and his hostess with a lover. What put a kink in the domestic bliss was Almina became pregnant. While most expectant women endlessly imagine the sex of their baby, Almina was obsessed with pigmentation: namely, would the baby bear the telltale Indian skin. In the latter contingency, Lady Almina rented a house where she could retreat with her infant and await the subsequent scandal and inevitable divorce. In 1898, her son, Henry George, was born with a light complexion; the baby's skin tone did not rule out Victor as the father since he was the offspring of a white mother. Whatever the genetic truth, Lord Carnarvon accepted Henry George as his son and heir. The couple was united in their efforts to keep the skeleton firmly locked in the depths of Highclere's capacious closets. The birth also meant the parting of the ways of Almina and the man she loved. The marriage survived, and two years later they had a daughter of unambiguous paternity, Lady Evelyn.

World War I proved Almina's finest hour when she channeled her out of control spending for a philanthropic cause. She transformed Highclere into a hospital and convalescence home and played the role of Florence Nightingale; the difference was that her lamp was the Rothschild riches. Lord Carnarvon gave his grudging approval and announced his new address as, "Carnarvon, Amputate, Highclere." Almina was enthusiastic about her project and assembled a team of beautiful nurses, clad in strawberry pink uniforms and makeup, who ministered to those returning from the trenches. Highclere patients—one the grandson of Alfred, Lord Tennyson—had their own red-lipped angel. Does *oblige* ever get more *noblesse*?

In 1918, Sir Alfred Rothschild died, leaving his house in Mayfair, fabulous paintings, and furnishings to his only child. At this time, Lord Carnarvon, obsessed with all things Egyptian, became entranced with the archaeologist Howard Carter's belief that in the Valley of Kings the boy-king Tutankhamun still slumbered undisturbed after three thousand years. With Almina's inheritance, the Carnarvons undertook the financial end of the expedition. When Carter discovered the tomb, a cable was immediately sent to Almina, who arrived in Luxor looking suitably ostentatious, her glamorous daughter in tow. When Carter first peered through the grate, he exclaimed, "I see wonderful things;" he was addressing Lord Carnarvon and Lady Evelyn. Soon the name of the pharaoh was everywhere—United States President Hoover named his dog King Tut. Because of Almina's largesse, the young pharaoh and his opulent lifestyle became as famous as the ash-imprisoned people of Pompeii. However, what added a bizarre postscript was Lord Carnarvon's misfortune in Egypt, where he died after the opening of the tomb. The event coincided with the lights of Cairo going out and with the passing of his beloved dog Susie in Highclere.

Arthur Conan Doyle, the creator of Sherlock Holmes, said it was the "curse" of the mummy; his comment inspired a host of Hollywood horror films. Lady Almina was to share in the curse.

With the demise of the Earl, possession of Highclere passed to Henry George, and Almina had to search for another home. Relations between Henry and his mother were tenuous due to the lingering uncertainty surrounding his paternity, his mother's affair with his friend Tommy Frost, and the fact she was loath to share her wealth. Her tightfisted attitude may have stemmed from her disappointment in the heir: while Lord Carnarvon had achieved international acclaim in the Valley of the Kings, Porchy's (his nickname from his title Lord Porchester) only distinction was he had cuckolded half the husbands of Berkshire.

After Almina left the estate where she had lived for almost three decades, she lavishly spent her fortune both on the worthwhile (she continued to fund further Carter expeditions) and the worthless, namely, a second husband. In the year she became a widow, Almina walked down the aisle with Ian Dennistoun, a bounder of all bounders. She had set him up in a cottage while her husband was off on his treasure hunt. He had been a Guards Officer whose promotion to Lieutenant-Colonel had been due to his first wife Dorothy's seduction of Sir John Cowans, a move undertaken not for passion but to further her husband's career. Dennistoun also proved useful for money laundering; Almina, after a life of free spending, was undergoing a financial pinch and sold the jewels and art she had received from poppa, a move designed to appease the taxman. To further complicate matters, Dennistoun's ex-wife, Dorothy, who had been denied alimony, came after him for support after she discovered her successor was Lady Carnarvon, infuriated she had volunteered her body for her husband's advancement only to be dismissed when he had bagged an heiress. Almina looked at her action as a shakedown and rather than pay, she allowed their fight to go public. The subsequent High Court case displayed very dirty linen. Almina found herself in the witness box; there, her adultery came to light, and the case blackened the name of everyone involved. Such was the uproar that King George V aired his disgust, but the country was captivated with the blue blood battle. The army dismissed Dennistoun, and Almina ended up paying the court costs of four hundred thousand pounds, far more than the sum Dorothy had requested. When hubby passed away some years later, Almina began an affair with his undertaker.

As the daughter of a Rothschild, the word *budget* had never been in Almina's vocabulary, which is why she managed to let a $100,000,000 fortune dissipate. To avoid insolvency, in a nod to the tried-and-true, she once more opened a nursing home. She chose a location in central London that she christened Alfred House after her father; patients likened the place to the Ritz Hotel. A hall porter in medals and a uniform greeted guests while Almina wafted around in her uniform. The trouble was she often forgot to provide a bill, both because she had never been concerned with money and she thought it in bad taste to ask for payment. However, as her coffers began to empty at an alarming rate, a new service was added to the repertoire of Alfred House. Despite the fact that pregnancy termination was illegal, a steady stream of well-to-do female patients began checking into the nursing home. Had Almina been caught, she would have faced imprisonment. However, high society willingly averted its gaze. Waugh described it as "Almina's abortionist parlour." What further lowered Almina's social standing was at age seventy, she took a thirty-years-younger lover, James Stocking, a heating engineer. The woman who had once been the crown jewel of society had descended to a hopelessly déclassé way of life. In addition, she was destitute. To make matters worse, her son outed her to the Inland Revenue over her past questionable dealings. Angry at the fact she had squandered the birthright of his inheritance that he desperately needed for the money-guzzling Highclere, he called her a "scheming swindler." He despised her so much he shut off her favorite room at Highclere.

At the age of seventy-five, largely due to the vengeful accusations of her son, the Rothschild-by-blood was bankrupt. She moved to a terrace house in Bristol, without the luxury of hot water, and survived on sporadic Highclere handouts. In 1969, she passed away in the shabby residence at age ninety-three, after choking on a piece of chicken. Her death ended a life that had proved as dramatic as that of *Downton Abbey*'s Lady Cora Crawley. To those of a superstitious bent, Almina's later-life misfortunes could indeed have been orchestrated by the revenge of the Egyptian boy-king, angered she had been the architect of disturbing his centuries-long slumber.

Almina's old age held ample fodder for nostalgia; the days she had been the chatelaine of Highclere, had played a role in opening the tomb of splendor and had played host to King Edward. But perhaps what tugged at her heartstrings the most was the memory of the stolen hours with Victor, when their musical accompaniment could have been the theme song from *Downton Abbey*, "Did I Make the Most of Loving You?"

Chapter 2

The Golden Lion
(1896)

Celebutantes derive fame for being famous, and some members of this tribe spend their lives clinging to the shirttails fashioned by their illustrious ancestors. One who refused to be cast in this mold was a 1920s flapper who did more than soullessly flap.

When one envisions the Cunard Cruise Ships, the image is of floating castles where the well-heeled dance the night away amidst jaw-dropping grandeur. However, in their history lurks tragedy: a German U-boat torpedoed one of Cunard's luxury liners, the *Lusitania*, bringing about America's entry into World War I. Another ghost haunting the line is the great-granddaughter of its founding father, the Canadian-born Samuel Cunard.

Nancy Clara was the only child of Sir Bache Cunard and Maud, his American heiress wife, who adopted the name Emerald; the couple's home was the thirteenth century estate Nevill Holt. The Baronet cared chiefly for foxhunting, fishing, and horseback riding, while his lady's passion was scaling the social hierarchy. In a bid to increase her prestige, Emerald championed Wallis Simpson in the hope of becoming a lady-in-waiting when her fellow American became queen. Due to Edward's abdication, this goal disappeared, leading to Emerald's narcissistic response, "How could he do this to me?"

The pampered child grew up alienated from her father and mother; she empathized with the foxes her dad hunted and the men her mom seduced. The only occasions Emerald noticed her daughter were the times the nannies brought her downstairs dressed as a Velazquez Infanta. Nancy's early pronouncement was, "I don't like her Ladyship."

Emerald's dowry of two million dollars (approximately five hundred million dollars today) had been chiefly undertaken to purchase the title of lady, but despite the high-end real estate, the couple separated in 1911. Although proud of her beautiful daughter, whom an admirer later pronounced "lovely enough to seduce a saint," Emerald shipped Nancy off to prestigious boarding schools in Britain, France, and Germany. Through her education, Nancy became fluent in French, Spanish, Italian, German—and loneliness.

The heiress returned home a rebellious teen, though mother and daughter seemed close when they embarked to Paris for a shopping spree for Nancy's debutante season. Emerald hoped her child, outfitted with an exquisite gown for presentation to the queen, would make a prestigious match. However, under the surface, tensions seethed. Playing a game of truth in which each player had to name the person they would most like to see enter the room, Nancy stated, "Lady Cunard—dead."

The unconventional heiress took the traditional route of escape: marriage to Sydney Fairbairn, a soldier on leave due to a battlefield injury. Sydney possessed the dual qualifications of physical attributes (something that pleased Nancy) and the lack of a title (something that displeased Lady Cunard). In November of 1916, the press took a break from coverage of the World War to report on the wedding of the heiress of two enormously wealthy parents. The union did not survive, and Nancy referred to its brief duration as "a detestable period." After Sydney returned to the front, Nancy fell in love with another soldier, Peter Broughton-Adderley; when he died in battle, she was inconsolable.

To assuage her grief, Nancy surrounded herself with the "Corrupt Coterie" writers, such as Somerset Maugham, W. B. Yeats, and George Bernard Shaw, who were spearheading a literary revolution. In 1921, she began an affair with Ezra Pound, undeterred by his marriage to Dorothy Shakespear. She also embarked on a dalliance with another famous poet, T. S. Eliot, who she met at one of her mother's galas. They had become acquainted when he rescued her from dancing with a smitten Prince of Wales, whom, to Emerald's chagrin, she found boring. Nancy felt an immediate attraction to Eliot as she was already seduced by his poem "The Love Song of J. Alfred Prufrock." She told the writer, "Your words got into my fiber." Richard Aldington described her in a short story as "a kind of erotic boa constrictor. She swallowed men whole. You could almost see their feet sticking out of her mouth."

Adrift, Nancy cast about for a new niche, and the heiress transformed into a bohemian flapper; she cut her long blonde hair into a bob adorned with plastered kiss curls on her cheeks, took to shorter dresses, and brandished a long cigarette holder. Unlike many heroines of the Jazz Age such as Zelda Fitzgerald, Nancy rejected her privileged upbringing. As a means of escape, she set her sights on the Paris that Pound described as the place for those who had "cast off the sanctified stupidities and timidities" and were looking for radical new horizons.

The following year, Nancy joined fellow denizens of the Lost Generation in France for, as she had penned in a poem, she longed to experience "strange people in faraway lands." Her famous name, beauty, and heiress status served as an entry visa into the avant-garde community of Dadaists and Surrealists. Nevertheless, being at their vortex did not free her from Prufrockian angst, and she became discontented with the shallow prestige of being the decade's "It Girl." Nancy turned to her customary standby—sex and alcohol—to tame her demons. Of the elixir of the bottle, she stated, "It smooths down the bitter silences and comforts the nerves, dissipates my shyness."

Another escape from spiritual emptiness was her founding of
The Hours Press, located in the Normandy countryside. Her
publishing house issued books by Pound and championed lesser-
known writers such as the twenty-three-year-old Samuel Beckett.

In the heady years of her 1920s heyday, Cunard became not only
a great patron of the arts but its muse extraordinaire: Eliot put
her in an early version of "The Wasteland," Neruda celebrated
her in his poems, and Beckett praised her "spunk and verve."
All three future Nobel laureates had romantic yearnings for the
heiress with a heart. Off the page, Nancy continued her erotic
quests; she embarked on an affair with Aldous Huxley who based
a character on her in his novel *Point Counter Point*. Huxley
became fixated on her to such an extent that his wife, Maria,
dragged him off to Italy. Nancy received house calls from James
Joyce and spent time in the Montparnasse cafes with Langston
Hughes, who called her "one of my favorite folks in the world."
William Carlos Williams kept a picture of her in his study and
pronounced Cunard "one of the major phenomena of history."
Cunard's unique blend of the literary and the erotic made her
the expatriate siren of Paris and led to the writer Harold Acton's
observation, "She had inspired (and probably slept with) half the
poets and novelists of the Twenties."

While Luigi Pirandello's characters were in search of an author,
Nancy Cunard was in search of an identity and used fashion as
artistic expression. She took to wearing turbans with gauze over
her eyes, and her trademark accessory was antique ivory and
ebony bangles that snaked up both of her slender arms from
wrist to elbow. Man Ray immortalized her in a photograph;
Brancusi captured her likeness in a sculpture.

The pivotal event of Cunard's life occurred in a Venice hotel
where she spied Henry Crowder, a black jazz musician from

Washington, DC. Later that evening she sent a gondola to bring him to her palazzo. Although the son of a poor family from Georgia was from another world, he spoke to her soul, and he was likewise mesmerized. He remarked he became "infatuated beyond all reason." Uncomfortable with the looks the interracial couple received from the Fascists, they returned to Paris where they were inseparable. Part of Henry's staying power, unlike his predecessors, was his ability to withstand her emotional and physical outbursts. When the New York writer Janet Flanner—half in love with Nancy herself—bumped into Henry and inquired about his bruises, he responded, "Just bracelet work, Miss Janet."

Henry brought Nancy emotional stability; however, his greatest gift was opening her eyes to the cause for which she would dedicate her life: finding windmills against which to joust. Not willing to be just a fashionable poor little rich girl and muse, Cunard became a tireless advocate for the disenfranchised and stated, "I've always had the feeling that everyone alive can do something that is worthwhile." When Henry returned to the States, she accompanied him and was the first white woman to stay in Harlem hotels. Her lover opened her eyes to the agonizing situation of the black man in America. She was now at the opposite end of the spectrum from Nevill Holt, a fact that proved shocking to society as well as to Lady Cunard. Emerald's only foray into the mingling of the races had occurred at a Strauss ball that she had attended in the company of Sir Jey Singh, Maharajah of Alway. After Emerald failed to break up the relationship, and with no hope of ever having a grandchild to carry on the Cunard name—Nancy had previously undergone a hysterectomy—the widowed lady cut Nancy out of her will. The final straw for Lady Cunard was when she heard the news of the interracial liaison from her rival, Lady Oxford, who breezed into lunch one day and inquired after Nancy, "What is it now—drink, drugs, or niggers?" Emerald went into a rage; Nancy responded by writing a diatribe against racism and her mother, sending it to Lady Cunard's friends. The act was one of literary matricide; mother and daughter never spoke again. The media also showed its fangs and portrayed Nancy as a depraved English aristocrat with a taste for black men; a barrage of hate mail followed, including one missive from the Ku Klux Klan. Inevitably their divergent backgrounds, the public condemnation, and Nancy's demons drove them apart, and she returned alone to Paris.

In the 1930s, Nancy wore liberal causes on her bangle-bedecked sleeve, and her chief one was a crusade against fascism. She wrote articles condemning Mussolini's invasion of Ethiopia and Franco's coup. In order to gain firsthand knowledge of Spain's civil war, she embarked to Barcelona. The former flapper publicized the plight of the refugees who fled to France, and she established a shelter. By the late 1930s, her Herculean efforts on behalf of the dispossessed took its toll, and she became painfully, rather than elegantly, thin. Cunard stood on the Parisian streets where she had once walked in grandeur, asking for contributions for "the bombed-out people of Barcelona."

Weakened by the Furies who had always pursued her, as well as by anorexia and alcoholism, Nancy left on a visit to Venice. Lost and alone, she stood on a palazzo balcony where the "It" Girl had once made the Twenties roar. Leaning against its railing, she poured a glass of champagne into the Grand Canal and whispered, "For Henry."

In 1960, after a lengthy alcohol-infused bender in London, the British authorities locked her in a mental hospital. After her release, a destitute Cunard spent five years subsisting mainly on liquor and cigarettes, ranting against racists. In 1965, in

Paris, just after her sixty-ninth birthday, a friend commented she "looked thinner than a Buchenwald corpse;" she was sixty-five pounds, much of it from the bangles, the last remnant of her bygone glory. Lying semi-comatose on her deathbed, she muttered something that sounded at first like "pain" but turned out to be "champagne." Her epitaph could have been one from her own newspaper article, "All that remains is a furious sense of indignation." *The Evening Standard* reported her death as "the sad, lonely farewell to a toast to the Twenties."

The girl who had been to the manor born had traveled far from her role as aristocratic heiress yet shared a link with the yachting empire founded by her grandfather. Nancy had lived her life as the embodiment of the Cunard flag—a flapping, golden lion.

Chapter 3

All the Difference (1898)

The name Guggenheim conjures the image of an iconic architectural sculpture whose walls showcase the apogee of artistic expression. The eponymous museum is the brainchild of its billionaire patron, but far more colorful was his flamboyant niece.

A many-splendored bank account allows an existence far removed from the realm of the rest of us, which proved the case with Marguerite "Peggy" Guggenheim. Both sides of her family were preposterously wealthy; her immigrant father, Benjamin, was one of several brothers of German heritage who, along with his father, Meyer, made a fortune from metals such as silver and copper that led to their women sporting diamonds as big as the Ritz. Peggy's mother, Florette Seligman, also a first-generation American, was an heiress of a banking family known as "the American Rothschilds" who founded New York's Temple Emanu-El. Peggy was born in one of New York City's grandest hotels where her parents lived before moving to their enormous mansion on the Upper East Side opposite Central Park; neighbors were the Rockefellers and President Grant's widow. Their home decorations erred on the side of ostentation: marble staircases, tiger-skin rugs, and everything Louis XVI. The children's dollhouses had crystal chandeliers. The Germanic Guggenheims were advocates of *kultur*, and their three daughters were privy to opera boxes, grand tours of Europe, and portraits from the brushes of the Old Masters.

However, under the storybook exterior, Peggy was miserable. Her adored father was seldom home, busy as he was with serial seductions, and her mother was emotionally distant. The upbringing of Peggy, along with sisters Hazel and Benita, fell to a series of sadistic governesses whose dreaded outdoor excursions left her with a lifelong dread of Central Park. Always precocious, at age seven her parents banished her from the dining table for saying, "Papa, you must have a mistress as you stay out so many nights!" It was a nod to "from out of mouths of babes." Soon after, Benjamin abandoned his family and moved to Paris and his French trysts; the following year, he decided to return home for Hazel's birthday only to perish on the *Titanic*. Fourteen-year-old Peggy never recovered from the tragedy. In a move that made Florette the embodiment of bad mothering, she blamed Hazel for her husband's demise. In later life, Hazel lost her two young sons when they fell from the roof of the Surrey Hotel. Fortune, at least the nonmaterial kind, and Hazel were not on speaking terms.

During the dismal period that followed Benjamin's death, the Guggenheim children had their first taste of the anti-Semitism that hovered outside their upper-crust enclave. In a town on the New Jersey Shore where Guggenheim's far wealthier cousins had vacation homes—one a replica of a Pompeian villa—a hotel turned them away because of its "No Jews Allowed" policy. Peggy felt satisfaction when she watched the offending structure burn down one summer. In middle age, Peggy stated, "My childhood was excessively unhappy. I have no pleasant memories of any kind."

What added to Peggy's sorrows was that along with the Guggenheim fortune, she had inherited their pronounced potato-shaped nose, an unflattering feature her two beautiful sisters did not share. She sought a rhinoplasty—but the art was still in its infancy; the doctor botched the painful procedure, and it was left even more of an eyesore.

Rather than revel in her rarified life, Peggy felt stifled and took her initial foray into bohemia when she obtained a job at an avant-garde bookshop, the Sunwise Turn. Through her cousin Harold Loeb, she met F. Scott Fitzgerald and Alfred Stieglitz, men she found far more intriguing than the straitlaced boys of her own milieu. In Stieglitz's gallery on Fifth Avenue, Peggy encountered modern art and had her first sighting of the work of Stieglitz's future wife, Georgia O'Keefe.

When her mother suggested she accompany her on a trip to Paris, Peggy readily agreed, anxious to meet the avant-garde painters. On the continent at age twenty-three, she was a well-heeled rebel ripe for adventure and love which she found in Laurence Vail, known as "the King of Bohemia." He paid her a visit when her mother was out and was taken aback when she acquiesced to his sexual advance. He immediately backtracked and said that as her mother might come back, they should wait till they could get a hotel. She fetched her hat. Her respectable New York escorts had been too proper for premarital sex, but ever since she had seen photographs of frescoes from Pompeii, she was entranced with all matters carnal. She said of the erotic art, "They depicted people making love in various positions, and of course I was very curious and wanted to try them all out myself." She shamelessly pursued Vail to the altar and was so unsure if he would be a no-show, she did not buy a dress. Peggy felt she was neither the possessor of beauty nor talent; all she could offer was money, something Vail was never loathe to accept. The affection-starved girl who had lost her beloved father lavished her love on her husband—who reciprocated with abuse. If she displeased him, he would walk on her stomach, hold her down under running water in the bathtub, or rub jam in her hair. Vail's novel contained an anti-Semitic portrait of his wife whom he caricatured: "in sleep she moves her lips as she dreams of sums." The tempestuous union produced a son, Sindbad, and a daughter, Pegeen.

The marriage expired three years later at a café in Saint-Tropez where Peggy met English intellectual John Holms. In the divorce, Laurence retained custody of Sindbad and Peggy of Pegeen; never the nurturing type, she once told Pegeen she would trade her for a Picasso. Peggy and John cohabited; their home, Hayford Hall, dubbed Hangover Hall by their Bloomsbury friends, became the site of furious rows fueled by alcohol, and Peggy again became a battered woman. She wrote in her autobiography, "He made me stand for ages naked in front of the open window (in December) and threw whiskey into my eyes." Freedom arrived when John passed away from a heart attack in 1934.

With two unhappy relationships behind her, Peggy decided to tread the road of noncommittal sex, and her carnal appetite was voracious—driven by emotional need and lust. Legend holds Guggenheim had gone through a thousand lovers as illustrated by an anecdote: when asked how many husbands she'd had, she responded, "Do you mean mine or other people's?" Her most thorough education in modern art came from Samuel Beckett, whom she had met at a dinner party hosted by James Joyce; when he arrived at her apartment, he lay on a sofa and asked her to join him. They spent a night and a day in bed, interrupted only by her demand that he go out for a bottle of champagne. During their relationship, Beckett enjoyed driving in her state-of-the-art sports cars, and through his contacts, she became the boho queen of the European art world. Whenever she pestered him about what he planned to do with their relationship, his invariable answer was: "Nothing."

Peggy latched onto the idea of showcasing her private collection in an art gallery, and even as the continent trembled on the brink of a world war, she plunged ahead with her cultural crusade.

She made a resolution to "buy a picture a day" and amassed canvasses by Dali, Braque, and Picasso in sharp contrast to her uncle Solomon who strictly adhered to the Old Masters. However, in her case, she encountered sexism. One afternoon she walked into Picasso's Paris studio seeking to purchase a painting. He dismissed her with the comment, "Madame, the lingerie department is on the second floor."

Guggenheim only admitted defeat weeks before France did the same when the Nazis goose-stepped into Paris. She finally realized that with her prominent—and Jewish—name she was a prime target. Nothing less than the occupation could have brought her back to the States which she associated with her unhappy childhood that she recalled as "one long, protracted agony." She asked the Louvre administrators to safeguard her paintings; they refused, stating her modern art was not worth the space. In desperation, she stored the works, all destined to carry multimillion price tags, in a friend's barn in the Vichy countryside. After living abroad for twenty-two years, she returned to the States along with her extended family: her ex-husband, his soon to be ex-wife, her two teenaged children, and the painter Max Ernst, a man she considered a relative as she already envisioned him as her third husband. When she had seduced the great surrealist painter, one of her former conquests remarked, "Max Ernst is now said to be Peggy Guggenheim's consort no 3,812." After she wed the broke artist, she commented, "I did not know if he was miserable because he was going to marry me or for some other reason."

Guggenheim established a New York Gallery, Art of This Century, in 1942, a time when no one was standing in line to buy avant-garde paintings. This fact did not faze the outlandish devotee of the new; at the opening, she wore one earring by Calder and one by Tanguy to demonstrate her equal regard for abstraction and Surrealism. Her establishment played a key role in Manhattan's displacement of Paris as the capital of modern art. On display were the canvasses of her latest discovery, Jackson Pollock, a carpenter in her uncle's museum. He was one of the rare artists who slipped through the patroness' net; he said that you would have to put a towel over her head to have sex with Peggy. With her beloved Lhasa Apso dogs trailing behind her, Peggy was a daily fixture at Art of This Century; at night, she threw wild parties attended by artists and guests such as Gypsy Rose Lee. Her marriage did not provide the satisfaction she derived from her gallery; unlike her art, she could not hold on to her men, and Ernst left her for the beautiful artist Dorothea Tanning.

After the war, Peggy determined to leave the country once more and set her sights on Venice. She purchased the eighteenth-century Palazzo Venier dei Leoni on the Grand Canal and lived in opulence amidst her modern masterpieces, servants, and eleven Lhasa apsos. She reigned in noble splendor and slept on an Alexander Calder sterling silver bed. Three afternoons a week the public roamed through her home to view her magnificent collection; there were even paintings in the bathroom, juxtaposed with wet stockings. She escaped the crowds by sunbathing nude on its roof. Guggenheim still courted the famous and hosted soirees with guests such as Yoko Ono, Tennessee Williams, and Truman Capote. Peggy, who took to sporting bat-winged sunglasses, continued her lifelong pursuit of paintings and penises; her wealth proved as intoxicating as a new-car scent for the possessors of testosterone. She resorted to gigolo-gondoliers and race car drivers for consorts.

In 1967, Pegeen, an alcoholic, depressed painter, committed suicide in her Paris home leaving behind four young sons. Her mother, informed of her death by telegram while vacationing in Mexico, never recovered. She said, "We were like two sisters, friends, having lovers. Her death has left me quite bankrupt." In tribute, a room of the palazzo became a shrine of her daughter's paintings of blank-faced dolls.

Guggenheim, the modern Medici of modern art, spent her final years devoid of company except for her fourteen dogs that inspired her nickname, "La Dogaressa." Her main activity was sailing the Grand Canal in her gondola, the last in the city to be privately owned. Instead of the traditional *cavalla* (seahorse shaped hardware), the ropes of her craft were tied to Lhasa Apso statuettes. She said, "I adore floating to such an extent I can't think of anything as nice since I gave up on sex, or, rather, it gave me up."

Peggy passed away from a stroke in 1979; she had directed her ashes to be interred in a corner of the Palazzo garden near the resting place of her beloved dogs. The Guggenheim fortune did not bring joy, but it did allow her to take Frost's road less traveled, a path that made all the difference.

Chapter 4

Indian Summer
(1901)

Voracious sexual appetites are traditionally associated with the possessors of testosterone, but history has proved there are Lady Casanovas. Catherine the Great was so hot to trot that a joke circulated in St. Petersburg asserting the canal that received the most use was Catherine's canal. Mae West's response to her maid informing her ten men were waiting at the door was, "Send one of them home. I'm tired." In a similar carnal vein, there was a British lady who could have given both the Russian empress and the American movie star a run for their money.

Edwina Cynthia Annette Ashley had a cocooned but lonely childhood as her parents lavished little time on her or her younger sister, Mary. When their mother passed away from tuberculosis, her death did not leave a significant impact on her daughters. Their father, Wilfred, a conservative Member of Parliament and future baron, remarried, and at his new wife's urging, sent Edwina to boarding school, one that she enjoyed as much as Jane Eyre did Lowood. Rescue arrived through her grandfather, Sir Ernest Cassel, a German-Jewish banker who had converted to Catholicism at the urging of his wife. After his daughter's death, he took Edwina under his wing, and she lived with him in Brook House, his Park Lane London estate. Grandpa's house had so many maids that one was employed full-time only to wash the flower-vases. The child became accustomed to footmen in livery, governesses, valets, chauffeurs, and a chef with four assistants. Their home was the most magnificent in Mayfair; Cassel had purchased the property in order to woo members of the aristocracy, a move calculated to distance him from his immigrant roots. His pastime was raising thoroughbreds, and at a race, Cassel achieved his greatest win: meeting the Prince of Wales. Cassel ended up as the future King Edward VII's financial advisor and confidant, thereby gaining entry into the upper echelons of the elite.

As a rich and desirable heiress, Edwina's marriage paved the way to the enclave of the blue bloods. The society darling met Prince Louis Mountbatten, whom the royal family nicknamed Dickie, at a ball hosted by Mrs. Cornelius Vanderbilt. His mother, Princess Victoria, was a granddaughter of Queen Victoria; Dickie was related to almost every king, prince, and grand duke in Europe. Their magnificent nuptials took place in 1922 at the Church of St. Margaret, Westminster Abbey, where the Prince of Wales served as the best man. Their honeymoon was spent in Spain as the guests of King Alfonso XIII and Queen Ena, while the Vanderbilts were ecstatic to serve as their Manhattan hosts. When the newlyweds returned to London, with his pedigree and her fortune, they became the "It couple" of the Twenties. From the cars—and sometimes airplanes—that alighted at Brook House stepped visitors such as Charlie Chaplin, Noel Cowart, Winston Churchill, and Douglas Fairbanks, Jr. One evening, King Edward VIII arrived with Mrs. Simpson.

As happens with couples from all walks of life, a wedding did not prove a prelude to a marriage of content. While ostensibly the Mountbattens were a perfect match, in actuality they shared few commonalities. His passion was the spoils of the good life; his lady, having always enjoyed luxury, was inured to its seduction. Furthermore, Edwina did not partake in her husband's other obsession: his position as First Sea Lord of the Royal Navy. So enamored was he of the Navy, he designed their bedroom after a ship's stateroom. Further problems dogged their marital vows when disharmony appeared in the boudoir. Initially, the inexperienced couple reveled in their mutual introduction to the horizontal life. The groom anointed his bride's breasts Mutt and Jeff—the nicknames World War I soldiers gave to their campaign medals—and the couple became parents of Patricia and Pamela. Part of their lack of physical chemistry may have arisen because the bisexual Mountbatten preferred male partners; while he was called Dickie to his family, in other circles, he was known as Mountbottom. When he resumed his duties as an officer, Edwina, described as one of the six best-dressed women in the world, shopped at Chanel, played bridge, and danced the Charleston until three in the morning, sometimes with Fred Astaire.

Motherhood did not provide the salve to her spiritual wasteland; though she loved her girls, she proved maternal nurture is not an instinct. After Patricia's birth, Edwina confided to her diary, "A divine little daughter. Too thrilling, too sweet," and then gave over her care to nannies while she partied in the south of France. Edwina possessed a razor-sharp mind, but because of the repressive nature of her era and class was unable to embark on a career and instead turned to amorous pursuits. At times, she juggled several lovers, and her bed, sheathed in pink satin sheets, became a variant of musical chairs. On one occasion, a maid at the Mayfair mansion was at her wit's end when the lady of the house bustled in from a shopping spree, and five gentlemen callers were awaiting her arrival. The frantic domestic said, "Mr. Gray is in the dining room, Mr. Sandford is in the library, Mr. Phillips is in the boudoir, Señor Portago in the anteroom... and I simply don't know what to do with Mr. Molyneux!" The inner circle—except for her husband who spent his time at sea—were aware of her hobby and referred to her lovers as Edwina's "ginks."

The most scandalous episode in her libidinous diary was her liaison with the bisexual West Indian cabaret pianist Leslie Hutchinson—the prototype for *Downton Abbey*'s royal gigolo Jack Ross. Leslie was performing, and Edwina, sitting in the audience with her husband and the Prince of Wales, was enamored. At another concert, as he played the piano, she took off her chiffon scarf, put it around his neck, and startled him with a passionate kiss. Following consummation, in appreciation of service rendered, she gave him a gold cigarette case, a signet ring bearing her coat of arms on the inside, and a diamond-encrusted penis sheath from Cartier. Their erotic romps ended when the newspaper *The People* proclaimed a woman highly connected and immensely rich was having an extramarital dalliance with a colored man. King George V ordered Edwina, who had temporarily moved to Malta where her husband was stationed, to return home to put a lid on the scandal. The couple was publicly invited to Buckingham Palace the following day, neatly papering over the cracks in their marriage. Later on, Mountbatten would admit, "Edwina and I spent all our married lives getting into other people's beds." The Mountbattens never contemplated divorce. His royal relations did not let divorced people set foot in the Royal Enclosure at Ascot, and without his wife's wealth, he would have been forced to live off his paltry officer's pay. After one of Edwina's transatlantic jaunts left American gossips in a feeding frenzy (she was supposed to be breaking up the Douglas Fairbanks–Mary Pickford marriage), the couple cut a deal: they would maintain separate beds but would remain deeply devoted friends.

Patricia and Pamela, although coddled with all the privileges that class, celebrity, and cash could bestow, were deprived of parental nurture, as dad was on the high seas and mummy was restlessly roaming the world. Edwina's companion on these adventures to Africa, China, and the Pacific was often Bunny Philips, who the children called Uncle. Compensation for their absences was lavish presents, and the girls wore handmade shoes from Paris and played with a miniature train set of solid silver. The children's menagerie of pets included souvenirs from their mother's exotic/erotic trips: a lion cub, a mongoose, and a pair of wallabies who fed on orchids and were never housebroken. In a nod to donning the maternal cloak, she took her children on a Continental tour and deposited them, along with nanny and governess, in a Hungarian hotel and then disappeared for months. After Edwina decided to retrieve them, she could not recall the name of the hotel. Ultimately, after retracing her route, there was a mother-child reunion.

Edwina's soulless odyssey came to a halt in 1947 when she became entangled in a pivotal moment in history. After attending the marriage of Queen Elizabeth II to Lord Mountbatten's nephew, Prince Philip, their lives were upended when the Atlee government appointed Mountbatten the last Viceroy of India. His job was to return the longtime star in the crown of the British Empire back to its own people.

Jawaharlal Nehru was a lonely widower; his only passion was his country's independence until he met the woman who proved the cliché that opposites attract. Though from different races, religions, cultures, and classes, they forged a magnetic connection, and Edwina relinquished her emotional virginity. However, unlike with her "ginks," she took pains to keep her extramarital affair discreet because Nehru's cause came first. On every possible opportunity, Nehru visited the monumental Rashtrapati Bhava, the Viceroy's sumptuous residence, for a rendezvous. On afternoons they would sit side-by-side on a bench, no space between them. Mountbatten often accompanied them to deflect attention from the affair. When duty drove them apart, she wrote Nehru, "I hated seeing you drive away this morning...you have left me with a strange sense of peace and happiness. Perhaps I have brought you the same?" Henri Cartier-Bresson's photograph of the three power players, taken in Delhi, serves as a metaphor for their triangular relationship: Viceroy Mountbatten dressed in white Navy attire looks off to the side, Nehru, in traditional Indian garb, is doubled over in mirth, Edwina smiles at her lover. Lord Mountbatten and Nehru shared more than a relationship with Edwina: they were both under monumental pressure on the best way to transfer power to a country rent asunder by virulent tensions simmering amongst Hindus, Muslims, and Sikhs.

In ten months, Mountbatten orchestrated the partition of India and the birth of Pakistan. Afterward, the British elite did what they had done for two centuries of rule: celebrated in grandiose style. On a balmy evening, Lord and Lady Mountbatten threw an extravagant party in the Mughal Gardens of Delhi to mark the extraction of the jewel of empire from Victoria's crown. Thousands of tiny lanterns hung from jacaranda trees as native princes in dazzling attire and British colonial officers wandered among the fountains and rose beds, sipping champagne and eating canapés. Nehru had been India's first Prime Minister for less than twenty-four hours; Pakistan was not yet a day old, and on the other side of the genteel enclosed gate, the continent was aflame with riots and enough blood to overflow the Ganges. The Viceroy had failed to appreciate that partition would lead to a million deaths.

Although flawless in the role of the perfect hostess, Edwina was apprehensive she would have to leave the man who had shown her the face of love, and the moment of separation arrived sooner than expected. After Gandhi's assassination—the activist Churchill had disparaged as "that half-naked fakir"— the British Prime Minister saw a newspaper photograph of the grieving Vicereine kneeling on the ground during the Mahatma's cremation. Sir Winston fumed she had gone over to the other side of the political fence and ordered the Mountbattens to immediately return to England. Edwina once more wore the mantle of poor little rich girl.

The separation was made bearable when Edwina visited India or Nehru was in England. He sent presents from wherever he traveled: sugar from the United States, cigarettes from Egypt, pressed ferns from Sikkim, and a book of erotic photographs from the Temple of the Sun in Orrissa. The couple, on the same page intellectually and spiritually, shared another commonality posthumously. In 1979, the IRA planted a bomb on Lord Mountbatten's fishing boat off the coast of Ireland, killing him, his fourteen-year-old grandson Nicholas, and the child's paternal grandmother; his daughter Patricia and Nicholas's twin brother, Timothy, sustained serious injuries. In a similar tragic vein, in 1984, Nehru's only child, Indira Gandhi, who was serving as Prime Minister, fell victim to an assassination orchestrated by her two Sikh bodyguards.

Edwina spent her last years emotionally adrift, miserable at the enforced separation of the man she loved and devastated at the tragic loss of her husband and grandson. She passed away from heart failure in North Borneo in 1960; on her deathbed were innumerable letters, written on fine blue paper, all from Jawaharlal Nehru. But their love story was not yet at an end. The Royal Navy took Edwina's body to its sea burial in the English Channel where her grief-stricken lover made a public declaration of his devotion; he sent his own Indian Navy frigate to cast a single wreath of marigolds on her watery grave. Late in life, Edwina discovered love—the real pearl beyond price—that allowed her a brief yet indelible Indian summer.

Chapter 5

What Profit a Man?
(1902)

A biblical passage segued into a modern morality tale, one whose sordid revelations opened a window on the denizens of the *Fortune 400*. In the words from the book of Timothy, "The love of money is the root of all evil."

Roberta Brooke Russell, the Queen Bee of high society, entered into the moneyed hive one Easter Sunday in New Hampshire. As is related in her memoir, *Patchwork Child*, her grandparents raised her "rather royally" in their Washington, DC, mansion while John, her father, a general, served a lengthy tour in the Orient. She adored him, but her relationship with her mother, socialite Mabel Howard Russell, was problematic. Brooke later recalled that to be with her was like being "in the midst of the blinding radiance that was mother." A few years later, the family joined John in his military postings to Hawaii, China, Panama, and Santo Domingo where there was an endless stream of governesses, embassy soirees, and tea dances, a childhood that made Brooke feel like a bird in an exotic cage. When the Russells arrived in Peking in 1910, some girls from the upper class still had bound feet; their society's *modus operandi* was to keep them docile and dainty in order to make them perfect wives for rich men. Her mother forced Brooke to wear high, tightly laced boots to keep her ankles slim; in a way similar to the Chinese, Mabel was raising Brooke to be a wife of wealth.

At age seventeen, Brooke returned to the States, where, at a Princeton prom, she met John Dryden Kuser, a member of a prominent New Jersey horse-set family. He was also an alcoholic, as well as addicted to gambling and floozies. Mabel, "dazzled" by his substantial fortune, was thrilled with the couple's 1919 wedding. But Brooke's introduction to sex was what she termed marital rape; John broke her jaw when she was six months pregnant. His rage stemmed from the unfounded belief that he was not the biological father of their son, Anthony, nicknamed "Toad." For eleven years, the couple lived in great luxury—and great misery. The marriage ended when John left his wife for the next Mrs. Kuser. The other woman earned Brooke's undying gratitude for taking the "perfectly horrible man" off her hands.

Post-divorce, Brooke and Tony left New Jersey and relocated to Manhattan. Although the six-year-old was upset at leaving his pony, he was relieved to escape from his abusive father. In 1932, Brooke met wealthy lawyer Charles "Buddie" Marshall, who left his spouse and children for her. Although Charles never adopted Tony nor treated him as his own child, Tony did eventually change his name to Marshall. This action angered Kuser to such an extent that he sued to disinherit his son from his trust fund and as grounds for terminating child support. Brooke wrote of the ensuing court battle, "I rather agreed with the judge—'people who fight over money never seem to me to deserve to have any.' " Because she was engrossed in her new husband, and as Tony physically favored her hated ex-husband, Brooke sent him off to boarding schools. Freed from child-rearing duty, the Marshalls sailed to Cherbourg aboard the steamer Europa. Summers were spent at a castle in Portofino, Italy, where Brooke met Max Beerbohm, Evelyn Waugh, and a shirtless Ezra Pound. The two decades she spent with Marshall were, she later said, the happiest of her life. Marshall died in her arms from a heart attack in 1952 on Thanksgiving Day.

Brooke's third trip down the aisle became the projectile that launched her into the stratosphere of New York's social register. Six months after she became a widow, she met the bearer of a gold-plated name: Vincent Astor. He had been a twenty-year-old when he inherited more than sixty million dollars from his father John Jacob Astor V—believed to be the country's first

millionaire—who went down with the *Titanic*. His grandmother
had been the famed Mrs. Astor who had developed the concept of
the top four hundred acceptable people of fashionable society—
based on how many people her ballroom could accommodate.
The name Astor connoted the highest society and lent its name to
the Waldorf-Astoria Hotel and Astor Place.

Brooke proved herself to be the social-climbing daughter of
Mabel when she married Vincent, an alcoholic recluse who
disliked her son. The wedding took place in a quiet 1953
ceremony at the Bar Harbor home of Joseph Pulitzer. Vincent's
peers—as well as his own mother—held him in such disdain
that he required a solitary seating for lunch at his club. Louis
Auchincloss remarked, "Of course she married Vincent for the
money. If she [had] married him for his charm, I'd have said she
ought to be put in an asylum."

Five years later Vincent died, thus ending a marriage his widow
referred to as her "fallow years." Although Astor had lavished her
with jewels and houses, he was so controlling he had not allowed
her to talk on the phone, entertain, nor go out with friends. Tony
had also been a casualty of his stepfather's misanthropy.

Brooke's life truly started when Vincent's ended. At age fifty-
seven, she inherited one of the country's oldest fortunes and the
administration of the Vincent Astor Foundation, both of which
made her the Grand Dame of New York. Before his death, he told
her he was leaving the trust to her, "You are going to have a lot of
fun running it, Pookie," and fun she had. Instantly recognizable
in her Chanel suits, ornate hats, pearls, and trademark gloves,
she visited every one of the organization's causes. One of the
jewels on Brooke's charitable tiara was the Bronx Zoo that
honored her by naming its first baby elephant Astor. The
christening might also have been a tongue-in-cheek nod to her

affiliation with the Republican Party. At her dinner party for
Ronald Reagan, the president-elect crawled under her table to
retrieve her diamond earring. Another recipient of her largesse
was the New York Public Library; in tribute, her gilt-edged name
is carved on its main entrance. Brooke had found a cause and
had no desire for a fourth husband. She disliked the notion of
"having anyone tugging at my sleeve at ten o'clock telling me
it's time to go home. I want to go at my own speed, and it's a lot
faster than theirs." She would no longer be a bird in any man's
gilded cage.

Almost every night—even in her nineties—she wore many-karat
diamonds and dressed in designer gowns. She especially loved to
dance and said, "When that music starts, it enters my blood like
a fever." Even in her tenth decade, she remained an unabashed
flirt. After David Rockefeller asked for a guest list for her
hundredth birthday, she suggested, "ninety-nine men and me."
Brooke joked about her horizontal life; she once remarked of
her many lovers, "When I can't fall asleep at night, I sometimes
start counting them, but I'm asleep before I get to the end of
the list." Beats counting sheep. If she did not go out for a night
in her town, she would invite people to one of her magnificent
homes: on Fifth Avenue, in Westchester County, and in Maine.
An invitation to one of her dinners, where a typical guest would
be Nancy Reagan, was a hallmark of the highest approval. The
itinerant soldier's daughter never made any apology for her life
of wealth, partially because she gave so much of it away. Unlike
Queen Victoria, Mrs. Astor was amused—always amused—until
she was not.

In her old age, the dowager doyenne disappeared from the
society pages that she had dominated for half a century. Most
assumed she had finally slowed down and was spending her

twilight years in her princely pleasure domes, in the company of friends and her beloved dogs. (In her unfailingly polite way, she asked for Sir Winston's Churchill's permission to name a puppy after him.) However, in her 104th year, her image appeared again in the media, but this time she was tabloid fodder in the eye of a lurid scandal.

In a life of many chapters, Brooke's final one became a saga of Greek tragedy. Her grandson, Philip Marshall, filed court papers charging his father, Anthony Marshall, with elder abuse by failing to provide care for his 104-year-old-mother and for using her fortune as his personal piggy bank. Some of the salacious tidbits were that although the socialite was no longer going out, her jaw-dropping jewels were—as adornments on Tony's third wife, Charlene, who had left her clergyman husband for Marshall. There was no way Brooke had lent them to her daughter-in-law; she never masked her loathing of her son's two-decade-younger wife, who a friend of Brooke's had dubbed Lady Macbeth. When Charlene presented her with flowers for her hundredth birthday—sent by Prince Charles—she received a look of undiluted dislike. Brooke had commented to her butler about her daughter-in-law, "She has no class and no neck." Philip, a Buddhist and a professor at Roger Williams University in Rhode Island, claimed his intention had not been to make his lawsuit a public can of worms: his only aim had been to protect his grandmother. However, when the press got whiff of this scandal, one that involved the haute monde, staggering wealth, and criminal activity, there ensued a feeding frenzy of schadenfreude. Anthony Marshall became the American Prince Charles, tired of waiting in the shadow of his elderly mother to take possession of his long-awaited birthright.

The court of public opinion vilified Tony for taking advantage of Manhattan's godmother, whose fairy dust had enriched the city with two hundred million dollars. His credibility was further weakened when Brooke's powerful friends—David Rockefeller, Henry Kissinger, and Annette de la Renta (wife of the famed fashion designer)—backed Phillip's charges. They claimed he made Brooke—still adorned in jewels and dressed to the nines—subsist on leftovers that she ate alone on a TV tray while sitting atop a urine-stained couch. A further accusation: she was kept from her beloved dachshunds—Boysie and Girlsie. Another damning finger was pointed in his direction when his mother's prized painting—one she had earmarked for the Metropolitan Museum at her passing—was found to have disappeared from her living room wall. Tony had sold it for ten million dollars and pocketed a two-million-dollar commission. Alarmed, her employees had installed a baby monitor in her room and eavesdropped on her conversations with her son and lawyer. They claimed while in the clutches of Alzheimer's, she had changed her will—making her son, rather than her charities—the chief beneficiary. Brooke claimed persecution by the men in the blue suits "who make me sign things." A judge revoked her son's guardianship, filed a criminal complaint, and Annette de la Renta assumed care of the once fiercely independent Mrs. Astor.

Tony's agenda may not have been fueled merely by a lust for material gain; it could also have been triggered by his desire to get back at Brooke who by her own admission had been "a lousy mother." She had not only always kept him at fur-bedecked arm's length; her famous name, wealth, and social standing had left her son in her shadow. The last Mrs. Astor had freely given of herself to her husbands, her charities, and her dogs, but she had always remained aloof to her only child.

Anthony Marshall became known as Crook Astor, and, when Anthony was age eighty-nine, a judge sentenced him to one to three years in prison. Like his father before him, Anthony cut off all ties with his son, whom he viewed as a Brutus. Brooke, in her twilight years, was not aware of the poisonous vapors from her fabulous fortune that had destroyed her family. Mrs. Astor had made it a point to try to mend burned bridges and had called a man she had stopped speaking to for many years. She explained, "I want to be at peace with all my friends when I die." Ironically, she had never resolved her own family feud.

At Mrs. Astor's funeral, Anthony said in an amalgam of the voices of an old man and a boy, "New York and her many friends have lost a wonderful person. But I've lost my mother." His tragedy, and Brooke's, was that he never had her in the first place.

A biblical injunction that has echoes to the last Mrs. Astor: "For what shall it profit a man if he shall gain the whole world, and lose his own soul?"

Chapter 6

The Porcelain Faces (1906)

The most indelible recluse in literature is Miss Havisham of
Charles Dickens's novel *Great Expectations*. When her fiancé
was a no-show at the altar, she spent her life in perpetual
mourning for what-could-have-been. Eventually, she resembled
a corpse in aging lace, entombed in her mansion of pain. A
modern Manhattan heiress echoed Dickens' tragic heroine who
became a prisoner entombed in her own Satis house.

The future recluse was the youngest daughter of a top-hatted,
Gilded Age mineral baron, Copper King William A. Clark, second
only in wealth to John D. Rockefeller. Upon the death of his first
wife, he took up with the four-decade-younger French-Canadian
Anna Eugenia LaChapelle. His five children learned of the new
Mrs. Clark from a newspaper headline; they were none too
pleased with their stepmother, many years their junior.

Clark County in Nevada took its name from the man who
presided over a mining empire and sold numerous lots of what
would later become downtown Vegas. At the same time, his
daughter Huguette was born in Paris and lived on the elite
Avenue Victor Hugo. A photograph of her at age four shows
the little girl, impeccably dressed in white, surrounded by her
doll collection.

The following year, the Clarks took Huguette and her older
sister, Andrée, to the grandest house in New York City, a six-
story, twelve-bathroom Fifth Avenue mansion. William custom
built the estate, one large enough to satiate his huge ego—it
was as oversized as the life-sized Zeus carved into its mammoth
fireplace. The estate boasted 121 rooms with ceilings made of
wood from Sherwood Forest, a five hundred seat theater, and
four art galleries awash with paintings by Rembrandt, Rubens,
and Degas. A private railway line supplied the family with coal;
the public dubbed the behemoth "Clark's Folly." William, who

had been born in a log cabin in Pennsylvania, used his fortune to purchase a seat on the Senate as casually as another man might buy a pair of shoes. Mark Twain remarked, "His proper place was the penitentiary, with a chain and ball on his legs." Although Clark was not a hero to the writer—nor to his butler, nor his ten servants and French chef—he was one to his adored daughters.

Along with the coal deliveries, the Grim Reaper paid a call; Andrée passed away from meningitis at age sixteen. Six years later William died and left his nineteen-year-old daughter an amount equivalent to $6.3 billion in contemporary currency. She later remarked that money was "a menace to happiness." As the patriarch had bequeathed his six children his mansion, they arranged its sale, and mother and daughter moved to a forty-two room Fifth Avenue apartment. The heiress graduated from Miss Spencer's Finishing School for Girls—where Isadora Duncan taught dance—and had her official coming-out party in 1926. With her beauty and billions, she could have been the flapper of the decade, on par with the other Gilded Age golden girls—the Guggenheims, the Vanderbilts, the Astors—but she preferred the solitary pursuits of painting and taking trips to France to acquire dolls.

Anna, who had risen from her youth as an impoverished teen to unimaginable wealth, may have entertained similar marital aspirations for her daughter; however, Huguette fell for William MacDonald Gower, a Princeton graduate of modest means, the son of her father's accountant. Although it was not a match that Anna desired for her daughter, she nevertheless was pleased the preternaturally shy Huguette had found love. Mrs. Clark spared no expense on the 1927 wedding held at the family's twenty-three-acre, forty-two room Santa Barbara mansion, Bellosguardo (Italian for beautiful lookout), perched atop a Pacific Ocean bluff.

Anna had been in charge of its construction and had veered from the excess of her husband, opting instead for staid elegance. She designed it in the eighteenth-century French architectural style, and its locale was a nod to its majestic site and its privacy, its only neighbors the gravestones of an old cemetery.

The couple bought a palatial apartment in the same Fifth Avenue apartment building where Anna resided when in New York; however, their union came with a nine-month expiration date. The last known photograph of Madame Clark, as she preferred to be known, captured her on the day of her 1930 Nevada divorce. The black-and-white image portrayed a somber Huguette in a fur-lined coat, her only jewelry a wristwatch and a simple strand of pearls. She charged desertion; William claimed the marriage had never been consummated. With the demise of her marriage, the heiress retreated further into her gilded shell.

Mother and daughter became modern-day Greta Garbos; the only Pied Piper that could coax Huguette from her cocoon was a Christian Dior fashion show where she would order scale replicas for the dolls who lined the walls in their own silk armchairs. The heiress had arranged one of them to be flown in from France as a first-class passenger; she had purchased two of them from Sotheby's Auction House for thirty thousand dollars.

In most respects, Huguette was not a chip off the block of her Copper King father—he was rapacious while she was generous, yet they shared a commonality. They were both avid builders, though the daughter's creations were on a far smaller, though no less grand, scale. She employed the finest craftsmen to create miniature dollhouses. One of these artists was from Bavaria, and he created masterpieces based on German fairy tales: *Rumpelstiltskin* with the scene of hay transformed to gold, Rapunzel trapped in a tower, Sleeping Beauty waiting to be awakened by her prince. Her collection grew so vast she employed, at ninety dollars an hour, an Austria-Hungarian immigrant to create furnishings. Once she called with an urgent concern—a ceiling had to be raised, "The little people are banging their heads!" A housekeeper was kept busy ironing the dolls' exquisite couturier dresses.

Mother and daughter, as artistically gifted as they were socially inept, filled their solitary hours with music. Anna strummed her harp while Huguette played on her four Stradivari violins, including one that had a carved wood image of Joan of Arc. Huguette's less highbrow activities were watching endless episodes of *The Flintstones* and *The Smurfs*, often while eating her customary cuisine of crackers and sardines.

The only people Huguette had ever let enter her ghostly heart were her father, her mother, and her sister Andrée, and when Anna passed away in her eighties, her only connection to another person vanished. She embodied the concept illustrated in the Alexander Pope quotation, "the world forgetting, by the world forgot," and rarely ventured outside for the next seventy years. The name and life of the mysterious recluse would have been forgotten had it not been for the convergence of a Google search engine and a journalist with a Sherlockian proclivity.

Bill Dedman was house hunting in Connecticut in 2009 when, out of curiosity, he Googled the most expensive home in the neighborhood. He was intrigued when a listing appeared for a twenty-four-million-dollar home on fifty-two acres in New Canaan called Le Beau Chateau, situated between properties owned by Harry Connick, Jr. on one side and Glenn Beck on the other. Intrigued, Dedman drove over and poked around the ivy-draped stone walls that edged the property. The home had a very unusual feature, even more unusual than a room dedicated to drying draperies. A caretaker from one of the estate's cottages mentioned he had worked there for two decades and that it had been unoccupied for sixty years. Dedman sensed a mystery and observed, "News is being committed here." Madame Clark had purchased it in 1951 and had added a master bedroom with an art studio above. On the stairs leading up to the enclave, every other spindle holding up the banister was in the likeness of a paintbrush. Upon further research, Dedman discovered Bellosguardo, the oceanfront palace that had aroused the acquisitiveness of the Shah of Iran; however, its owner had not agreed to its sale, although she had never once set foot on the property for half a century.

The mysterious land baroness had also disappeared from one of the largest apartments in Manhattan, leaving as its only occupants upwards of a thousand dolls and their elaborate miniature homes. The journalist became immersed in the trail of his own investigative "Rosebud," one that led to New York's Beth Israel Hospital.

In 1991, Suzanne Pierre, Huguette's former secretary and her closest relationship approximating a friendship, grew concerned she had not been able to reach Madame Clark by phone and sent over a doctor to the apartment which occupied an entire Fifth Avenue floor. Despite its splendor, it existed in a time warp; the rotary dial telephones still identified the exchange number as "Butterfield 8." The décor was not the type preferred by another resident in the same apartment building: Martha Stewart. In this baronial expanse sat an emaciated centenarian, wrapped in a filthy bathrobe, disfigured by untreated skin cancer that had eaten away parts of her lip and eyelids. Several months later, plastic surgery had restored her face, and the heiress received a clean bill of health. Nevertheless, rather than return to Bellosguardo and its ocean breeze, to her apartment overlooking Central Park, or to Le Beau Chateau enveloped in pristine grounds, she remained in her fourteen-by-twenty-four-foot hospital room for twenty years. Her new quarters' view was of an air-conditioning unit, and her room was located next to a janitor's closet. To protect her privacy—though the public no longer remembered her name—she took the precaution of registering under the alias of Harriet Chase. The austere room's only hint of its occupant's improbable wealth was the presence of her fine French dolls; they were valued at two million dollars, but to their owner, they were her pearls beyond price—her surrogate daughters.

Had life gone according to Madame Clark's desire, she would have died as she had lived, hidden from prying eyes. Ironically, her very act of disappearing, and the enormous interest her life and half-billion-dollar fortune generated, put her in the epicenter of a media storm. Her story's dramatic elements—robber baron father, empty estates, and echoes of Miss Havisham—provided tantalizing drama, especially when it took on another entangled thread.

Huguette had cheated death—the Clarks had unused passenger tickets on the *Titanic*—but the Grim Reaper finally caught up with her at age 105. Her casket lay in the Clark family tomb in the Bronx, where she was united with Andrée and her parents. After her relatives, descendants from William's first marriage, learned the lifelong Francophile had left them nary a franc of her five-hundred-million-dollar estate, they claimed that when she had signed her final will, she was, to paraphrase the words of King Lear, "not in [her] perfect mind." They cited her obvious preference for a hospital room instead of Gatsby-worthy mansions and launched a *j'accuse!* lawsuit against her accountant, Irving Kamsler; Kamsler had once been known in AOL chat rooms as a former prisoner with the user name "IRV1040" and was a registered sex offender after having been caught in an Internet sex sting. Her attorney, Wallace Bock, had accepted Mrs. Clark's gift of a dollhouse worth more than ten thousand dollars for his granddaughter, and after the September 11 attacks, Huguette had donated $1.5 million for a security system to the settlement in Israel in which Bock's daughter and her family lived. Another accusing finger was pointed at her Filipino nurse, Hadassah Peri, who was, thanks to her employer, the beneficiary of a bequest of thirty-nine million dollars, several homes, a Lincoln, a Hummer, and a Bentley.

Her estranged family painted Huguette as a madwoman whose attic was a hospital room, while others viewed her as a Boo Radley who preferred to be shut away from a hurtful world. No one can know what lay in the ghostly heart of Madame Clark. However, the closest autographical glimpse was when she shared her favorite eighteenth-century French fable: its moral was that it was better to live unobtrusively as a cricket than glamorously as a butterfly. In the end, the only ones who truly mourned Huguette's passing were those of the unblinking, non-judgmental eyes, the possessors of porcelain faces.

Chapter 7

King Midas's Granddaughter (1912)

One American heiress would have fared far better if she had learned the lesson of the British Fab Four's lyric, "I don't care too much for money, money can't buy me love." What her fortune did buy was false friends, materialistic husbands, and a life punctuated with sorrow.

The quintessential poor little rich girl, Barbara Hutton, was born in New York, the granddaughter of Franklin Winfield Woolworth. The son of a poor potato farmer, his five-and-dime empire (the Walmart of its era) made him one of the world's wealthiest men. His eponymous skyscraper, the first on the New York skyline, was paid for in cash, and for many years it had the distinction of being the tallest in the world. During its opening extravaganza, a reporter overheard the following exchange: "How did he do it?" one charwoman asked another. Her response, "With your dime and mine." His stratospheric fortune was not able to slay his daughter Edna's demons, and she poisoned herself in despair over her husband's philandering. Barbara, at age five, stumbled upon her mother's lifeless body in their suite at the Plaza. The death deprived the child of maternal love while bequeathing her one-third of a sixty-million-dollar inheritance, one billion dollars in contemporary currency. The suicide thrust the little Woolworth heiress into the headlines, and for the rest of her life, she remained a tabloid staple. She lived in a gilded cage of bodyguards, servants, nannies, and private railroad cars. Her father, who preferred gambling and womanizing, was mostly an absent figure, and she grew up plump, reticent, and lonely. Various relatives took her in, and she lived for a period with her aunt, cereal heiress Marjorie Merriweather Post.

Although shy, she wasted no time in pouncing on any object or person that caught her fancy. At age seventeen, she was emotionally needy and seduced her tennis pro instructor and then her bodyguard. Later conquests included a one-night stand with James Dean who declined her offer of becoming her boy toy and living in unimaginable luxury. He told her, "I'm the wrong guy for you. I can never belong to anybody, even myself." She had a longer liaison with one of the world's richest men, Howard Hughes, of whom she remarked, "The charming thing about Howard is that he isn't charming." Ok.

At age eighteen, Ms. Hutton had her debutante party, and the glittering guests included the Astors, the Rockefellers, and stars such as Maurice Chevalier. The price tag for the affair was eighty thousand dollars, an unimaginable extravagance for 1930, the year after the Wall Street crash. Twelve million people were out of work, and thousands of women toiled for a pittance at Woolworths. The salesgirls went on strike, picketing outside the swanky Pierre Hotel where Hutton had a suite of rooms. They held placards contrasting their lives with Barbara's. The public viewed the extravaganza as the French version of, "Let them eat cake." The heiress responded, "Do people realize I have no more to do with running the Woolworth stores than I have [with] the running of the British Empire?" When Barbara publicly stated, "Living well is the best revenge," it hurt the retail behemoth. Customers were reluctant to spend their hard-earned nickels at a business that had such an unsympathetic figure as its prow. She became the object of further ire when she renounced her American citizenship in a move calculated to lessen her taxes. Later, during World War II, in an effort to save the life of a one-time lover and future husband, she sent money to fascist contacts in Europe that led the FBI to investigate the heiress as a Nazi sympathizer.

The venue for the ball was Manhattan's Ritz-Carlton, and Barbara's doting but distant grandfather arranged for it to be an affair to remember. The glittering soiree entailed four orchestras, two hundred waiters, and two thousand bottles of champagne, Prohibition notwithstanding. Never one to skimp— the Woolworth patriarch had installed a two-million-dollar pink marble stairway in his sixty-two-room home, Winfield Hall— there were one thousand seven-course midnight dinners. The press compared the occasion to the maiden voyage of the *Titanic*. A year later, British society hosted the heiress when she visited the Court of St. James.

In 1932, the actor David Niven met the walking Fort Knox and described the twenty-year-old Barbara as "a petite, snub-nosed blond, very pretty American girl... She was a gay and sparking creature, full of life and laughter." In 1965, Paul Bowes visited Barbara in her estate in Tangiers and said, "Her complexion was powdery, and her arms were as thin as toothpicks. She had difficulty remembering the names of all her husbands." She was also forty-two million dollars poorer, several times divorced, and addicted to Coca-Cola and drugs. What happened to the five-and-dime princess in thirty-three years? What had transformed the storied life that had included masquerades in Venice, tangoes in Tangiers, and diamonds as big as the Ritz?

Barbara took the well-worn path of American heiresses who trade their wealth for titles and left for Europe on the prowl for a blue blood. On the continent, she fell for a Russian royal, Prince Alexis Mdivani. Her father felt the prince was hungry for the Hutton bank account. He sent his daughter on a trip around the world to discourage the romance, but Mdivani followed her to Bangkok. "It's going to be fun being a princess," the twenty-year-old bride exclaimed before the civil ceremony in Paris. It wasn't. Five years later, after lavishing two million dollars on hubby, the heiress and the prince divorced in Reno. Barbara married other titled men: Count Kurt Haugwitz Reventlow of Denmark, Prince Igor Troubetzkoy of Lithuania, and Baron Gottfried Von Cramm of Germany, an international tennis star. In between, Ms. Hutton sandwiched in a three-year term of wedlock to Hollywood film star Cary Grant, a union the press dubbed "Cash n' Cary." Unlike the others, he never asked for money as good-bye payola. She gave him his walking papers on the grounds of mental cruelty; namely, he was more interested in his career than in her. Barbara claimed Grant was the husband she loved the most. With the departure of Grant, she stated, "My money has never brought me happiness. You can't buy love with money." Grant's take on the marriage was, "Barbara surrounded herself with a consortium of fawning parasites—European titles, broken-down Hollywood types, a maharaja or two, a sheik, the military, several English peers, and a few tennis bums. If one more phony earl had entered the house, I'd have suffocated."

One of her most colorful spouses was the notorious playboy Porfirio Rubirosa; perhaps he had a surfeit of pheromones, as he had previously tied the knot with Doris Duke. Their 1953 nuptial was held amidst Zsa Zsa Gabor's proclamation that he would really have liked to jilt Hutton for her. While the new Mrs. Rubirosa took the slight with a smile, the marriage broke down in three months. The marriage cost Hutton a string of polo ponies, a Dominican Republic coffee plantation, and a plane; what she gained was public humiliation. After the demise of her sixth marriage, she declared it was her last, "You can't go on being a fool forever." But in 1947, she again took vows with Prince Troubetzkoy. Ill health plagued her during their time together, and she underwent major surgery for a kidney ailment and an intestinal disorder. Like her others, the union collapsed, and in 1951, she obtained a divorce in Paris. Despite all her disappointments, hope sprang eternal. She said, "I've had happiness, and I'll have it again."

In between the weddings and the beddings, there was the shopping. The black belt of consumption acquired a jaw-dropping collection of jewelry made with historical connotations that added panache. Some of her gems had belonged to Marie Antoinette and Empress Eugenie of France; others hailed from the House of Fabergé and Cartier. The forty-carat Pasha Diamond was a pièce de résistance; after Barbara's passing, Sotheby's auctioned many of her possessions in multimillion-dollar bids. She treated upmarket jewelers Cartier, Asprey, Van Cleef, and Arpels the way other people treated her grandfather's five-and-dime stores. Hutton's archrival was Doris Duke, and the two spent their lives in a high-society claw fest. Barbara was by far the freer spending of the two—she referred to her rival as cheap—and Hutton never turned her back on an indulgence. On one occasion, spying a large rock crystal chandelier in Doris's home, actor Errol Flynn quipped, "Doris, what are you doing with one of Barbara's earrings?" The Gold-Dust twins, as they were known, were fascinated by psychics and faith healers; big-dame hunters pursued them from Hawaii to Hollywood to the Riviera. Barbara's generosity also outweighed Doris's. Nobody who met Hutton walked away the poorer; how she loved to shower others with the Woolworth fountain.

To salve her marital wounds, Barbara traveled to exotic locales and acquired a number of luxurious homes. She spent the equivalent of twenty million pounds on building Winfield House in London's Regent Park (now the US ambassador's residence). Another exquisite property was a sixteenth century, fifteen-room palace called Sidi Hosi in Tangier, Morocco. Hutton filled her real estate trophy with Middle Eastern art and

antiques, including a million-dollar jewel-encrusted tapestry.
As she craved company, her home was the venue of legendary
parties; her guests were European aristocrats. Ever restless,
Hutton changed abodes even more rapidly than husbands.
The only constant in Barbara's life was her only child, Lance,
born in London, the son of the Danish count. After his birth,
the Countess developed serious health problems, and the boy
became the rope in a tug-of-war custody battle. Heavily guarded
during his childhood because of the threat of kidnapping, he
inherited a fortune when he turned twenty-one. He married
Cheryl Holdridge, a former Walt Disney Mouseketeer in 1964,
after his divorce from actress Jill St. John.

Barbara's later years were a dizzying downward descent. Lonely
and in ill health, she took to self-medicating with alcohol and
drugs, and as with her shopping, she did so on a grand scale.
She had experimented in her teens with the barbiturate-based
tranquilizer Seconal, along with her cohort in experimentation,
her cousin Jimmy Donahue. His claim to infamy was although he
was a practicing homosexual, he had an affair with the Duchess
of Windsor that led an acquaintance to quip, "She married a
king, but screwed a queen."

Despite her half dozen failed attempts at wedded bliss, loneliness
led to husband number seven. She stated of the marital
conundrum, "All the unhappiness in my life has been caused by
men. I think I'm pretty timid about marriage, but I'm also too
timid to live alone, and life doesn't make sense without men."
Her final rendezvous at the altar was in 1964; it was also her
most exotic. She became the Princess Doan Vinh Na Champassak
in a civil ceremony at her walled estate near Cuernavaca, Mexico.
The Laotian prince, a painter and a chemist, was three years his
wife's junior. Miss Hutton, her son at her side, wore a green and

gold sari type gown, a gold ring on each big toe, and gold anklets. The soles of her feet were painted red. When they separated late in 1966, there was talk of a four-million-dollar parting gift. Old habits die hard. The prince said, "She gave me more than four million dollars. She gave me love." A more visceral loss was Lance, who was by then a daredevil racecar driver and died in 1972 at age thirty-six in the crash of a small plane in Colorado.

Of all her palatial residences, Barbara's Sunset Boulevard was the penthouse of the Beverly Wilshire Hotel. Her former beauty—that Doris Duke had so envied—was no more. Miss Hutton, who had been termed "fat as butter" during her teens, had spent a lifetime in strenuous dieting; in lieu of a healthy diet, she subsisted on cases of Coca-Cola mixed with alcohol, usually vodka, as well as intravenous megavitamin shots laced with amphetamines, supplemented with a cocktail of drugs including codeine, Valium, and morphine. A cataract surgery had left her with impaired vision, and a fall in Rome had left her with a damaged hip. Retainers carried her everywhere. The quintessential poor little rich girl, now bedridden and alone, died of a heart attack in the penthouse of the Beverly Wilshire Hotel. In her once too-great-to-be-real bank account, there remained $3,500. In a further disconnect from her glittering former life, the mortuary referred to her as Barbara Doan.

Barbara's final resting place was the Woolworth family vault in New York's Woodlawn Cemetery which houses the McMansions of the dead. The pharaoh of the five-and-dime constructed a marble Egyptian themed mausoleum whose pillared entrance is guarded by stone sphinxes.

Although Woolworth's tomb is a nod to ancient Egypt, metaphorically he was a modern King Midas. As a boy, his greatest desire had been for wealth, yet when he achieved his dream, as with his mythological counterpart, it brought desolation in its wake. Barbara Hutton, as King Midas's granddaughter, paid a high price.

Chapter 8

Lucky Strike
(1912)

The Duchess of Windsor famously observed that a woman can never be too rich or too thin. The formula seemed to have worked for her as a king renounced his crown on her behalf. And yet, money can come with a hefty price tag.

When the fifty-four-year-old tobacco tsar James Buchanan Duke was on the threshold of becoming a father, he summoned twenty-four doctors and a battalion of nurses to his five-story Fifth Avenue mansion, Manhattan's grandest. *The New York Times* heralded Doris's arrival with a headline: "The Million Dollar Baby." The words were a jeweled cross she would bear all the days of her life. Her doting dad raised Doris in a cosseted cocoon, one far removed from his modest North Carolina roots. His cigarette empire cornered the market, and his little girl's shoes bore her name embossed in gold leaf; she wore coats of mink, sable, and ermine that hung in room-sized closets. Even Doris's dolls sported designer dresses. The child had a number of hired retainers: a nanny, maid, laundress, nurses, three bodyguards, and a chauffeur for her own Rolls Royce. Her bedroom walls displayed original Gainsborough paintings; when Duke first saw the painting *Blue Boy*, he was disappointed to discover the artist had died and could not paint a portrait of his darling daughter. In contrast, the air hung heavy with the odor of ammonia as her father was a germophobe. Birthdays parties were extravaganzas at the family's 2,700-acre New Jersey estate, Duke Farms, where an entire circus, replete with clowns, acrobats, and elephants, performed.

While the public marveled at the Dukes' storied lifestyle, the little princess nursed secret sorrow. Her mother, Nanaline, though not the stuff of which a Disney villainess is made, held her at arm's length. She never formed an emotional attachment to Doris, though she remained devoted to Iman Walker, her wastrel son from her former marriage. Doris recalled, "I would look at the way she caressed her furs and diamonds and wish she felt the same way about me." Duke's fear of kidnapping threats, along with Nanaline's insistence that her daughter only associate with the bluest blood types, cultivated a breeding ground of isolation. Doris was even alienated from her retinue; Nanaline had observed that the servants of European royalty did not speak to their employers, and it became a rule she reinforced in her Fifth Avenue fiefdom. The tobacco tycoon passed away when Doris was twelve, and the last three words he whispered to her from his deathbed were: "Trust no one." That advice, along with her mother's prediction that no one would ever look at her without seeing her bank account, darkened her days.

Although James Duke had made one of the world's great fortunes on a product that contributed to the scourge of lung cancer, he also used his wealth for philanthropy and bequeathed Trinity College in North Carolina forty million dollars. In appreciation, the school changed its name to Duke University, and at his interment, the students formed an honor guard; its football team acted as pallbearers. The main beneficiary of his will was Doris, who inherited one billion dollars in today's currency, making her the most celebrated heiress in American history. In contrast, his "grieving" widow—there were rumors she had hastened his demise—received a stipend of $100,000 a year. The financial situation altered the mother-daughter dynamic; when Nanaline attempted to sell Duke Farms, a teenaged Doris successfully sued. She loved the home where she dined on one hundred thousand gold place settings and bathed in marble tubs with water that flowed from gold spigots. In the same year, when visiting Rough Point, her thirty-room summer "cottage" in Newport, Rhode Island, she told a reporter, "I am no different from anyone else. Really."

At age eighteen, Doris was one of nine American debutantes, along with Campbell soup heiress Charlotte Dorrance, presented at Buckingham Palace to King George V and Queen Mary. Doris distinguished herself both by her fortune and her towering height of six feet one inch. Men on both sides of the Atlantic were entranced by her blue-green eyes, her wavy blonde hair, and her fabulous fortune. Gold-diggers viewed her as a walking Fort Knox.

Doris felt a walk down the aisle would free her from the grasp of her mother, furnish her with the male affection she had lost with her father's death, and satiate her ravenous carnality. She later remarked, "Every member of the Duke family is oversexed. It's in the genes. The government should test our chromosomes." At age twenty-two, Doris married Jimmy Cromwell, sixteen years her senior, whose first wife had been Delphine Dodge, heiress to the automobile dynasty. The venue was the library of the Fifth Avenue Duke mansion, because in it Doris felt the presence of her father, who could give her away in spirit. Had the room really served as the setting for a séance, it would have reverberated with the words "Trust no one." The ten-minute proceeding was traditional with the exception that Doris had stricken the word "obey" from her vows; afterwards, the Cromwells embarked on their honeymoon—an eleven-month world cruise. The bride's dreams of marital bliss dissipated on her wedding night as she waited in her negligee, and Jimmy, rather than engage in impassioned lovemaking, inquired as to what he could expect as his annual income. She told him to go to hell, and he left for the ship's bar. Jimmy's sexual disinterest may have stemmed from his preference for a partner who did not share his wife's anatomy. To deflect blame, he pointed a finger at his wife and called her a sexual Frigidairess; for her part, Doris's opinion of Cromwell was, "Jimmy was no endowment. He wasn't even a

small annuity." The heiress loved seeing the world—especially
the Taj Mahal—but said she would have traded it "for a good
romp." The newlyweds had an audience with Gandhi, and, in
comparison to the Mahatma, Jimmy appeared an even more
pompous fool. On their honeymoon, Doris fell out of love with
her husband and fell in love with Diamond Head, Hawaii. She
purchased five acres overlooking the Pacific and built a home
she christened Shangri-La after the mythical kingdom in *Lost
Horizon*, one where no one ever grew old. The ocean lapped
against the estate's Moorish steps, ceiling-high goldfish tanks
graced the walls, and two stone camels stood guard by its front
door. To make up for the lack of marital passion, Doris, who had
a black belt in shopping, acquired endless luxury items.

As the mistress of her own home, Doris began an affair with
Hawaiian surfing legend Duke Kahanamoku; she later said one
Duke taught her about love and another taught her how to make
love. When she left the island, she became romantically involved
with Errol Flynn in Los Angeles and started another liaison with
an aristocratic Member of Parliament in London. In 1939, the
wages of her carnality were pregnancy. She understood that
the child, although it was Duke's and not Cromwell's, would
result in a lifelong tie with a man she despised. In New York, she
underwent an illegal abortion. A year later, she again became
pregnant and in Honolulu gave birth to her daughter, Arden,
who survived for twenty-four hours. The doctors informed Doris
that due to complications, she would never again give birth.

The loss left a gaping wound, one she could not fill by material
acquisition, by innumerable sexual partners, or by making it
onto the world's best-dressed list—she was second behind the
Duchess of Windsor. The fashion house kings—Balenciaga, Dior,
and Givenchy—personally created her couturier outfits. In 1940,

the debutante turned undercover agent and went by the code name Daisy. She had named herself after the leggy Daisy Mae Yokum from the Li'l Abner cartoon. The position introduced her to General George Patton with whom she had a sexcapade on the Russian front; she claimed his polished leather boots aroused her. "Daisy" spent four days with "Georgie" at a chateau that had once belonged to Emperor Franz Joseph of Austria. She mentioned that the general was as powerful in the boudoir as he was on the battlefield. However, as Patton had a wife and several mistresses, Doris was again on the prowl. In Rome in 1945, she told a journalist, "All that money is a problem sometimes. After I've gone out with a man a few times, he starts to tell me how much he loves me. How can I ever be sure?"

In Italy, Doris met the Dominican Don Juan Porfirio Rubirosa, a Trujillo political assassin turned playboy, owner of a legendary anatomical advantage. Along the Riviera, he was known as "toujours prêt"—"Mr. Ever Ready." To this day, "Rubirosas" are what Parisian waiters call their pepper mills. Doris bought another big-ticket item when she paid "Rubi's" actress wife a million dollars to leave him, and a sexually sated Doris remarked it had been worth every penny. A biographer wrote, "He kept her well-laid and she kept him well-paid." Doris's editor, Carmel Snow, for whom Doris worked during a stint at *Harper's Bazaar* at a salary of fifty dollars a week, arranged for a prenup when Doris tied the knot with her Latin lover, since Ms. Snow was well aware of Rubirosa's reputation as a fortune hunter. While Doris's first marriage had lasted seven years, her second—despite the magnificent member—was a mere one year in duration. Cromwell had received nothing in his divorce from Doris, in contrast to Rubirosa who walked away with an annual allowance equivalent to $2,250,000, a coffee plantation, a string of polo ponies, several race cars, and a Paris mansion. He later married

Barbara Hutton, heiress to the Woolworth fortune; he met his end when his Ferrari crashed into a tree.

Doris used to say that you can't buy a person, but you sure can rent one for a while. And rent them she did. The heiress became the nonfictional *Forrest Gump* who interacted with the famous. She fraternized with First Ladies: toured with Eleanor Roosevelt, dined with Jacqueline Kennedy, and "loaned" Imelda Marcos five million dollars. The designer-dressed heiress met celebrities Elizabeth Taylor, Elvis Presley, and Greta Garbo—"the most boring woman in the world"—and held court with Andy Warhol in Studio 54. Doris hobnobbed with Citizen Hearst and the movie crowd in San Simeon Saudi, and arms dealer Adrian Khashoggi gave her a gift of two camels she named Princess and Baby. When Newport officials explained having them on her lawn violated a city ordinance, she moved them indoors, where camel dung soiled her precious Persian carpets. She said of her pets, "The only real love I ever had was from my father and my animals." Doris also added to her real estate jewels when she purchased Rudolph Valentino's former home, Falcon's Lair, from Gloria Swanson. Duke Ellington jammed in its velvet-lined music room; at Duke Farms, Martha Graham gave Doris private dance lessons, and in her Park Avenue penthouse, she unsuccessfully tried to seduce Rudolph Nureyev. One person with whom she never socialized was her estranged mother. All contact had been broken off when Nanaline told Doris her biological father had in actuality been her Nordic butler. In 1966, a devastating incident occurred; Doris accidentally caused the death of her friend Eduardo Tirella after her car slammed him against the gate on Rough Point. The inquest cleared the heiress of his death but left her traumatized and reclusive.

In 1988, a desperately lonely and poorly aging Doris adopted
Chandi Heffner, thirty-five, a belly dancer and former adherent
of the Hare Krishna religious group whom she had met at a
dance class in Hawaii. Doris felt Chandi was the reincarnation of
Arden, her lost little girl. Maternal feelings ended in 1991 when
Duke sought to disinherit Chandi amidst concern she was trying
to poison Duke to hasten her access to her promised inheritance.
Doris bitterly declared the adoption the biggest mistake of her
life. The hurt engendered by the episode was the final blow in a
life devoted to looking for love in all the wrong places.

In later life, Doris desperately desired the eternal youth promised
by Shangri-La. Her fortune bought her estates, husbands, and
lovers, but the Beatles had it right: "Money can't buy you love."
In a nod to the butler-did-it trope, when Doris died at Falcon
Lair, suspicion fell on Doris's Jeeves, one Bernard Lafferty, a
ponytailed, pill-popping alcoholic Irish butler with a penchant
for Cartier, Giorgio Armani, alcohol, and male lovers. The
caregiver refused to take her to Duke Hospital and may have
expedited her demise—in cahoots with her physician—with
an overdose of morphine injections. Lafferty had her body
immediately cremated; there was no autopsy. In a suspicious
twist, before her passing, she had left him five million dollars
as well as a five-million-dollar annual stipend as executor of
her $1.2 billion estate. In order to avoid a legal entanglement,
Chandra Heffner received sixty-five million dollars.

Despite all her riches, Doris once revealed, "I am living proof that
money cannot buy friendship." Despite her father's deathbed
warning, Doris failed to be careful who she trusted. The tobacco

heiress, who enjoyed splendor—from champagne to camels—was a tragic figure; like those of the source of her wealth, her dreams of fulfillment went up in smoke. The name of the cigarette that paved the way for her destiny can serve as an ironic metaphor for her life—*Lucky Strike.*

Chapter 9

Round Midnight (1913)

While viewing the Palatial Chateau Ferrières outside Paris, Wilhelm I commented, "Kings couldn't afford this. It could only belong to a Rothschild!" The anecdote illustrates the wealth of the family whose coffers surpass that of royalty. In a move that shocked others in her milieu, one of the dynasty's daughters turned her back on her rarified life, seduced by a siren song.

The Rothschild family rose from ghetto dwellers to be Europe's power elite when their banks financed monarchs and governments. The dynasty's coat of arms is an eagle whose talons clutch five golden arrows, each representative of one of founder Mayer Rothschild's sons, who established branches of the family bank in Frankfurt, London, Paris, Vienna, and Naples. Nathaniel Charles Rothschild, known by his middle name, was a nineteenth-century British heir who married Baroness Rozsika Edie von Wertheimstein, daughter of a Transylvanian baron. Their home, Tring Park (now Waddesdon Manor), was the crown jewel among half a dozen ostentatious country estates. Charles worked in his London bank where he felt as attached to his work as Sisyphus did to his rock. Although he did not have to pursue gainful employment and would have much rather indulged his obsession with insects, he subscribed to the Rothschild motto: *Concordia, integritas, industria*, or "Unity, integrity, industry." Rozsika enjoyed her role as chatelaine of the grand estate and as mother to children Nathaniel Mayer Victor (called Victor), Miriam Louisa, Elizabeth Charlotte (nicknamed Liberty), and their youngest, Pannonica. Although she claimed her name derived from a species of butterfly, Charles had christened her after a rare Hungarian moth. In either contingency, she was known as Nica.

Within the hallowed walls of the Rothschild manor, footmen carried cherry trees to the table so that the family might have fruit straight from the branch, and an army of servants catered to their every whim. If the walls could have talked, they would have testified to its owner's eccentricities; on its endless acres, emus, giant tortoises, and kangaroos roamed. Charles's brother Victor liked to water-ski in a Schiaparelli silk dressing gown; another brother, Walter, drove a team of six zebras.

Life in Tring Park was not all wine, roses, and cherry trees. Charles suffered from a mood disorder and alternated from not speaking for days to being unable to stop talking. In 1923, he locked himself in a bathroom and slit his throat. Liberty shared his psychological demons and lived under a cloud of schizophrenia. Nica became the wild child and sneaked friends into Tring's attic where they indulged in wine-soaked revels. Rozsika sent her daughter to a Parisian finishing school to tame her wild ways, but it did not have the desired result. The teen claimed lascivious "wig-wearing lesbian sisters" ran the place.

Nica did find something to her liking when a London musician piqued her interest in flying; by age twenty-one, she had her pilot's license and her own plane. Despite her nonconformity, she agreed to a debutante party—an event attended by Winston Churchill—where the beautiful heiress dazzled in strings of emeralds and diamonds. Restless, Nica felt she existed in a gilded cage, a waiting room for her future as a society matron and mother.

Three years later, Nica met Baron Jules de Koenigswarter, a French-Jewish diplomat, at Le Touquet airfield in France. He was smitten as he watched her alight from her plane which she had just flown across the English Chanel. On their first date, he took her straight from lunch for a flight in his Leopard Moth aircraft. At thirty-one, he was a decade older, a widower with a son, but they bonded over their mutual love of aviation. Although the Koenigswarters were not in the same stratosphere as the Rothschilds (who was?), he possessed sufficient credentials—one being his ability to put up with Nica—and her family approved the match. Three months later, they were married in New York City, and immediately after the ceremony, the bride headed to Harlem's Savoy Ballroom. The couple took up residence in Chateau d'Abondant, a seventeenth-century mansion, where they raised their children, Patrick and Janka, who were mainly left in the care of nannies. The baron was controlling, but Nica was used to that from her parents. She transformed into the prototype of a dynastic matriarch, with her days filled with choosing daily menus, managing her extensive staff, and acting as hostess to distinguished guests.

Life continued in this metronomic fashion until the Nazis were on the verge of goose-stepping into France, prompting Jules to join de Gaulle's Free French forces in the Congo. Although Nica was a prime target as both a Jew and a Rothschild, she refused to leave until 1940 when she took the last train out of Paris. The move most likely saved her life as the baron's mother, his extended family, and Rozsika's Hungarian relatives all perished in the Holocaust. Nica was drawn into the war effort, and after depositing her children with the Guggenheim family on Long Island, she took passage on a Norwegian freighter and joined her husband in the resistance.

With the defeat of Germany, the baron entered the French diplomatic service, and they lived first in Norway and then Mexico. The couple had three more children: Berit, Shaun, and Kari, but without the romance and adrenaline of war, the marriage floundered. She did not fit comfortably into the role of an ambassador's wife and was often absent or late for official dinners. The baron retaliated by smashing her records, and the children were lulled to sleep by the sound of smashing vinyl and servants gossiping about the goings-on. In the hope that absence would make the heart grow fonder, Nica left for a vacation in Manhattan, a city with which she felt kinship.

The baroness was on the way to the airport to return to Mexico from New York when she paid a visit to her brother's music tutor, jazz pianist Teddy Wilson. He inadvertently altered her destiny when he played a recording of Thelonious Monk, the high priest of bebop. For Nica, the music illuminated the darkness; it spoke of freedom. Enthralled, she played the record twenty times and missed her flight. Instead of catching another, she rented a suite at the Stanhope Hotel on Fifth Avenue, where, to the management's dismay, she kept an open house for impoverished African American musicians—social pariahs in that period. This situation did not sit well with the hotel's segregationist policies. However, her illustrious name, blue blood title, and bottomless pockets made them turn a deaf ear. Never one for slumming, Nica bought a blue Bentley, sported a leopard-skin coat, and drank Chivas Regal from a flask. She became a fixture in Greenwich Village nightclubs where alcohol and cigarettes were acceptable; what was not acceptable was jazz and jazz musicians. In 1954, discovering Monk was in Paris, she flew to meet her idol and declared he was the most beautiful man she had ever seen.

Nica became the patron of the struggling musicians and raised eyebrows as she broke time-honored taboos of race, religion, and class. The highest raised eyebrow of all was from Jules, who was infuriated with Nica's lifestyle which he considered not seemly for a mother, diplomat's wife, or for a Rothschild. Nevertheless, anxious to avoid a scandal, and as his wife was an heiress, he fumed in silence until an event forced his hand.

In 1955, saxophone genius and heroin junkie Charlie "Bird" Parker arrived at Nica's suite, desperately ill, with no other place to go. Although she understood the impropriety of letting him stay, as a Jewish refugee from Hitler, she did not consider sending him away. While watching a variety show on television, he died on her sofa. Although there had been no foul play or romantic involvement, in the 1950s the fact that a black jazz musician had died in a blue blood residence sent the press into a feeding frenzy. One headline ran: Bird in the Baroness's Boudoir. The Rothschilds were aghast and, metaphorically, aimed the five heraldic golden arrows in her direction. Koenigswarter filed for divorce and in a classic understatement said, "Jazz didn't do my marriage any good." He received custody of the children, a judgment Nica did not contest. After hearing Monk's recording, she realized she had to break with her former "bullshit" life. The incident also severed her ties with the Stanhope, and she relocated to the Algonquin. When that hotel likewise did not prove to be a lasting love connection, she bought a house in New Jersey with a fabulous view of the Manhattan skyline, the former residence of Marlene Dietrich's husband, film director Josef von Sternberg. Her home, Catville, was so called because of the "jazz cats" who flopped on her couches as well as the residency of no fewer than 306 felines, all named after musicians. Many had been strays who Nica had rescued by scooping them up in the Behop Bentley; she had also used it in a drag race with Miles Davis down Seventh Avenue. With her typical humor, Nica described Catville as "the only house on the block without a For Sale sign."

As the patron saint of jazz musicians and because of her relationship with Thelonious—whose parents had christened him after a Benedictine monk—Nica became renowned as the bebop baroness. And, just as her father had been obsessed with insects,

the unstable Monk became the great project of her life. She paid
his bills and put up with his drug addictions and schizophrenia.
In appreciation, he immortalized her in his songs, ones that
were slated to define their era. However, her quick action during
an incident on the way to a performance in Delaware proved to
be the true measure of her devotion. In 1955, the spectacle of a
white woman and a black man in the South driving in a Bentley
caught the eye of a trooper, who pulled them over. During a
search of the car, the officer discovered marijuana in the trunk,
and in the ensuing fracas, the police treated Thelonious as a
punching bag. Although the contraband belonged to Monk, Nica,
aware that a conviction would mean the loss of his cabaret card
which allowed him to perform, served as the scapegoat, claiming
it was hers. She spent the night in jail and received a three-year
sentence that the court dismissed on a technicality.

For twenty-eight years, Nica catered to the musician's
eccentricities and breakdowns and unstintingly used her
wealth on his behalf. In his last years, his psychological health
deteriorated, exacerbated by marijuana and heroin, and he
took up full-time residence in Nica's Jersey home, along with
a -Steinway piano, a gift from his patroness. She remained
his pillar until his 1982 death; at his funeral, Nica and Monk's
widow, Nellie, sat side-by-side, and mourners paid their respects
to each of them as if they were both widows. They had shared a
triangular relationship, implicitly understanding the larger-than-
life Monk was too much for any one woman. The baroness said of
her idol, "He could make you see the music inside the music."

One of the lingering questions that remains about the enigmatic
baroness was whether she and Monk had been lovers or it had
remained a platonic relationship. On that topic, Nica was for

once circumspect. Monk, when asked about this issue, stated his wife was his "black bitch" and Nica was his "white bitch."

Long estranged from her relatives, Nica's great-niece, Hannah Rothschild, became intrigued with the woman the Rothschilds had expunged from the family tree. Hannah phoned her great-aunt and requested a meeting. "Wild," was Nica's response, "Come to the club downtown after midnight." The seventy-one-year-old baroness was adorned with a pearl necklace and a magnificent fur coat—symbols of the life she had left behind—as she held court, a ravaged version of her former beauty. She was smoking a cigarette in a long, black filter and drinking whiskey from a chipped china cup. In answer to Hannah's question of *Why*, Nica, swaying to the music, replied, "Remember, there is only one life."

During the heyday of bebop, Nica had produced a volume entitled *Three Wishes: An Intimate Look at Jazz Greats*, a collection of photographs compiled of the musicians in their off-hours. Alongside the snapshots were the responses to the baroness's question: "If you were given three wishes to be instantly granted, what would they be?" Miles Davis's was, "To be white!" Pianist Sonny Clark's was, "All the bitches in the world," in contrast to Thelonious Monk's, "To have a crazy friend like you." If Nica had included her own portrait, she would not have needed to pen her wish—her life was the fulfillment of her dream. The rebel Rothschild remains a mysterious figure, as hauntingly elusive as the bebop ballads she worshipped.

Pannonica Rothschild passed away in 1988 from a heart attack, and her final request was for her ashes to be scattered over Catville. She specified the time of ceremony to be held for the occasion—which was also the name of the recording that had changed her life: "Around Midnight."

Chapter 10

She and Trouble (1920)

When the Tin Man made his request, the Wizard of Oz tried to dissuade him with the admonition, "Hearts will never be practical until they can be made unbreakable." Nevertheless, Dorothy's companion persisted as he understood having a heart—for all its residual pain—is what makes existence bearable. The simple woodcutter understood a lesson a haughty queen never fathomed.

The woman who scoffed at the notion all men are created equal, Leona Mindy Rosenthal, was born on the Fourth of July in Brooklyn. Her parents, Russian/Polish Jewish immigrants, struggled to support their four children on father Morris's job as a hatmaker. When the Depression hit, Morris sent Leona to live with her uncle for six months, an experience that left her with a feeling of abandonment. Leona took an after-school job selling Eskimo Pies in Coney Island; as a teen, she quit Hunter College in the pursuit of her definition of happiness—financial independence. She changed her name to Leona Roberts to bypass anti-Semitism and allegedly modeled for Chesterfield cigarettes.

In 1940, caving into parental pressure, she married attorney Leo Panzirer and moved to Flatbush where she had her only child, Jay Robert Panzirer. The couple divorced in 1950, and then she married, divorced, and then remarried businessman Joe Lubin. Although wedlock allowed her to move to a six-room apartment in Riverdale, New York, despite their two attempts, it did not provide lasting holy matrimony. Leona, finding herself in the unenviable position of a single mother with no independent means, moved in with her mother. In a bid to better herself, Leona took a job at a New York real estate firm where she became one of the city's most successful female agents and managed to sell something other than just primo properties.

Leona's coup was landing Harry Helmsley, the King Kong owner of the Empire State Building and other crown jewels of Manhattan. Accounts of their meeting vary. Leona's version was that she met her future husband when he "heard of my reputation," and she said when he called, she had told him with characteristic chutzpah, "You can't afford me, I'm in a bad bracket now." A more plausible scenario is Leona, girded with mascara-caked eyelashes, prowled for Helmsley at a 1969 industry dinner at the Waldorf-Astoria. Harry Helmsley, in his sixth decade, had amassed two passions: business and waltzing. At work, he was a dull number cruncher in a nondescript suit, but in a tuxedo on the dance floor, he was a stooped Fred Astaire. His handicap was Eve, his retiring Quaker wife, who preferred to remain home in Westchester County. Soon Leona and Harry were dancing to "Raindrops Keep Fallin' on My Head," and like Eliza Doolittle, Leona could have danced all night.

Weeks later, Leona was ensconced in a Helmsley holding, Gallery House, that doubled as an upscale love nest. In matters of real estate, Harry had no peer; in matters of the heart, he was a babe in the woods. Nevertheless, as he was still not ready to leave his wife of thirty-three years, Leona let slip that a man in Georgia had sent her a diamond ring—and had given her an ultimatum she had ten days to answer his proposal. Harry responded on bended, arthritic knee, and in 1972, the Helmsleys tied the knot in his grandiose penthouse with its view of Central Park and Harry's new Park Lane Hotel. At the age of fifty-two, Leona Mindy Rosenthal from Flatbush was a bona fide billionaire. For their honeymoon, they cruised to Cannes on a 136-foot yacht, where Leona realized her fantasy of standing aboard a ship with her chiffon gown billowing in the wind.

While the old song states, "First comes love, then comes marriage," with Leona, it was the other way around. At the onset of their relationship, it was the endless green that had served as pheromones for her, but Harry turned out to be the only person Leona ever let into her tightly guarded fortress of a heart. The Helmsleys became the first couple of the Big Apple—which was logical, as they owned most of it. They reigned from their ten-thousand-square-foot duplex with a living room on each floor, a swimming pool, a greenhouse, and a terrace with a four-way panoramic spread of Manhattan. They also owned Dunellen Hall, a twenty-eight-room mansion in Connecticut; a lakefront condominium in Palm Beach; and a mountaintop hideaway near Phoenix. A minimum of twelve pictures of Leona were in every room; it is unlikely Morris would have been able to make a hat sufficiently big to fit his daughter's head. To ferry them between their various pleasure domes, a four-million-dollar, one-hundred-seat jet with a private bedroom stood at the ready.

To the Helmsleys' horror, a year after their wedding, a nightmarish episode intruded into their rarified existence. They were in their Palm Beach home when Leona awoke in the dark to find an intruder, wearing a gas mask, in their bedroom. She nudged her husband, "Wake up, darling. We have company." Rather than risk the thief making off with their property, the naked Helmsleys gave chase, and the burglar stabbed both husband and wife. After the home invasion, bodyguards were added to the Helmsley payroll. However, the assault carried one unexpected boon. Jay flew to his mother's side, thereby ending a five-year estrangement. After the reconciliation, Mrs. Helmsley brought him into the empire.

The highlight of the Helmsleys' social calendar was their annual March 4th gala for Henry's birthday, an over-the-top bash where Manhattan's glitterati, including Barbara Walters, Frank Sinatra, Gregory Peck, and Laurence Rockefeller—minus rival land baron Donald Trump—wore "I'm Just Wild about Harry" buttons and the birthday boy sported his own: "I'm Harry." The power couple adorned their penthouse to create Harry's Bar, overflowing with caviar and champagne; florists festooned the pool with gardenias, and a sixteen-piece orchestra completed the ambience. To its strains, the king and his queen waltzed to the Eubie Blake song referenced on the buttons while Leona mouthed, "And Harry's wild about me." At the witching hour, balloons—emblazoned with the lyric—descended from the ballroom ceiling. In reciprocity, on the bicentennial Fourth of July, Henry lit his Empire State Building in red, white, and blue. His act was not a nod to America's independence, but rather to a far more auspicious occasion—his wife's birthday. He said of the hundred-thousand-dollar cost of the light show that it was cheaper than a diamond necklace. Never shy of PDA, she playfully called him, "My pussy-cat. Snooky, Wooky, Dooky."

As a further love note, Harry christened a new hotel acquisition the "Harley"—a blend of their names. And, if this were not adorable enough, he made his wife a pivotal player in his Helmsley Palace Hotel chain advertising campaign. In a series of ubiquitous ads in *The New York Times*, the Pan Am in-flight magazine *Clipper Travel*, and other glossies, the Missus, sporting a diamond tiara and a gold lamé gown that revealed more than a hint of décolletage, descended a gilded staircase. The caption beside her face-lifted features: "It's the only palace in the world where the queen stands guard." Their hotel's gift shops featured gilt-trimmed playing cards featuring pictures of Her Majesty. Ah, the perks of the one percent.

In private, the grinning monarch was a despot of the
nonbenevolent variety. A perfectionist, she proved a royal pain
and held her army of employees to her exacting standards.
For any infractions, it was her version of, "Off with their
heads!" During her blitzkrieg inspections, she unleashed her
fury on hapless heads—especially homosexual ones—with
tirades composed of the sort of venom which God reserves for
warmongers. Terrified employees devised an alarm system to
alert each other when she left her penthouse on the way to one
of her hotels. A journalist referred to her as "the Lady Macbeth
of the lodging industry." Those who toiled in the boot camp of
Dunnellen Hall fared no better. Friends of a contractor who had
never been paid for installing a thirteen-thousand-dollar custom-
made barbeque said he had six children to support. Leona's
response, "Why didn't he keep his pants on? He wouldn't have
so many problems." These let-them-eat-cake incidents led to the
Helmsleys' dethroning.

Apparently, the country was no longer wild about Harry—and
Harry's wife. Disgruntled employees alerted *The Post* of their
employers' unorthodox habit of charging personal items—a
million-dollar marble dance floor above a swimming pool, a
$130,000 stereo system, a $45,000 silver clock in the shape
of the Helmsley Building, a $210,000 mahogany card table,
and even a twelve-dollar girdle—as hotel operating costs. The
raindrops kept falling on the Gordon Gekko heads when the IRS
charged them with evading $4,000,000 in income taxes. A judge
ruled that Harry, by then debilitated by a series of strokes, was
incompetent to stand trial. In her characteristic manner, Leona
quipped when he appeared with an unzipped fly: "Don't brag,
darling!" So many disgruntled Flying Monkeys queued up to
testify—about everything from withholding wages to cheating
at backgammon—that one man likened the mob to "Yankee

Stadium on the day the World Series tickets go on sale." Mayor Ed Koch called her "the Wicked Witch of the West," and Donald Trump proclaimed she was "a horrible, horrible human being." Leona responded, "I can't wait to read Trump's new book, especially chapter eleven." The most damning courtroom remark came from a maid who claimed Mrs. Helmsley had remarked, "We don't pay taxes. Only the little people pay taxes." The phrase shadowed the hotel magnate for all the remaining days of her life. Leona's defense attorney asked the jurors not to condemn on the criteria of personality, saying, "I don't believe Mrs. Helmsley is charged in the indictment with being a tough bitch." The public warmed itself on a tabloid bonfire built on the pyre of the woman dubbed "the Queen of Mean." Even *Newsweek* captioned her photograph: "Rhymes with Rich." Upon the announcement of a guilty verdict, huzzahs rang from the peasantry, and the police escorted the sobbing Marie Antoinette off to serve twenty-one months. The sentence was carried out on Tax Day: April 15, 1992, the date Leona had to report to prison. On the long lonely nights sans Harry and the Palaces, she must have been visited by her own ghosts of Christmas Past. Although Leona had become Manhattan's punching bag, Harry remained *semper fidelis*— ever faithful. When an interviewer asked what he considered his greatest achievement, he replied, "Marrying Leona." On the night of her incarceration, he ordered the lights turned off in the Empire State Building.

After her 1994 release, as former friends were now not so wild about Harry, the couple became reclusive, mainly residing in their Scottsdale, Arizona, estate. When Harry passed away in 1997, Leona was inconsolable, saying, "My fairy tale is over," and she roamed her huge estates alone. His will left her a property empire that controlled much of the Manhattan skyline. After Jay's passing from a heart attack, her relationship with her daughter-in-law, Mimi Panzirer, soured when Leona evicted her and Leona's own grandson after her son's passing, explaining that the company owned the property and Jay was no longer a Helmsley employee.

Leona had never been a dog lover; she had once told a man his dog Katie would make a nice coat. Since Leona was starved for affection, she purchased a four-pound Maltese she christened Trouble. The puppy left the pet store in a Mercedes Benz stretch limo, and from that point on, one was never seen without the other. The pup was a tiny terror who bit employees and dined on gourmet meals. The princess, as she demanded her pooch be called, prowled the halls with a diamond studded collar around her neck. A second pup, Double Trouble, did not fare as well, and Leona banished him from her empire.

The man behind the curtain in the Emerald City had observed, "A heart is not judged by how much you love but by how much you are loved by others." If the Wizard's words proved prescient, at Leona Helmsley's 2007 passing, ironically due to heart failure, she greatly failed his litmus test. Her will revealed that from her billion-dollar-plus holdings, two grandchildren received ten million, two not a penny, and her later life confidant, a Maltese, was the recipient of twelve million. However, what her last will and testament did not reveal was why the queen had been so mean. Only she knew. She and Trouble.

Chapter 11

Was It Worth It?
(1922)

The Prince of Denmark lashed out at Ophelia for wearing makeup that he equated with female deception, "God has given you one face, and you make yourself another." A twentieth-century cosmetic empire was likewise associated with duplicity that not even its most artful of concealers could camouflage.

Women browse the cosmetic aisles, to capture attention, to recapture youth. Although the major names on the packages are iconic, most customers are unaware of the histories behind the labels. Every time a woman pulls out a compact, she pays silent tribute to Polish Jew Maksymilian Faktorowicz, cosmetician to the Russian royal court, founder of Max Factor. Nineteen-year-old Tom Lyle Williams watched his sister, Mabel, apply Vaseline and coal dust to her eyelashes, and Maybelline was born. And the world's behemoth of a cosmetic company began with Eugene Schueller, the chemist son of a baker. His genius: an instinct for knowing what makes women feel beautiful. In 1907, while experimenting at his kitchen sink in his two-bedroom apartment, he developed the first hair dye that offered a variety of shades, which he christened Aureale—the future L'Oréal. "This little bottle holds a huge industry!" he declared. "One day millions of brunettes will want to be blonde." When a fair-haired Jean Harlow made golden tresses a fad by smoldering in the Hollywood hit *Platinum Blonde*, his prediction proved prescient.

Eugene's pianist wife, Louise, passed away when their only child, Liliane Henriette Charlotte, was five, and as the little girl was jealous of the women who circled around her wealthy father, his affection only extended to his daughter. At age fifteen, Liliane dabbled in the family business as an apprentice, her only hands-on encounter with the business that made her the heir to a fabulous fortune. The company was already a force to be reckoned with and distributed products in seven countries.

Schueller acquired a chic Left Bank apartment and the trappings of wealth. During the Nazi occupation, he also donned the mantle of collaborator in order to enrich his company's coffers; its German headquarters was a confiscated Jewish property. Later Liliane defended her beloved papa with her explanation, "He was a pathological optimist who hadn't the first idea about politics and who always managed to be in the wrong place."

In 1950, Liliane, a great beauty, wed Andre Bettencourt—another man who happened to be in the wrong place. He had worked alongside Schueller in La Cagoule, a virulently anti-Semitic group that busied itself with pastimes such as firebombing synagogues. L'Oréal's' Nazi past sadly answered Ophelia's question in *Hamlet*, "Could beauty, my Lord, have better commerce than with honesty?"

The Bettencourts settled in an Art Moderne mansion in Neuilly-sur-Seine that became a mecca for Paris's beau monde where politicians, financiers, and artists mingled under dazzling chandeliers and priceless art-adorned walls. In this milieu, Liliane and Andre raised a daughter, Francoise, born in 1953. As with her mother before her, an English governess was in charge of her upbringing; Liliane was never close with her daughter and described her as "a cold child." With Andre at its helm, and with Liliane as chief shareholder upon the death of Eugene, L'Oréal acquired Helena Rubenstein, Maybelline, Lancôme, Ralph Lauren, and the Body Shop. With these plum packages and shares in the Swiss firm Nestlé, Liliane reigned as the ultimate Forbes-worthy heiress—to the tune of $39.5 billion.

In a nod to breaking with the family's link to anti-Semitism, Francoise, the product of a staunchly Catholic household, converted to Judaism when she married Jean-Pierre Meyers, whom she met at the chic Alpine ski resort of Megève. Andre was fond of telling people his daughter had "married an Israelite who likes us a lot." Her two sons, Jean-Victor and Nicolas, had the unique heritage of a maternal grandfather who was a German collaborator and a paternal grandfather, a rabbi, who had been murdered in Auschwitz. Andre, who had written during the war, "The Jews their race is tainted with Jesus' blood," had long recanted, blaming his sentiments on the vagaries of youth. Whenever one pointed a *j'accuse* finger at the House of L'Oréal, Liliane kept her immaculately painted lips sealed.

By most accounts, the Bettencourts enjoyed a happy marriage in their mega-mansions; however, unlike other well-known heiresses whose notches on the crotch made appearances in the society pages, the world's richest woman preferred the sanctity of the shadows. Her reticence may have been because of her innate shyness, fear of being a bull's-eye draw for kidnappers, or apprehension of resurrecting a painful past.

After the 1997 passing of Andre, his eighty-seven-year-old widow intended to spend her twilight years in luxury and privacy, flitting between her luxurious homes: a sumptuous mansion in the chic Paris suburb of Neuilly-sur-Seine, a luxury property built by her father overlooking the coast of Brittany, and D'Arros, an isolated Seychelles Island enclave, purchased from Prince Shahram Pahlavi Nia of Iran. But the best-laid plans of mice and heiresses went awry when her tranquil twilight collided with the clatter of skeletons tumbling from her hangar-sized closets. The regal Bettencourt was appalled to find herself in a scandal dubbed L'Affaire Bettencourt, one far afield from her golden rule: never complain, never explain.

The other key player in what became France's greatest blood feud-cum-soap opera would surely surpass any *Reader's Digest Most Unforgettable* entry. The chapter began with Francois-

Marie Banier, a sixty-year-old photographer, who possessed
Oscar Wilde's level of wit and charm—as well as the Irish writer's
sexual persuasion. His surrogate family included the names of
legend: Salvador Dali, Yves St. Laurent, Pierre Cardin, Mick
Jagger, and Johnny Depp and captured on film Samuel Beckett,
Princess Caroline of Monaca (complete with shaved head),
Lauren Bacall, Catherine Deneuve, and Truman Capote. As a
fashion house guru, Banier coined the name of Dior's cologne
Poison. He loved names and celebrity widows; it soon became
obvious he also loved money.

The widow Bettencourt grew lonely for companionship
something which Francois graciously provided. She dubbed
him her "enfant cheri," and in return, Liliane gifted him—*Mon
Dieu!*—$1.3 billion in the world's greatest goodie bag: paintings
by Picasso, Matisse, and Mondrian, an island in the Seychelles,
life insurance policies, and cash. What punctured Banier's
fortune-filled balloon was the Bettencourt butler. In the Paul
Simon lyric, "What the mama saw, it was against the law," and
what the butler saw he also deemed illegal. Surreptitiously, he
began taping exchanges between his boss and her BFF, using a
tiny recorder hidden on his cocktail tray. He presented these to
Francoise—along with the tidbit that her mother was planning
to adopt Banier—and the authorities charged him with *abus de
faiblesse*, exploitation of the elderly. Mrs. Meyers' opinion of
the photographer was exemplified by the name of Dior's cologne
Poison. Besides the exploitation, Francoise was hurt because her
mother paid more attention to her companion than she had ever
lavished on her own daughter. She also sought to have Liliane
put under court-ordered guardianship. The French press had
a field day—the two most reclusive and wealthy women in the
world facing off, with the art-world enfant terrible of French
society in the middle, filled reams of print.

Liliane was infuriated and vowed nuclear war against her
daughter to whom she swore never more to exchange a word.
She raged Francois had committed the ultimate sin: airing the
family's dirty laundry in public and as they were her billions,
bequeathed her by her father, she could do with the fortune as
she wished. Liliane explained that without Francois-Marie's
friendship, charm, and intelligence, she would have been
imprisoned in the stiff, boring life of an elderly billionaire.
The heiress further explained her largesse by stating that
Francois's "friendship brought me intense pleasure, and we did
laugh like mad." She went on the attack in the press, stating of
Bettencourt-Meyer, "My daughter could have waited patiently
for my death instead of doing all she can to precipitate it."
Her attorney said he believed the case was less about money
than about a dysfunctional mother-daughter relationship.
He observed, "That Madame Bettencourt should have the
misfortune of finding the brilliant Mr. Banier more amusing
than her own daughter—and between you and me, that's no
surprise—is not for this court to decide." Banier, the Svengali
at the eye of the storm, was detained for thirty-six hours for
questioning; when asked about the multimillion-dollar gift of the
Seychelles Island, he testified he had never wanted it "because
of its mosquitoes and sharks." The court of public opinion
thought Monsieur Banier the shark, as lethal as the maritime
predator. However, he had his high-profile defenders such as
Karl Lagerfeld, the king of Chanel, and fashion designer Diane
von Furstenberg. Their contention was it was the daughter, not
Banier, who had violated the unwritten code of the Parisian beau
monde: keep up appearances above all else. The scandal took its
toll on Bettencourt, whose skeletal frame appeared lost under the
weight of her massive pearl earrings.

With mother and daughter at war, it fell to Francois's son, Jean-Victor Meyers, to serve as a diplomat between the two; it must have been daunting to be a twenty-something peacemaker and to assume the helm of a multibillion-dollar company. The fact that he looks like a top European model, is heir to one of the world's largest fortunes, and has access to every cosmetic and perfume one could desire, makes him a target for female Baniers.

Into every heiress's life some rain must fall, and after a drought-free life, Liliane endured a torrential downpour. Besides the famous family feud with her daughter and the humiliation of appearing in the world press as a senile cash-cow, more storm clouds hovered. In the midst of having to prove her mental fitness, it came to light she had been the first investor in a fund managed by René-Thierry Magon de la Villehuchet who committed suicide in Manhattan after he lost $1.4 billion to Bernie Madoff, twenty-two million of which had belonged to Liliane. Although the amount was paltry for Bettencourt, she was dismayed at the further mention of her name in the international press. And it was only to get worse.

The butler's tape proved as damaging to Bettencourt as the Watergate tapes were to Nixon. Not only did it reveal Banier's ever-escalating demands for gifts, it also pointed a finger at French President Nicolas Sarkozy, whose love of luxury earned him the moniker "the bling-bling president." His First Lady Carla Bruni, former lover of Mick Jagger, was none too averse to the green herself. The tape indicated Sarkozy was accepting huge envelopes of cash in exchange for the government's decision not to scrutinize Bettencourt's taxes. With the publication of these titillating excerpts from the tapes, which dripped phrases such as tax evasion and campaign-finance violations just as Banier's trial was set to start, any hope of public relations damage control flew out the suddenly wide-open windows of Liliane's Art Deco mansion. The heiress was further transformed into a modern Job with the publication of *Ugly Beauty* and *Bitter Scent*, which resurrected the back story of its fascist-fancying founder. The scandal manifested the French novelist Honore de Balzac's observation, "The secret of great fortune...is a forgotten crime." Given the storms buffeting the House of Bettencourt, Liliane became the French Lear, mumbling, "How sharper than a serpent's tooth it is to have a thankless child."

L'Oréal's famous catchphrase, "Because I'm worth it," can be converted into a tagline for Ms. Bettencourt. Considering the associations of her billion-dollar empire, which entailed a Nazi past, a bitter family feud, and exploitation, leads one to muse: *Was it worth it?*

Chapter 12

The Beautiful and the Damned (1922)

In the opening scene of *The Graduate*, a family friend offered Benjamin Braddock advice: "I just want to say one word to you. Just one word: plastics." While the fictional Mr. McGuire suggested the synthetic held the key to success for the family of the inventor of plastic, in real life, the substance molded a fate that could have sprung from the hand of Hades.

This saga of madness and mayhem had its genesis in the early years of the twentieth century. Leo Hendrik Baekeland, a Belgian immigrant chemist, invented Bakelite working in his barn in Yonkers, New York. He referred to his brainchild as "the material of a thousand uses," and it became the staple for everything from telephones, toilets, and artificial limbs, to chunky bracelets popularized by Coco Chanel. Bakelite also played a crucial role in the creation of the atomic bomb. Leo appeared on the 1924 cover of *Time Magazine* and thus began a dynasty of deep pockets.

The 1960s desperate housewife who would make Wisteria Lane seem a drama-free zone was Boston-born Barbara Daly. From her parents, she inherited her beauty—titian hair and chiseled features; however, her DNA may also have carried psychological instability. Her mother, Nini, had suffered a mental breakdown before her daughter's birth; when Barbara was ten, her father, Frank, poisoned himself with exhaust fumes in his garage as his son, Frank Jr., looked on from a window. He later followed his father's lead and died when he crashed into a tree.

When Barbara was in her late teens, mother and daughter took up residence in Manhattan's Delmonico Hotel, the cost of which was financed by Frank's life insurance payout. The address was one of the city's most expensive, but they hoped it would provide Barbara a fertile hunting ground for an eligible husband. To their mutual distress, a relationship with John Jacob Astor failed to lead to holy matrimony.

Barbara was one of New York City's most beautiful women and appeared on the pages of *Vogue* and *Harper's Bazaar*. The magazine exposure led to a Hollywood screen test she hoped would make her a silver screen siren. Her aspiration did not pan out, though it did lead to a friendship with fellow aspiring actress Cornelia "Dickie" Baekeland, who introduced Barbara to her younger brother.

By the third generation, the plastic fortune had produced Brooks Baekeland, who started out as a brilliant student before abandoning physics for writing just before he would have completed a PhD at Columbia. He became a writer who never wrote, a fact that filled him with self-loathing. He was strikingly handsome, entertaining at dinner parties, and a possessor of a dazzling bank account. Brooks boasted he had "fuck-you money," a variation on his grandmother's adage: "One of the uses of money is that it allows us not to live with the consequences of our mistakes." Brooks was the poster boy for the evils of easy money, and he was intimate with a number of the Seven Deadly Sins.

Although Barbara's IQ never matched Brooks', she was savvy enough to lure him into matrimony by informing him she was pregnant. However, besides the nonexistent baby, she kept another secret: she shared her parents' mental instability. Shortly before the couple's meeting, Barbara had been a patient of the celebrated New York psychiatrist Foster Kennedy. Later, the doctor revealed that during their therapy sessions, his patient had unnerved him to such an extent he hoped she would never have a child. A short while later, the phantom pregnancy became a real one and produced Anthony Baekeland.

Barbara raised Anthony, whom they called Tony, in a fashion that placed the letter "s" before the word "mother." By the time of her son's birth, her relationship with her husband was strained, and she felt her son would serve as a marital anchor. The intent and effect of Brooks' parenting was mainly to keep his only child at arm's length. Part of his negativity toward his wife and son stemmed from his own sense of impotence; he was aware he was the under-motivated, over-leisured scion of a grandfather in whose accomplished footsteps he could never follow.

Ostensibly, the Baekelands enjoyed an enchanted life, and their social milieu was the moneyed, American dolce vita set; Barbara proved a nimble social climber. She became a culture vulture and entertained the celebrated in her lavish home. The *crème de la crème* were drawn to their lavish dinner parties, lured by Baekeland's famous forebear and his beautiful wife, which were hosted in their enormous wood-paneled living room on the Upper East Side. The seating cards at these dinners carried the names Salvador Dali, Tennessee Williams, and Dylan Thomas. They came in equal measure for the finest of food and the risqué after-dinner dessert: at one gathering, the men hid behind a screen, obscured from the waist up, and removed their trousers; wives had to guess which bottom belonged to which husband.

One of the points on which the warring Baekelands agreed was their belief that Tony was a child prodigy, and he was the centerpiece of their strange soirees. On one occasion, Barbara and Brooks had Tony read aloud from the Marquis de Sade's erotic writings. Another time Brook described how his son had pulled the wings off a fly to see how that would affect its balance. While Brook thought it showed his son carried the scientific genes of his great-grandfather, most viewed it as sadism, and several posh schools expelled him.

Battling boredom, the Baekelands relocated to Europe and became jet set nomads, hoping on the continent to attain the happiness that had eluded them back home. They rented villa after villa in fashionable resorts, and, wherever they hung their hats, Barbara was careful to leave a bowl full of visiting cards in plain view, carefully arranged so others could see that luminaries such as James Joyce, the Duchess de Croy, or the Prince de Lippe had been their guests. In some of their residences, Greta Garbo would pop in for drinks, and in Cap d'Antibes in the south of France, they were pleased that their neighbor was Freddy Heineken, the Dutch beer baron. Guest William Styron was enchanted with Tony and pronounced him a young Adonis. Tony often had play dates at various beaches with celebrity children such as Princess Yasmin, daughter of Rita Hayworth and the Aga Khan. He amused himself at the seashore by playing with crabs, which for him meant tearing them apart.

A teenaged Tony sought release from his psychological torment and took to painting; his portraits often displayed a decapitated Barbara. His parents remained in denial until, on a vacation from boarding school, he informed them he was homosexual; they reacted as if they had touched a live wire. Brooks was appalled and began to refer to Tony as "her son." In 1967, the family was vacationing in the Spanish town of Cadaqué where Tony met Jake Cooper, a handsome young Australian. He was known by the epithet Black Jake and lived on an abandoned farm with a hippie entourage who were into magic mushrooms and black magic. The twenty-one-year-old Tony was hypnotically drawn to Jake's circle and readily bought their friendship when he paid for their drugs. Tony also fell in love with the leather-clad Cooper. Frantic, Barbara convinced him to return with her to their home in Switzerland. Mother and son were stopped at the border because Tony did not have his passport, and in the ensuing scene, replete with Barbara kicking and spitting at the immigration officials, the police arrested them, and they spent the night in jail. As they were led off in handcuffs, Barbara chillingly remarked, "Here you are, darling, at last manacled to Mommy."

The family dynamics were a Petri dish where unsavory elements were fermenting. One of its ingredients was Brooks' wandering eye, and in 1963, he fell in love with a British diplomat's daughter fifteen years his junior. When he asked for a divorce, his wife's response was to take an overdose of pills. She survived, and her husband gave up the girl, not wanting to be complicit in his wife's demise. To prove she was still attractive to other men and to make her husband take notice, Barbara had her own affair with a Spanish physicist. However, this backfired when Brooks offered her a generous annual allowance if she would grant him a divorce, now that she had her own lover. She declined and spiraled even further into an emotional abyss.

Tony, still grappling with his sexual preference, brought home a French girl named Sylvie, whom he had also met in Cadaqués. Barbara was ecstatic and repeatedly told the young woman that if she married into the Baekeland family, she would be an heiress. Sylvie was happy to oblige; however, she set her sights on the father rather than the son, and Brooks readily reciprocated. When Barbara discovered the affair, she underwent another botched suicide. Sylvie, frantic that Brooks would give her up, also attempted to take her own life. When both his wife and lover survived, Brooks chose his mistress.

The betrayal fractured his wife and son's ever-fragile psyches, and in the summer of 1969, they ended up in Majorca, in a home loaned to them by an Austrian archduke. The estate was a cliffside villa, and it became the place where the woman who had charmed the heirs to the Astor and Baekeland fortunes seduced another wealthy man—her son. She embarked on the incestuous relationship in the hope of curing his homosexuality.

The role of acting as his mother's de facto husband played havoc with Tony's mental state, and his behavior became increasingly bizarre. Under these conditions, Mother Dearest and son rented a penthouse in the tony section of Chelsea, London, known as Cadogan Square. At this point, it was difficult for the Baekelands to lower the bar on family dysfunction: they had dappled in adultery, divorce, drugs, and incest, yet more horror lurked.

One afternoon in 1972, Barbara had lunch with her Chelsea neighbor, a Russian princess; when she returned home, she became embroiled in a ferocious fight with her twenty-six-year-old son, with whom she had maintained her Oedipal relationship. An enraged Tony released his pent-up fury and plunged a knife into his mother's chest. Afterwards, he made two phone calls—one for an order of Chinese food, the other for an ambulance. By the time the paramedics arrived, Barbara Baekeland was deceased. Tony told the police, "It was horrible. I held her hand and she would not look at me. Then she died." He claimed the murderer was Nini Daly, his grandmother, who was currently in New York. Barbara's Siamese cat, Mr. Wuss, was cowering under the bed. When Brooks learned of the mummy-murder, he told Sylvie, "She's again found a way to get at me."

The heir was found guilty of manslaughter with diminished mental capacity and sent to Broadmoor, a Dickensian hospital for the criminally insane. When friends came to visit, he always inquired after his mother's health. After several years, a well-connected family friend, who believed Tony's issues had died along with his mother, orchestrated his release. Brooks, who had married Sylvie with whom he had a son, believed his firstborn should remain permanently behind bars. Tony returned to the States and lived with his Grandmother Nini. Tony spent most of his time indoors, playing morbid music in front of a shrine to

Barbara; it consisted of candles and her photograph, with her ashes as the centerpiece. Six days after he moved in, he opened the door to the maid and told her to call an ambulance—he had stabbed his eighty-eight-year-old grandmother. He had wanted to have sex with his grandmother, and upon her refusal, he had slashed her eight times. A judge convicted him of attempted murder and sent him to prison on Rikers Island, where other prisoners preyed on the trust fund inmate. Denied bail, he returned to his cell, where "the material of a thousand uses" found one more. Tony died—either from suicide or murder— from suffocation brought about by a plastic bag that covered his face; the material behind the fortune that had made the Baekelands one of America's most envied, and most tragic, families. Their story bears witness to the sour side of la dolce vita. Brooks never wrote the great American novel, but his life with Barbara could have been encapsulated by the title of the F. Scott Fitzgerald novel *The Beautiful and the Damned*.

Chapter 13

The Swan Princess (1924)

Some people are deeded more dramatic lives than others. The peaks of their biographical landscapes are higher, their valleys lower. While most biographies can be covered in one slim volume, tempest-tossed individuals require a memoir of many volumes. The road less traveled was taken by an heiress who left her famous name on the posteriors of America.

Long before Paris Hilton unwittingly participated in a steamy sex video, the gossip columnists of yesteryear focused on a woman born into an American dynasty synonymous with privilege. The railroads that opened up the American West had made Cornelius Vanderbilt the tenth richest man in history. His likeness stands at the entrance of Grand Central Station in New York City in the form of a twelve-foot, four-ton bronze statue. His home was a 130-room Fifth Avenue palace situated where Van Clef & Arpels and Bergdorf Goodman currently stand. While the billionaire's talent was acquiring money, his great-grandson, Reginald Claypoole Vanderbilt, dissipated it on women, gambling, and liquor. Reginald passed away at age forty-four, having exhausted his liver and most of his twenty-five-million-dollar inheritance. He left behind his widow, twenty-year-old Gloria Mercedes, and his eighteen-month-old daughter, Gloria Laura, whose birth had merited a *New York Times* headline. Chauffeurs ferried her in a Hispano-Suiza to country weekends spent in the company of British royalty. However, her mother Gloria's maternal instinct chiefly centered on her daughter's five-million-dollar trust fund, equivalent to fifty million in contemporary currency. Reginald's will left everything solely to his children: Cathleen from his first marriage and Gloria from his second.

Mrs. Vanderbilt treated her child with affection but was a shadowy presence. The merry widow, accompanied by her identical twin sister, Thelma, Lady Furness (who was married to a British viscount, one of Britain's wealthiest men), trolled the beaches of Biarritz and Cap Ferrat on the prowl for another trophy husband. As her mother flitted around the glittering capitals of Europe, sometimes on the arm of Rudolph Valentino or Maurice Chevalier, little Gloria's German nurse, nicknamed Dodo, picked up the slack.

Gertrude Vanderbilt Whitney, one of New York City's wealthiest women and founder of the Whitney Museum of American Art, was infuriated with her gadabout sister-in-law and petitioned the courts for custody of her ten-year-old niece. Gloria was devastated at the news, mainly because her lavish lifestyle depended on the interest from her daughter's trust fund, and she refused to relinquish her parental rights. The judge warned her, "There will be so much dirt by the press that it will drag you and the child through a mire of infamy that will cling to her as long as she lives." It was a price Mrs. Vanderbilt was willing to pay.

In the autumn of 1934, the public on both sides of the Atlantic readied for a close-up of an outrageous episode in the lifestyles of the rich and famous. The tawdry trial captivated a world seeking diversion from the Great Depression. This battle of the blue bloods provided a peephole into the world of wealth as well as a dose of schadenfreude while American royalty was proven not to be immune to life's slings and arrows. The national audience was riveted by the lurid allegations that Gloria was the lesbian lover of the Marchioness of Milford Haven. Dodo claimed her employer soaked her feet in champagne, and even more damning, described her as "a cocktail-crazed dancing mother, a devotee of sex erotica, and the mistress of a German prince." Mama Vanderbilt lost custody of both child and purse strings. Her twin also fared badly. In order to support her sister at the trial, Lady Furness had flown in from England, leaving behind

her lover, the Prince of Wales, a liaison that had previously
led to her divorce. Before her departure, she had entrusted the
care of the future King Edward VIII to Wallis Simpson—a task
Mrs. Simpson took to heart. When Thelma discovered Wallis
had stolen the royal heart, the woman scorned retaliated by
proclaiming the five feet, seven inches tall Edward, known as
the Little Prince, should be known by that epithet for another
reason. Her remark helped explain the current lore that the
talented Mrs. Simpson had won the future king's heart with her
"ability to make a matchstick feel like a cigar." Had it not been
for the custody battle of the century, England might have avoided
a constitutional crisis borne of Edward relinquishing his throne
for his lady.

Little Gloria, dressed in a fur coat and with eyes downcast to
avoid the glare of flashbulbs, went to live with (as she called
her) Aunt Ger. Her new life was the opposite of her former: her
mother had been an absentee parent but had been affectionate
when present; her aunt, although a constant presence, was aloof.
While the rest of the country was financially bankrupt, the poor
little rich girl was emotionally adrift. In 1985, Gloria tried to
come to terms with these lonely years by writing the first of her
four memoirs, *Once Upon a Time: A True Story*. She recounted
that the reason why she had spent so much time in the attic was
because that was where the maid pressed her mother's clothes,
and by knowing what dresses belonged to her mother, she was
able to tell the difference between her mother and her twin
sister. In response to the court's allegations that she was an unfit
parent, Mrs. Vanderbilt had rationalized, "Mothers are busy with
the duties their social lives entail." However, as Mrs. Whitney's
lawyer had pointed out, these duties entailed massages, fittings,
hairstyling, and dressing for lunch and then for dinner. The
dream of maternal love was apparent from the dedication page

of Gloria's memoir of her childhood, which read, "And to the memory of my Mother. Always."

Gertrude managed to keep the two Glorias apart, but when Gloria was seventeen, she permitted her ward to go on a two-week vacation with her mother in Beverly Hills. "Suddenly," she recalled, "the door of the cage was open and out I flew." Instead of being chaperoned to tea dances with eligible heirs at the Plaza, she spent nights at the Mocambo, squired by Hollywood stars. She had also caught the roving and rapacious eye of Pat DiCicco, Howard Hughes' gofer and sometime procurer. Gloria was mesmerized by the film-star handsome man who favored white on white suits and all-night card games. An introduction to Howard Hughes followed. At thirty-six, Hughes was an uber eligible bachelor renowned as a pioneer aviator, filmmaker, and multimillionaire, who was still decades away from his infamous fate as a paranoia-driven recluse marooned at the top of his own Las Vegas hotels. At his home in Santa Monica, he constantly played a record of *Moonlight Sonata* as a mode of seduction. He escorted her to dinners where he always ordered the same meal—steak, peas, and a baked potato. Gloria reminisced, "I was crazy about him and would have married him in a minute. But then, I would have married anybody in a minute because I wanted to get out." Desperate not to return to Aunt Ger, Gloria saw a husband as the only escape route.

When Hughes wanted more variety in women than he did in dinners, Gloria married DiCicco in a Santa Barbara church with Errol Flynn as an usher. The union finally brought about a meeting of minds between her aunt and her mother: both were aghast. Gloria was delighted. She said, "What can one say about a first marriage, except that it's wonderful?" As it turned out, she had merely traded one prison for another. DiCicco's first wife, actress Thelma Todd, had been murdered in 1935 in an unsolved crime in which he was rumored to have played a part. He called Gloria Fatsy Roo, and on their wedding night, they never made it to the marital bed; he stayed all night in the next room playing gin rummy with Zeppo Marx. He also beat her into unconsciousness by banging her head against the wall. As she would do throughout her life, Gloria found a new love interest before disposing of her old.

While still married, Gloria met Leopold Stokowski, a world-famous conductor and the producer of the soundtrack to Disney's *Fantasia*. The veteran ladies' man already had two ex-wives and had once had an affair with Greta Garbo. The press labeled him Stokie; he referred to himself as "maestro." Viewing age as no impediment, the sixty-two-year-old white-haired conductor and the twenty-year-old raven-haired beauty married before the ink was dry on her Reno divorce. Their ten-year relationship resulted in sons Stanislaus (Stan) in 1950 and Christopher in 1955. Leopold turned out to be as pompous as he was talented and hinted he was a descendant of the Hapsburgs; in fact, he came from a Cockney background. The incident that gave her the courage to leave her narcissistic spouse was a one-night stand with Marlon Brando. She remained circumspect about the encounter except to share, "I didn't have any long philosophical discussions." She mentioned that he kept a large portrait of himself in his bedroom from his role as Napoleon. She was smitten; Brando was not. Nevertheless, his virility gave her the impetus to disentangle herself from Leopold, and she took solace in an affair with Frank Sinatra—of whom she wrote that he burst upon her like a firecracker—who was on the rebound from his divorce to Ava Gardner. When the crooner left to croon elsewhere, fashion photographer Richard Avedon introduced her to Sidney Lumet, the film director of *Network*, which led to a third trip down the aisle. Their seven-year marriage, during which they partied with celebrities such as Marilyn Monroe, Rita Haywood, and Salvador Dali, failed to provide the grand passion for which she yearned, and she guiltily took her leave.

Gloria, realizing wedding confetti did not equate to the elixir of happiness, became a designing woman in the 1970s when she marketed fashion jeans that displayed her famous name on the derriere and her trademark swan on the front. Her logo may have been inspired by her being one of Truman Capote's flock of "swans"—his designation for the famous society beauties who inspired his character Holly Golightly in *Breakfast at Tiffany's*. The writer, known as the tiny terror, wrote of these women, "They were blessed with that best of beauty emollients, a splendid bank account." In one year, her denim empire brought in ten million dollars. Ms. Vanderbilt explained her reason for becoming a designing woman by quoting the Billie Holiday lyric, "Mama may have, Papa may have, but God bless the child that's got his own." She also found romantic success at last with her fourth marriage to Wyatt Cooper, the love of her life. Equally enamored, he explained his wife's allure: "She has the freshness of Snow White and the glamour of the Wicked Queen." He proved a wonderful father both to his two stepsons and the two boys he and Gloria had together: Anderson and Carter. However, Gloria was to experience the truth of the Shakespearean pronouncement that "When sorrows come, they come in battalions." Due to family dynamics, Christopher cut off all contact with his family—an estrangement that has continued for forty years. Added to this heartache was another: in 1978, Wyatt suffered the last in a series of heart attacks and died in the operating room at age fifty. A decade later, while Carter was visiting his mother, he—despite his mother's pleas, made on her knees with outstretched arms—plunged off her fourteenth-floor balcony. When Anderson once asked her how she had survived, she responded, "I had an image of myself that at my core there was a rock-hard diamond that nothing could get at, nothing could crack." Her explanation showed her steely determination, though one suffused with sadness. What helped soften these kidney punches to her soul was that Stan gave her three grandchildren and Anderson became a beloved and respected CNN talk show host. He and his mother referred to each other as best friends. Anderson went public with a comment to Howard Stern that he wanted no part of her two-hundred-million-dollar fortune as he feels inherited wealth is a curse.

In a nod to the idea that one is never too old to try something new—or something racy, in her eighth decade, Gloria expanded her repertoire of achievements from gracing the derrieres of America to gracing the spine of her novel *Obsession*. Her book— with an endorsement by her friend Joyce Carol Oates—is the tale of a woman who becomes entranced by her dead husband's affair with a dominatrix. The publication led Carter to quip, "The six most surprising words a mother can say to her son: 'Honey, I'm writing an erotic novel.'" The steamy work has led to yet another incarnation—as sexual guru to the postmenopausal. *The New York Times* stated it "may be the steamiest book ever written by an octogenarian;" the *New York Post* described it as "elegant, unadulterated smut." When two of her waspy friends cautioned the book would tarnish her reputation, she replied, "Oh, goody!"

Because of the sensational 1930s trial, the death of her husband, and the suicide of her son, if Americans were given an auditory Rorschach test with the words "poor little rich girl," odds are the response would be "Gloria Vanderbilt." Yet this answer is not an accurate assessment of the heiress who embodied the Duchess of Windsor maxim, "You can never be too rich or too thin." In her nineties, Gloria appeared as immune to the ravages of time as the portrait of Dorian Gray. Through the power of persistence, she took life on her own terms and reigned as a legendary swan princess.

Chapter 14

Prince Charming (1931)

In the German Grimm Brothers' *Sleeping Beauty*, Aurora pricks her finger on a spindle and falls into an enchanted slumber until aroused by the kiss of the handsome prince. In the twentieth-century American version, Sleeping Beauty did not awaken and may even have been sent into an eternal sleep by the hand of her own dark prince.

If ever there were a female counterpart of the poetic figure Richard Cory, it was the woman who began what promised to be an enchanted life as Martha Sharp Crawford. She was born in a railway carriage between White Sulphur Springs, West Virginia, and New York, leading to her nickname, "Choo-Choo." The family fortune derived from her father, George Crawford, founder of Columbia Gas & Electric, who was seventy-five at the time of his daughter's birth, decades older than his twenty-eight-year-old wife, Annie-Laurie. The Missus was no slouch either in the well-heeled department: her father was Robert Warmack, founder of the International Shoe Company. Martha was George's only child, and he left his four-year-old a 1935 fortune of seventy-five million dollars.

Sunny—as Martha was called because of her disposition—grew up in Manhattan, where a chauffeur-driven Rolls Royce transported her from her Fifth Avenue zip code to the exclusive Chapin School. Summers were spent with her mother and grandmother on the family estate, Tamarlane, in Greenwich, Connecticut. At her debutante ball, the public was entranced by the teen with the Grace Kelly beauty and the dazzling wealth, a flesh-and-blood fairy princess. In the 1950s, she became the precursor to Paris Hilton: rich, blonde, a fixture of upper-crust Manhattan and Newport, Rhode Island.

Sunny passed university entrance exams, but, as academia held no appeal, Annie-Laurie took her on countless tours of Parisian couture houses. The society girl made it onto Vogue's list of the ten best-dressed women. Mother and daughter frequented European country house sporting parties where American heiresses and penniless Continental aristocrats made mutual matches of convenience. In 1957, while visiting the Tyrolean country club Schloss Mitersill, Sunny met its tennis pro, Prince Alfred von Auersperg. Despite the insignia on his family's coat of arms, he was short of schillings. After their marriage, the couple settled in Austria, where their home bordered a golf course. However, despite the blending of green new-world money and blue old-world blood, as well as children, Alexander and Annie-Laurie (nicknamed Ala), cracks appeared in their relationship. The handsome husband often absented himself for big game safaris in Africa and in pursuit of other trophies—such as the Italian film star Gina Lollobrigida, with whom he had a widely publicized affair. After seven years, when Alfred failed to lose his itch for other women, Choo-Choo decided her marriage had gone off the track and filed for divorce. Auersperg settled in Africa to pursue big game hunting and managed to lose his million-dollar divorce settlement when Emperor Bokassa confiscated it for his country's coffer. The prince was later involved in a car accident that left him in a vegetative state until his death.

At a London dinner party, Sunny succumbed to the charms of fellow guest Claus von Bülow, a debonair aristocrat. Claus had been christened Claus Cecil Borberg but had changed his last name to von Bülow when his Danish father, a drama critic and Nazi supporter, had been convicted as a collaborator; Claus had distanced himself from the shame by adopting his maternal grandfather's surname. A Cambridge educated lawyer, he greatly impressed J. Paul Getty and became the billionaire's personal assistant.

In 1966, Sunny traded her Austrian playboy prince for the
Danish-born man-about-society. It seemed a likely match: Claus
had the manners; Sunny had the manors. They celebrated with
a ball attended by two hundred thirty guests at Claus's flat in
London's Belgrave Square, decorated like an eighteenth-century
Indian palace. Sunny still preferred the United States as her
chief zip code, and the couple lived in her multimillion-dollar
fourteen-room Fifth Avenue Manhattan apartment overlooking
Central Park. Summer vacations were spent in a Georgian Rhode
Island mansion on Millionaires' Row, nestled on ten acres
overlooking the Atlantic. The couple had one child together,
Cosima, and John Paul Getty served as her godfather. Their 1904
estate, Clarendon Court, had originally been named Claradon
Court by railroad executive Edward C. Knight after his wife Clara
and had served as the setting for the 1956 musical *High Society*
starring Frank Sinatra, Bing Crosby, and Grace Kelly.

Sunny von Bülow had an enchanted life as a beautiful titled
heiress, blessed with a charming husband and three children.
The family's chief residence was Newport, Rhode Island, where
the great mansions stand like sentinels at the edge of the sea,
flaunting their wealth at the waves. Sunny's daily regimen: she
awoke at eleven, shared an hour of phone conversation with
her mother, and then the chauffeur ferried her to exercise class;
she shopped, had lunch, changed into her lounging clothes, and
watched television with Claus. Occasionally, she would appear at
parties, sheathed in a designer gown. She retired early, sharing a
bed with Claus and their four Labradors.

There is a saying it is not wise to let too much light into the
castle, and this aphorism was accurate when it came to the von
Bülows' pleasure domes. By 1980, Claus, who appeared uxorious,
had followed in his predecessor's shoes by bedding a bevy of

beauties; even worse, one of these liaisons had also slipped into the realm of romantic adultery. The mistress who wanted to become the Mrs. was Alexandra Isles, a socialite and sometime soap opera actress, and she was putting the screws to her lover to terminate his marriage. In this instance, the wife was not the last to know, and the distraught Sunny turned to self-medicating her pain with pills and alcohol. She resented her philandering spouse as it was the Crawford money that had put his elegant clothes on his back and his money-hungry lover in his arms. The mansion doubled as a mausoleum as the von Bülow marriage merely went through the motions.

In 1980, Sunny was found lying comatose on her marble bathroom floor, a syringe by her hand. The doctors said she would never regain consciousness, a condition induced by an overdose of the insulin she took to control her hypoglycemia (low blood sugar). People assumed her coma had been the result of a terrible accident until Sunny's mother and two oldest children pointed an accusatory finger at Claus. Acting on their suspicions, Alexander hired a private investigator who discovered a black bag in Claus's locked closet that included an insulin-tainted needle. Based on this evidence, authorities charged von Bülow with attempted murder. The prosecution claimed his motive was financial; Sunny had shared with her son her desire to file for divorce. According to a prenuptial agreement, Claus would receive nothing in that contingency; if she died during their marriage, he would inherit fourteen million dollars of his wife's seventy-five-million-dollar fortune, as well as her palatial properties and a $120,000 annual stipend. Another incentive: with his wife out of the way, he would be free to marry his mistress. The sign above the entrance of Clarendon Court could have read: Home Sweet Homicide.

The trial was among the most sensational of the 1980s. News media from around the world were mesmerized by the drama of the American sleeping beauty heiress who lay in a perpetual twilight zone and the European husband accused of delivering the kiss of death. A further thread of the web was that the two older royal children and their grandmother were infuriated with Cosima, who sided with her father, even when Laurie-Annie cut her out of her ninety-million-dollar will. The drama had every prerequisite for an orgy of headlines: enormous wealth, adultery, and an allegation of attempted murder.

The tragic tale became the first major criminal trial televised in the United States. Network executives discovered that real-life courtroom drama, in which the sets and the actors came gratis ended up generating higher ratings than soap operas. In steamy testimony that mesmerized the country, there were allegations from Truman Capote that Sunny was "a psychological wallflower," a drug addict and a drunk. Claus's attorney claimed the coma had been self-induced by a binge of drugs and sweets, including a "sugar bomb" of eggnog, twelve fresh eggs and a bottle of bourbon. Countering these allegations, the prosecution put Sunny's maid on the stand; she claimed that von Bülow had ignored her pleas to summon medical help. Claus's stepchildren implicated him in the attempted murder, as did his former mistress, although Alexandra did retrieve his wedding band so that he could wear it during the trial.

Claus's closest friend said, "The problem with Claus is that he does not dwell in the Palace of Truth. You see, he's a fake. Claus is trompe l'oeil." Of the media circus lapping up every lurid detail, von Bülow simply stated, "The case has shown that wealthy people are also ordinary people." After five and a half tempestuous days of deliberation, the seven men and five women delivered their verdict—that the superbly tailored defendant was guilty; the murder weapon: a hypodermic needle filled with a lethal dose of insulin. The judge sentenced him to thirty years in prison. When asked, post-conviction, how he felt about Newport, Claus responded, "The same way, I suppose, Mrs. Lincoln felt about the Ford Theater." The verdict was a stunning end to the sensational case that had set a Raymond Chandler plot against a Scott Fitzgerald backdrop. When released on one million dollars bail, without skipping a heartbeat, Claus once more slipped into the role of a man-about-town. Rather than maintain a low profile, one evening at a restaurant, when someone at the next table had a heart attack, Claus leapt to his feet shouting, "It wasn't me! It wasn't me!"

For his appeal, von Bülow hired celebrity lawyer Alan J. Dershowitz—later part of O. J. Simpson's Dream Team—who obtained an acquittal. His legal stratagem was to show that the evidence gathered by the private detectives hired by Alexander, and then turned over to the authorities, should have been inadmissible in court. He argued that the rich cannot be permitted to decide what evidence should be made available. The jury agreed and acquitted Claus. Dershowitz wrote of the case in *Reversal of Fortune*, whose title encapsulated the life of the heiress born with a silver spoon that became so drastically tarnished. In the televised version, Jeremy Irons, as the debonair Dane, offered the line, "What is another name for fear of insulin?" followed by his own response, "*Claus*trophobia." Two years later, Claus's stepchildren filed a fifty-six-million-dollar civil suit against him that was resolved on the condition that he divorce the comatose Sunny and renounce any claim to her fortune. The settlement also restored Cosima as a recipient to one-third of the one-hundred-million-dollar estate of her grandmother. Claus von Bülow agreed and moved to London.

Sunny von Bülow spent the rest of her life curled in a fetal position in a Manhattan nursing home. The Auersperg children—who had the singular misfortune of having both their parents in irreversible comas—continued to visit, played classical music in case she could on some level hear it, and arranged for her hair and nails to be done on a daily basis. Her hospital sported designer Porthault sheets, and several paintings from her New York apartment hung on the walls. Fresh flowers arrived every day, and they placed photographs of her children, and the grandchildren she had never met, around the room. Their dearest hope was that Sunny, in Lazarus fashion, would awaken. After twenty-eight years, Sunny passed away in 2008, and the secret behind her coma died with her. Her final resting place is in a cemetery near Newport, next to her mother, in her former sanctuary by the sea. The heiress's life that had started as a fairy tale ended as a Greek tragedy. Unlike the Grimm Brother's Aurora, for this sleeping beauty, there was no awakening from the kiss of her Prince Charming.

Chapter 15

Amazing Grace (1937)

Somerset Maugham, who lived for years in the Riviera, once famously remarked, "Monaco is a sunny place for shady people." His observation proved prescient in an incident that could have well been gleaned from his novel, *Of Human Bondage*.

The marriage of the American film star Grace Kelly to Prince Rainier put his principality on the jet set radar, and the princess used her star power to burnish its image. However, the fabled kingdom, despite its pink fairy-tale palace, has walked hand in hand with notoriety ever since its ruling family took over more than seven hundred years ago when the pirate Francois Grimaldi, disguised as a Franciscan monk, seized control in a coup.

Although Prince Rainier and Princess Grace, along with their children Albert, Stephanie, and Caroline, had been tabloid staples for years, Monaco's second most wealthy and powerful family at first led largely private lives. The genesis of their dynasty began in the 1880s when a poor Italian stonemason, Jean-Baptiste Pastor, arrived penniless from the Liguria region of Italy. He enjoyed a comfortable lifestyle as a contractor until 1936, when Louis II, Prince Albert's grandfather, anointed him the master builder of the country's first football stadium. Their association signaled the start of a professional and personal relationship between the two men. After World War II, Jean-Baptiste's son Gildo amassed what was then inexpensive waterfront property, and in the 1950s, he built luxury apartments with harbor views that became sanctuaries for the one percent enamored of the Riviera's ostentatious lifestyle. Pastor's properties became the havens of the world's rich and royal, including many tax refugees from other well-heeled zip codes. Upon Gildo's 1990 death, he left his real estate empire to his three children, Victor, Michel, and Hélène, contrary to Ligurian tradition in which daughters were not eligible to inherit. After the passing of her brothers, Hélène controlled Pastor's holdings which had grown into a multibillion-dollar enterprise. In recognition of her financial stature and her association with the royal family, Monaco's elite dubbed her "la vice-princesse."

Despite her fortune and close ties to the Grimaldi dynasty, Hélène chose to remain in the shadows. Although the name J. B. Pastor is emblazoned on the construction cranes that dot the Monaco waterfront high-rises, her own rarely appeared in the newspapers. She was uninterested in attending high-society events and preferred to immerse herself in managing her innumerable properties. The value of her financial portfolio was a closely guarded secret, but as the owner of three thousand of the principalities' waterfront apartments, her fortune was in the rarified neighborhood of twenty-five billion dollars. She became even more reclusive after her two marriages ended in divorce. Her first, when she was eighteen, was to a Polish barman in the employ of Aristotle Onassis, Alfred Ratkowski, with whom she had a daughter, Sylvia, in 1961; her second was to a dentist, Dr. Claude Pallanca, with whom she had a son, Gildo, in 1967.

Consistently clad in Chanel business suits and known for her taciturn manner, she managed her crown jewels of prestigious addresses along the Avenues Princesse-Grace and Grande-Bretagne from the Gildo Pastor Center. Photographs of her father adorned the company's headquarters, from which she employed a staff of forty. After work, she customarily returned to her majestic apartment in the Trocadero, one of her buildings, a home she shared with Belle, her large, white Pyrenean shepherd. Her outings consisted of taking Belle for walks; Hélène dispensed with a bodyguard as she felt her low profile exempted her from being publicly perceived as a walking treasury. The real estate mogul also felt immune from kidnapping as Monte Carlo had one policeman for every one hundred residents and more closed-circuit security cameras per square foot than any other country. Crime in the crème de la crème city is virtually nonexistent, ensuring the omnipresent Ferrari convertibles and their bejeweled owners can shine resplendent when exiting the casino at midnight.

Besides her dedication to her family firm, the heiress was a devoted mother to Gildo, who was the co-founder, along with Leonardo DiCaprio, of a Formula E style electric car racing team, as well as the owner of the electric car brand Venturi. She also loved Sylvia, though their relationship proved contentious. Sylvia Ratkowski-Pastor, known as Sisi, like her mother, was a worker not a socialite. She had married an industrialist in Turin, Italy, and had a daughter. However, her life was altered dramatically in 1986 when on a visit home, she met the Polish-born Wojciech Janowski. He had a job in the Casino de Monte Carlo, the legendary gambling mecca immortalized by a James Bond film. He worked as a glorified bouncer—pacing the floor to spot cheats and other troublemakers. As Sylvia's marriage had collapsed, she moved in with Janowski who raised her child as his own. In 1997, they had a daughter, a fact that helped him to distance himself from his poor Polish past, an autobiographical omission he preferred. The couple's relationship never set well with Hélène, who could not abide her common-law son-in-law. Her animosity may have been due to of her first ill-advised marriage to a Pole, because she felt her heiress daughter could have set her sights higher, or because she had uncovered something unsavory about his past. She had once confided to a friend about her de facto son-in-law, "I know a lot of things about him. He's somebody *terrible*. One day, I will tell you everything." This situation resulted in mother-daughter issues, already exacerbated by Sylvia's belief that Hélène had always favored Gildo.

Hélène sensed her child's antipathy and told a confidant that her daughter didn't like her. However, as Janowski was the parent of one granddaughter and surrogate father to another, Hélène bit her lip and grudgingly held her peace. Partly because of her mother's dislike of her partner, despite living together for twenty-eight years, Sylvia and Janowski never married. Nevertheless, it appeared that though Hélène did not trust Wojciech, Sylvia did, and she gave herself to him heart, body, soul, and checkbook. The erstwhile penniless immigrant had access to Sylvia's allowance to the substantial tune of $650,000 a month. In addition, he lived rent-free in Sylvia's vast penthouse apartment with a harbor view, in an elite Pastor-owned high-rise, Le Schuylkill (named after the river in Princess Grace's hometown of East Falls, Pennsylvania). Other funds enabled them to purchase additional residences in London and Switzerland, a yacht, the use of private jets, and deluxe family vacations. Because Janowski had attained super-rich status, honors were forthcoming: he became the honorary consul of Poland in Monaco, and French President Nicolas Sarkozy decorated him with the Legion of Honor for his charitable work. However, inside their rarified world, heartache made daily appearances. Hélène, so mild-mannered in public, phoned her daughter each day, beginning at dawn, and the calls were heated. Sylvia often complained to friends of her mother's rantings which left her in tears. She also mentioned that Hélène was "extremely cold."

Despite all Hélène's wealth and power, 2012 proved her annus horribilis. Gildo, at age forty-seven, suffered a massive stroke that left him paralyzed and unable to speak. If this blow had not been devastating enough, doctors diagnosed Sylvia with breast cancer. The third sorrow was that a week after her son's hospitalization, her brother Michel, known as "the boss of

Monaco," passed away, leaving Hélène the last surviving sibling. These horrors led her to remark to a friend, "Sometimes I wonder if there is a God."

On May 7, Hélène departed the L'Archet Hospital in Nice with buoyed spirits; Gildo's condition had improved to such an extent he was going home. The heiress climbed into her black Lancia Voyager minivan, where her longtime chauffeur Mohamed Darwich waited to drive her back to Monaco. Because Belle took up the entire back seat, Hélène sat in the front. Moments later, in a surreal act that created bedlam in the crowded street, a young man fired into the car with a sawed-off shotgun, hitting Mohamed and the heiress, with bullets lodging in the face, neck, chest, and abdomens of the victims. Mohammed died on impact; Hélène clung to life for four days. When questioned about the attack, she said she had no idea who was behind it as she had no enemies. On May 21, she passed away; Sylvia was her last visitor.

The news of the attack consumed the international media, especially in Monaco. Prince Albert and his wife attended the very private funeral, and circling helicopters prevented the paparazzi from taking aerial photographs. The predominant question that baffled both the media, and the French and Monacan investigators, was the identity of the assassins and the motive. Initially, the police felt the murder was the calling card of the Italian and Russian mafia who wanted to muscle in on Monte Carlo real estate, the priciest in the world. Others speculated the hit was the handiwork of a Pastor tenant who had clashed with the iron-willed landlady. When the truth came out, it was something that rivaled anything that had been presented at the year's Cannes Film Festival.

The reason why a street in Nice had been transformed into a scene of terror was a result of Sylvia Ratkowski-Pastor's breast cancer. When Janowski learned of the diagnosis, he was panic-stricken, and not just with concern over Sylvia. If she were to die, then the monthly allowance would cease; Hélène would evict him from Le Schuylkill like a delinquent tenant. He was under no illusion that Hélène would show mercy, and as he and Sylvia had never made their union legal, he would have no legal recourse to her estate. Janowski had started life as a penniless Polish immigrant and had no desire to end up in that situation again. For financial self-preservation, he decided to arrange Hélène's murder, and she had to predecease her daughter. In addition, with Hélène's death, he would be able to get his hands on a multibillion-dollar fortune rather than making do with a paltry $650,000 monthly allowance.

Janowski, who always had minions do his bidding, did not carry out the act himself. Instead, his personal trainer, Pascal Doriac, commissioned two small-time hoodlums from a Marseilles slum who, when captured, pointed the finger of blame at the honorary Polish consul. After four days in custody, Janowski admitted to having paid $260,000 to get the job done. He claimed his motive was not monetary but rather for love. He stated, "The emotional abuse of my wife by her mother had gone on since the day I met Sylvia. You can't imagine the times I've had to pick Sylvia off the floor. The idea of killing Hélène grew in me whenever I saw my wife destroyed every night." He attempted to portray himself as a saint rather than as a sinner. The public looked at his mea culpa as camouflage for wanting to lay his hands on the deceased's billions. When questioned about the murder of the chauffeur, he explained his death had been merely collateral damage, carried out "as a diversion and to muddle things up and make people question who was the real target."

When news of his confession leaked, the upper crust of Monaco
was appalled that one of their own could have been involved
in such a heinous crime. A society lady, Elizabeth Ann Croesi-
Notari, honorary consul to the Dominican Republic, gasped,
"And to think that we used to kiss each other on the cheek."
At least she and her charmed circle took solace that he was,
in the end, a Polish immigrant. In reference to the suspect's
charming façade and his cold-blooded act, the authorities
dubbed Janowski Janus—a reference to the ancient Roman god
with two faces. Sylvia, who the authorities had arrested as a
suspect but later cleared, was in a "state of abject shock," which
was understandable after the murder of her mother, her own
incarceration, and her companion's complicity. She swore off
any future contact with the man with whom she had lived for
nearly three decades. Their teenage daughter suffered horribly:
her father had killed granny. What added an additional note of
horror was it was the victim's own money that had been used
to pay her killers. In the end, the murder of Hélène Pastor and
her chauffeur turned out to be what had been assumed from
the beginning: a "crime crapuleux," a criminal act sparked by a
motive as old as the Monaco hills: money.

Janowski soon retracted his confession, stating that he had not
understood "all the nuances of the French language." He also
claimed that the police had "done everything to me but tear out
my fingernails" to coerce his confession. He was taken to an
isolated cell in Marseille's notoriously squalid Les Baumettes
jail to await his trial. During the ensuing months, he was an
incarcerated Janus—looking back at his days of opulence,
looking ahead to his future in a brutal prison. After a five-week
trial, the judge determined the Polish honorary consul was
anything but and pronounced a life sentence. After the verdict,

Sylvia remarked, "I've lost *maman*. I've lost Wojciech. I have nothing left."

The opening sentence of *Casino Royale* can serve as a metaphor for the moneyed corruption of the principality: "The scent and smoke and sweat of a casino are nauseating at three in the morning. Then the soul erosion produced by high gambling—a compost of greed and fear and nervous tension—becomes unbearable." The high-profile homicide, committed by someone with family ties to the deceased, showed the world that the fairy-tale kingdom was not immune to a dark knight, a man who, unlike Monaco's Hollywood princess, was far removed from the state of Amazing Grace.

Chapter 16

The Wounding Thorns
(1938)

Sultan Shahriya, angered after his wife dabbled in adultery, ordered her execution. To avoid further humiliation, every night he married a virgin whom he beheaded the next morning. Scheherazade, one of his hapless brides, devised a plan to escape her predecessors' fate. During pillow talk, she spun such fantastic tales that the king delayed her death. After 1,001 nights, the Sultan fell in love, and Scheherazade lived out her natural life span. The ancient Persian tale had real-life implications for a modern-day *Shahbanou* (Persian for Shah, meaning Queen).

Farah, the woman who would be queen, was born in Iran, the only child of Captain Sohrab Diba (Persian for silk) and Farideh Ghotbi. The captain's father had been the Persian Ambassador to the Russian Romanov Court. The sole trauma of Farah's idyllic childhood came at age nine with the sudden death of her father from cancer. Her grief was made even greater as her family had hidden his illness to spare her worry. His passing left his wife and child in straitened circumstances, and they left their large villa for an uncle's cramped apartment. As a teen, Farah studied at the Sorbonne's Ecole d'Architecture. In France, Farah had a rendezvous with a destiny that rivaled the tales of *One Thousand and One Nights*.

The Pahlavi dynasty was not of an ancient lineage; it originated with Reza Shah Pahlavi, the first Shah of Persia, who changed the name of his empire to Iran. The patriarch took his surname from the ancient Persian language. In 1959, his successor, Mohammed Reza Pahlavi, met Farah at the Iranian embassy in France. He was taken with the twenty-one-year-old beauty and was intrigued when she had the moxie to complain how their country's reduction of scholarship funding created a hardship for its students studying abroad. She recalled of their first meeting, "I wrote a letter to my mother saying he has such beautiful eyes but very sad eyes." The encounter turned into a royal romance despite their nineteen-year-age difference, her status as a commoner, and Mohammed's two failed marriages. His first wife was Princess Fawzia, daughter of King Fuad I of Egypt. The teenaged couple united two great Muslim lands, and during their wedding, fireworks lit up the sky over the Nile. She bore their daughter, Princess Shahnaz; however, when there was no further pregnancy, as the Shah needed a male heir to inherit the peacock throne, she returned to Egypt. The next Shahbanou was Princess Soraya, a daughter of Iran's powerful Bakhtiari family. He adored her; however, just as Napoleon had to end his union with Josephine because she was barren, the same fate befell Soraya. The story of her divorce inspired a French songwriter, Francoise Mallet-Jorris, to write "Je Veux Pleurer Comme Soraya" (I Want to Cry like Soraya). What helped dry her tears was a more than generous settlement. When she passed away in Paris, she left behind a fifty-million-pound fortune that included a Rolls Royce, her 22.37 carat diamond engagement ring, and a lavish Parisian apartment. Farah became Mohammed's third consort, and her youth, beauty, and elegance, coupled with her royal status, made her the eastern Princess Diana.

The couple were married in the Marble Palace in a Shiite Muslim ceremony. On her head rested a Harry Winston creation: a four-pound tiara whose centerpiece was the sixty-carat pink Noor-ol-Ain (Eye of Light) diamond, one of the largest in the world. Yves St. Laurent created the wedding gown, including a fur-lined hem on the bridal dress with the color blue sewn in for good luck. In keeping with tradition, the bride set 150 caged nightingales free. In one photograph, her mother stands beside the bride, also awash in diamonds, no doubt far from displeased that her daughter had caught the catch of catches. Wherever she went in

Iran, people cheered; President Charles de Gaulle liked her more than any other first lady, including Jacqueline Kennedy.

Farah escaped the fate of her two predecessors when she gave birth to a son and heir, Crown Prince Reza, ten months after tying the imperial knot. An honor guard marked the moment by firing their guns, and there was dancing in the streets. A second son, Prince Alireza, and daughters, Princess Farahnaz and Princess Leila, followed. Among other lavish perks, the children enjoyed their private zoo stacked with deer, antelope, monkeys, lions, and an Indian elephant, a gift from Indira Gandhi.

The Shah was a complicated man; on the one hand, he believed in the divine right of kings, while on the other, he strove to modernize his country. As part of his White Revolution, he worked to emancipate women, and the empress was a symbol of their newfound freedom. Unwilling to be just a beautiful face with a tiara, she was the first Iranian queen to be named as regent in the event her husband died before the crown prince turned twenty. The empress was the patron of twenty-four organizations; she donated blood, established the first self-sustaining leper colony, and went on to visit its residents. Under the rule of the royals, a certain class of Iranian women played volleyball on the shores of the Caspian Sea in bikinis—a world away from the enforced modesty of the shawl.

The Shahbanou founded the Tehran Museum of Contemporary Art, where she assembled the greatest collection of art outside of Europe. The masterpieces included the Impressionists (Monet and Renoir) at an estimated cost of one hundred million dollars. Today, the gallery—which includes works by Gauguin, Toulouse-Lautrec, Picasso, Dali, Pollock, and Lichtenstein—is valued at three billion dollars. During its construction, she met Salvador Dali, Marc Chagall, and Henry Moore. In 1976, Empress Farah commissioned Andy Warhol to paint her portrait. The queen and the pop artist had met at a White House dinner hosted by President Gerald Ford in honor of the Shah. Warhol's portrait portrayed her with blue eye shadow and pink lipstick, against a vivid yellow background. In an article about his commission, he wrote, "I had the best time. It was just so up there. So *glamorous.* She was really, really kind and so beautiful." During their reign, Frank Sinatra and Yehudi Menuhin performed, and theaters screened *Midnight Cowboy.* Although many applauded her liberalism, others blamed Farah and her Westernization for the rise of Ayatollah Khomeini.

Before long, the streets became the arena for less than laudatory displays of public sentiment. Pahlavi's White Revolution alarmed conservative Iranians who feared that imported films, clothes, and customs endangered their Islamic faith. When the economy weakened in 1977, the simmering discontent became a flood that threatened to wash away the monarchy. Mohammed used the Savak, his dreaded secret police, as the antidote to dissenters.

Despite the blue fur hem and the freeing of the nightingales, Farah's luck deserted her. With strikes paralyzing the country, the Pahlavis left Iran for a vacation that turned into permanent exile. They would never be able to go home again; the revolutionary government had ordered the execution of the Shah and the Shahbanou. Mohammed's staff did not have the opportunity to flee, and the Islamic clerics had them executed. Farah said that saddened her.

Ousted from the Marble Palace, they became royal refugees. In Farah's memoir, *An Enduring Love: My Life with the Shah*, she waxes eloquent on her early days in exile. Traveling with what she claims were only fifteen suitcases, none of which, she wanted it to be known, contained the Iranian crown jewels or priceless paintings, the Pahlavis embarked on a desperate odyssey. Every country that opened their doors to the pair received a barrage of threats from enraged Islamic radicals. In desperation, they became royals in search of asylum. They went first to Egypt, then to Morocco as guests of King Hassan II, then to the Bahamas, and then Mexico. They headed to the Caribbean, where they were granted temporary refuge in the Bahamas on Paradise Island. The Shah offered to buy the island for $425 million, but the officials rejected his offer. Despite rumors that Mohamed and Farah had escaped with one hundred million dollars and were known to be generous, old friends turned their backs in fear. Farah wrote of the days when she had to eat the bitter bread of banishment, "People change when you are not in power. I lived hour-to-hour, day-to-day. But I had to survive for my children. You can lose your position, your possessions, your country, your loved ones, but you shouldn't lose your dignity or your courage."

In 1979, they came to the United States for Mohammed's cancer treatment. His wife had been kept in the dark over his illness, an echo of what had transpired with her father. In fury at America for helping the Shah, thirteen days later, militant Iranian Muslims invaded the US Embassy in Tehran and took hostages to demand the Shah's extradition, the return of his plundered wealth, and a confession of American crimes in Iran. Upon his release from the hospital, Mexico blocked his return. The family went to Panama and then departed once more to Cairo, where Mohammed died at age sixty, a king without a country. However, he remained a king with a fortune. His holdings have been estimated at more than twenty billion dollars, although much of the imperial wealth remained in Iran and could not be liquidated after the revolution. Farah's fairy-tale life had become a living hell.

With Mohammed's death, President Sadat granted the devastated widow asylum and the use of the Koubbeh palace in Cairo, but his assassination the next year ended this refuge. At this juncture, President Reagan told them they were welcome in the United States, where the family finally settled in the upscale town of Greenwich, Connecticut. One would have assumed that this sanctuary was to be the last chapter in Farah's One Thousand and One Nights, but the gods were not yet finished with her.

Farah had been extremely worried about her youngest daughter, Princess Laila, who suffered from low self-esteem, even though her beauty had led to her walking the Parisian catwalks as a Valentino model. Among her afflictions were anorexia, depression, and insomnia. Her mother's friend discovered Laila's emaciated body in a five hundred pound per night London hotel room; her death was the result of an overdose of prescription drugs and cocaine. In the nightstand was a photograph of her family watching television in their palace in Tehran. Laila's funeral was in the Cimetière de Passy, Paris; in attendance were members of the French royal family and her mother, her face etched in grief. Alireza had been extremely close to his sister as well, and her passing cast a lingering shadow. He had received his bachelor's degree from Princeton and a master's degree from Columbia and was studying for his PhD at Harvard. His credentials had earned him the designation of being "one of the world's most eligible princes." Despite his privileged life, in 2011, Ali committed suicide with a shotgun in his Boston home. His final wish was for his ashes to be scattered in the Caspian Sea. Seven months later, his girlfriend gave birth to their daughter, Iryana Leila. Farah recognized her as a full member of their family and as a Princess of Iran.

Farah Diba Pahlavi, the survivor of many storms, lives alone in
a vast apartment overlooking the River Seine in Paris. The floors
display fine silk rugs, there are displays of Persian antiquities,
and handmade bonbons are offered by a silent maid in a starched
pinafore. "Exile is very hard," she has said, and she would know,
after living it for twenty-five years. She could also be referring
to the hardship of having only two personal assistants; in the
olden, golden days, she had sixty. In her remembrances of things
past in her memoir, she recalled her lost land through rose-
tinted glasses. She painted an adoring portrait of Mohammed,
a statement that leaves hanging one question: if the Shah was
the wonderful ruler she claims he was, why were five hundred
thousand people waiting at the Tehran airport to welcome
his archrival, the Ayatollah Khomeini, back from exile? She
also dismissed the torture and murders committed by the
Savak secret police with the literary equivalent of a wave of
the hand. However, she did concede that Mohammed's desire
for modernization was too far-reaching for a country mired
in the Middle Ages, that his rule was too authoritarian, and
that "perhaps we should have been more humble." Humility
had never been their strong suit. In 1971, in the ancient city of
Persepolis, they threw what has been described as the greatest
party in history to celebrate the 2500th anniversary of the
Persian Empire. Maxim's of Paris catered the affair; Baccarat
provided the goblets. Elizabeth Arden created a new line of
cosmetics christened Farah. The party price tag: two hundred
million dollars.

While watching television in her Parisian apartment, she
discovered that Fundamentalist vandals had slashed her Warhol
portrait; the damaged masterpiece could serve as a metaphor
for her fractured country. Her pronouncement was, "They are
stupid. Instead of tearing it, they could have sold it!" The clerics

had banished the billion-dollar collection to the basement of the Tehran Museum of Contemporary Art as they deemed the artistic creations the products of the decadent, depraved Western world. There was no way that Renoir's *Gabrielle with Open Blouse* would have passed the regime's censors. The Moore sculpture in the garden bears the mark of a bullet. However, even four decades after the revolution, the empress in exile remains optimistic that light will overcome darkness. She stated, "The seeds you plant and love never perish."

At eighty, the woman who was empress remains elegant as ever, her Nefertiti-esque makeup only slightly toned down from when she sat for Andy Warhol. Every year Farah visits her husband's tomb in the Al-Rifai mosque in Cairo. She remembers him as an adoring husband, a memory that contrasts with less laudatory accounts by others portraying him as a philanderer whose view of women was chauvinistic. He had remarked, "In a man's life, women count only if they are beautiful, graceful, and know how to stay feminine. Women have never produced a Michelangelo or a Bach or even a great cook."

Farah explained she finds comfort for her life's vicissitudes in the words of Hafiz, a celebrated Persian poet: "Pay no heed to the wounding thorns."

Chapter 17

A Facial Attraction (1940)

In some worldly scenarios, soap operas can play second fiddle to reality, especially when plot elements include family fortunes and oversized personalities are part of the dramatis personae. Fact triumphed over fiction in the case of a surgically enhanced cat lady, a dynasty with Nazi associations, and a trove of treasures.

The Wildensteins are an obsessively secretive family of French-Jewish art dealers stretching back five generations whose name has long been renowned as one of the most prestigious and powerful in international circles. When the Germans goose-stepped into Paris in 1942, they escaped the swastika and opened a Manhattan gallery which their paintings, including Old Masters and Impressionist canvasses, made into a miniature Louvre. Daniel, the family patriarch, valued his treasures and secrecy, and he kept his two sons, Alec and Guy, in line with his exacting standards by controlling the plentiful purse strings.

Through an unlikely 1977 encounter, a woman left an indelible scratch in this rarified milieu. Jocelynnys (she preferred Jocelyn) Dayannys da Silva Bezerra Perisset was born in Switzerland, the only child of a middle-class family. Her father, Armand, sold sporting goods in a department store, and his daughter made use of his products as she was an athlete—both an ace shot and a pilot. At seventeen, she began dating Cyril Piguet, a Swiss movie producer, and through him, she traded laid-back Lausanne for Paris. On a vacation in Africa, she fell in love with the continent, drawn in by its exotic animals. It was there she met big game hunter Alec Wildenstein. Saudi arms dealer Adnan Khashoggi proved a matchmaker when he invited the Swiss knockout to stay at his ranch in Kenya, which was also where the Wildensteins had Ol Jogi, their sixty-six-thousand-acre spread. Her first date with Alec took place when he had to put down a lion at a neighbor's ranch and Jocelyn asked to accompany him.

Afterwards, they rode a motorcycle to a hilltop and discovered they shared commonalities—love of the Serengeti and lions as well as the mutual loss of their dogs, both of whom had been German short-haired pointers. At the scenic spot, they had their first kiss, one Jocelyn called "quite intense." Alec found her physically intoxicating, and she was equally intoxicated by Alec, who was heir to his father's five-billion-dollar fortune. Their romance was a love affair made in safari heaven.

When Jocelyn returned to Paris, she visited her hair salon Karita, as she did every Tuesday, and Alec arranged for thousands of white orchids to fill every available spot. He flew in from his home base in New York, and on their fourth date, over dinner chez Au Pied de Cochon, he proposed. She recalled, "He didn't ask me; he told me. I was not about to argue with that." The news of his oldest son's engagement did not please papa patriarch—especially amidst rumors Jocelyn had worked as a courtesan and did not share their Jewish religion. Despite parental disapproval, a year later they eloped to Las Vegas, and a rabbi officiated at the ceremony in the Hilton Hotel. Daniel did not care to fly to the wedding in his private Gulfstream IV jet and likewise absented himself from a second ceremony in Lausanne.

The new Mrs. Wildenstein stepped into a world of unimagined luxury: they transformed Ol Jogi into an African Versailles replete with a private zoo consisting of a giraffe, a leopard, lions, and a white rhino. Two lions roamed in a bulletproof glass-enclosed cage. Other refinements were fifty-five artificial lakes, a swimming pool with rocks and waterfalls, a golf course, a racetrack, and a tennis court, all maintained by a staff of 366. Other places to lay their hats included a private Virgin Island compound; a 150-year-old castle, Chateau de Marienthal (reportedly the largest private residence in metropolitan Paris);

and a house in Lausanne. Their marital base was a five-story New York City townhouse with an indoor pool inlaid with tiles depicting dolphins. A sitting room held ten Pierre Bonnard paintings, valued at one hundred million dollars. Another decorating touch was a unique glass-topped coffee table whose base held antique swords and a velvet-handled rifle that had belonged to Marie Antoinette. The couple kept a menagerie consisting of five Italian greyhounds, a pet lynx, a black leopard, and a monkey, May Moon. The other two-footed occupants were Alec Jr. and daughter Dianne who, on her seventeenth birthday, received a three-million-dollar home addition in Ol Jogi. Determined that his trophy wife should always eclipse her rivals at social events, Alec purchased for his Cinderella a one of a kind Chanel dress that cost $350,000 for a New Year's Eve party, and he dropped ten million dollars on visits to Cartier. Each household had a chef—Jocelyn claimed she was domestically challenged; it was "lifestyles of the rich" on steroids.

After the children left for college, Jocelyn feared her husband's eye was wandering to human big game trophies. As Alec loved exotic cats, in a bid to remedy her marital malady, she went under the plastic surgeon's knife to appear "more feline." When she emerged from the doctor's office, a patient fled from the waiting room. Similarly, after Alec saw his mutilated wife, he screamed in horror at her resemblance to the lions in Ol Jogi. Her rubbery mask had journalists posing questions: Can she close her eyes to sleep? Do her ears wiggle when she smiles? (If she can even smile.) Bizarrely, rather than show nip-and-tuck remorse, she became addicted to cosmetic surgery and spent four million dollars in her quest to appear purr-fect. Clinging to a version of fantasy that she may have mistaken for truth, she professed that she came by her looks through genetics, "If I show you pictures of my grandmother, what you see is these cat eyes and high cheekbones." Her husband, who suffered from the public stares, bemoaned her fixation: "She has the impression you fix a face the way you fix a house. I must say I have trouble recognizing her up close." Her mask-like facial features led the *New York Post* to dub the socialite "the Bride of Wildenstein" and *New York Magazine* to label her "the Lion Queen." What Daniel labeled his daughter-in-law remains in the Wildenstein family vaults next to the old and new Masters. Remarkably, Jocelyn's otherworldly face was not to be the strangest thing in the Wildenstein saga.

In 1997, Jocelyn was at Ol Jogi attending to her mother, who was suffering from Alzheimer's, and her father, who was dying of pneumonia. Despite repeated pleas to help her through this rough patch, Alec did not join her, not even for his father-in-law's funeral. What happened next can be viewed as From Russia With Sex. When Jocelyn and her two bodyguards stepped off the elevator in her Manhattan home that led to the third-floor bedroom, she saw Alec holding a towel around his waist with one hand and gripping his pistol in the other—a semi-automatic, not the Marie Antoinette model. She had walked in on him and a nineteen-year-old naked blonde Slavic model. Hubby grabbed his girlfriend, who was scared out of her wits—either by the weapon or the woman with the terrifying face. Jocelyn, meanwhile, phoned the police and screamed that her husband was threatening her life. His explanation was he had mistaken the two bodyguards for burglars; he added that his wife had set up the whole scenario to portray him in a bad light as he was demanding a divorce.

Despite his protestations, Alec departed his townhouse in handcuffs and spent sixteen hours in custody while cellmates gawked at the prisoner clad in an Armani suit. The following day, the art world's wealthiest and most secretive family became tabloid fodder. A further woe was that the girl in his bed was not his girlfriend Yelena Jarikova, but rather another Russian model. When Yelena discovered this tidbit, she was so infuriated Alec had to buy her a Mercedes to calm her down. The gift proved a satisfying salve as Yelena had only recently immigrated, and, in her country, she had been so impoverished she had never eaten fresh fruit or vegetables. Jocelyn told him she would forgive him, but Alec's rejoinder dashed her hopes, as he preferred his Russian paramour: "I don't think I was ever in love till now." Daniel was furious at the public fallout; although he'd had his share of extramarital activities, they had been discreet. He was beside himself that his son had been caught with his pants down, in his own home, by his wife, no less—and that the scandal had hit the papers (mainly because the press never missed a photo op involving the eerily photogenic Jocelyn). Daniel's ire focused on his daughter-in-law, and he vowed she would walk away with nothing. He felt safe declaring economic war on Jocelyn since he held the purse strings.

Alec, despite a lifestyle that rivaled that of a drug kingpin, was on paper merely an employee of the family empire; hence, the only way Jocelyn could get money was to sue her father-in-law, a legal impossibility. Daniel blitzed her credit cards, cut her telephone lines, and locked most of the rooms in the house that was in his name. The socialite said she was not just cut off financially but socially as well. She groused that erstwhile friends of the couple, such as financier Nathaniel de Rothschild and his parents, Liliane and Elie, kept her at arm's length. There appeared to be no "Hakuna matata" on her horizon. However, Alec was wrong if he thought she would slouch away; after all, cats have claws. Jocelyn, who used to water-ski on Africa's crocodile-infested Zambezi River, girded herself for battle. Of Alec's proposal, she had said, "I was not about to argue with that," but this time, she was going to argue and to fight for her spoils of war. Her method of attack was to strike through the tabloids, the reclusive family's Achilles' heel. After nineteen years of marriage, Jocelyn had a powerful trump card: dirt on the dynasty. Salacious tidbits included their unpaid taxes—to the tune of millions— and information revealing the Wildenstein fortune had derived from a Nazi collaboration that had looted works of art from Europe's Jews. Many priceless paintings that had vanished in the Holocaust had mysteriously resurfaced in the Wildenstein vaults. The art world was revolted and riveted. One collector commented, "Jocelyn could be the thread that unravels the whole sweater."

In court, the wife scorned claimed she needed a million a month to run her household because years of dependence on servants had left her bereft of the ability to light a stove, make toast, or boil an egg. Alec's lawyer parried by saying that as an employee of the family firm, Alec only made a $175,000 annual salary. The amount was contradicted by his recent jaunt to Kenya to take a breather from his marital woes. In Ol Jogi, he'd had a craving for sushi, something not readily available in Africa, and he, along with Yelena, had flown his Gulfstream IV jet to deliver Nobu Matsuhisa, a world-renowned Japanese chef, along with a week's supply of raw fish, to the Serengeti. He made a point of missing his wife's television appearance during which she aired the family's dirty laundry. He stated, "I never look at her. She's crazy. You can't stop crazy people." But apparently while she may not have been crazy like a fox, she was crazy like a feline. After a lengthy court hearing, the Mrs. received $2.5 billion plus $100 million annually for thirteen years. The judge, however, stipulated that the money not be used for further facelifts and advised her to buy a microwave. Acrimonious about his alimony, in consolation Alec married a young Russian model (who was neither Yelena nor the one his wife had found in her bed). He decamped to Europe to concentrate on Ecurie Wildenstein, the family's extensive French racing interests. In answer to the question if Jocelyn was able to smile, after the judge's ruling, presumably she did—at least as best she could considering her mask-like face.

After the divorce, Jocelyn decided to remain in the States where she embarked on another of her allotted nine lives—as a cougar cat lady. She is currently in a relationship with designer Lloyd Klein, thirty years her junior. They spend a lot of date nights in Hollywood, an appropriate playground, as it is both the place where reality and fantasy blur and the cosmetic capital of the world. And Jocelyn still attracts stares. The attention derives both from her aging feline features and her attire; though in her seventh decade, she dresses in skintight black leather pants and sports a long blond mane. Hopefully, her new beau will not ultimately feel the way her ex-husband did—that Jocelyn Wildenstein did not prove to be a feline facial attraction.

Chapter 18

The Book of Ruth
(1941)

A passage from the biblical Gospel of Mark poses the question, "For what shall it profit a man if he shall gain the whole world and lose his own soul?" A twentieth-century man turned a deaf ear to this advice, and in the process, he sacrificed his soul— along with his wife's—the dethroned Park Avenue Princess.

Another religious quotation, this one from Saint Teresa of Avila, states, "Answered prayers cause more tears than those that remain unanswered." This truth was something Ruth Alpern learned, a lesson that came with a steep price tag. She was born into a Jewish family in Queens, the daughter of Saul, an accountant, and Sara, a housewife, younger sister to Joan. After years of saving, her parents moved from their Brooklyn apartment to a modest clapboard house in Laurelton. However, the Alpern daughters' wish-upon-a-star desire was to live in the affluent suburb of Belle Harbor, where doting dads did not worry about the cost of weddings. The girls attended Far Rockaway High, where Ruth, a beauty, a cheerleader, and an honors student, was known as "Josie College," a 1950s yearbook colloquialism that pegged her as preppy, bright, and going places.

The defining moment in Ruth's life occurred at age fourteen when she met sixteen-year-old Bernie Madoff who lived two streets away. The freshman and the junior were so inseparable their classmates referred to them as "eggs and bacon." No one was surprised when the sweethearts married at the Laurelton Jewish Center immediately after graduation.

The couple started with five hundred dollars and rented an eighty-seven-dollar-a-month one-bedroom apartment in Bayside, Queens, where they lived with their schnauzer, Muffin. Bernie had endured his father's bankruptcy, and that horror provided the fuel that drove his desire for financial success.

Ruth and Bernie attended college, and Bernie worked as a part-time sprinkler installer. After they completed their degrees, Ruth devoted herself to raising their sons, Andrew and Mark, while Bernie began an eponymous investment firm. His earliest champion was his father-in-law, Saul, who, before retiring to a condo in Florida, entrusted his money to Bernie's care. The young financier became a wunderkind, and, with the sun never setting on a bad day at Bernard L. Madoff Investment Securities, people ponied up their savings. Improved finances allowed the family to relocate to a bigger apartment in Great Neck, Long Island, and then to a ranch house in Roslyn. The girl who had once dreamt of moving to the right side of the tracks in Queens began to collect properties as other women do charms for their bracelets: a beach house in Montauk, a penthouse in Manhattan, an apartment in France, a mansion in Palm Beach. Other perks of being Mrs. Midas were a 10.5 carat diamond ring, a $36,000 Russian sable coat, and a yacht christened *Bull*.

Contrary to Bob Dylan's lyric, "I'm helpless like a rich man's son," in Ruth's *tsoris*-free life, Mark graduated from the University of Michigan and Andrew from the Wharton Business School. When their sons shopped for homes, they did not have to contend with the privations of starter digs; they settled into mansions, compliments of the Bank of Bernie. Queens resounded with the wails of mothers whose daughters had attended Far Rockaway High—why hadn't they snagged Bernie?

Life for Mrs. Moneybags was a dizzying agenda of flitting between her various pleasure domes, each decorated with the best of everything. When living on the West Coast, Ruth frequented the Palm Beach Country Club; its initiation fees are in excess of three hundred thousand dollars. On her New York home turf, she embarked on the life of a Manhattan moneyed matron: hair appointments at the Pierre Michel Salon, where Giselle—a colorist profiled in Vogue—applied foils to attain the shade of Soft Baby Blonde. To further Ruth's quest of sipping from the Fountain of Youth, one of the duties of a manager in the Madoff London branch was to keep Ruth supplied with Boots No 7 Protect & Perfect Beauty Serum. Ruth maintained her one-hundred-pound frame by boycotting carbohydrates; after she had consumed her allotted portion, she poured copious amounts of salt on her food to prevent furtive bites. Despite being a nucleus of the glitterati herself, Ruth's North Star remained her husband. In Stepford style, she devoted herself to making his life comfortable: she dressed in the clothes he found flattering and would not tolerate hearing a word against him. When someone kibitzed that Bernie was a "shyster," the feisty girl from Queens emerged; her nails turned to talons. She decorated their Xanadu properties to his exacting standards and made sure his boxer shorts were custom-made with buttons up the side as he disliked elastic. Ruth led a charmed life—until her handsome prince transformed into a dark knight.

In December 2008, Bernie confessed to his family that his financial kingdom consisted of smoke and mirrors and that he had been running a sixty-five-billion-dollar Ponzi scheme. Allegedly, Ruth asked, "What's a Ponzi scheme?" The truth of whether or not she knew lies in the gray domain of conjecture; however, Andrew and Mark understood all too well. The sons, in an embodiment of the first syllable of their surname, went into survival mode. They feared that as they worked in the family firm and enjoyed jet-setting lifestyles, the eye of suspicion would land on them and the sins of the father would be visited on the sons. To deflect guilt, they contacted the FBI and slammed out the door of the family penthouse, forever departing their vanished world. One can only imagine the torture Ruth endured while awaiting the morning arrival of the police who would sever her from the side of the man for whom she had lived for the previous fifty years. The seven-million-dollar art-filled home, replete with a thirty-five-thousand-dollar Persian carpet, $104,000 silverware, and an Impressionist painting, had dissolved into smoking guns of guilt. Like Fitzgerald's Gatsby, Ruth's list of enchanted objects began to diminish.

Bernie left jail on a ten-million-dollar bond and spent hours in front of the television, eyes streaming tears. On Christmas Eve, pilloried in the court of public opinion, alienated from their sons, with the loss of their fortune and prison looming, the Romeo and Juliet of corporate greed lay down on their canopied bed—with God knows what thread count sheets—and swallowed handfuls of Ambien. Fifteen hours later, they awoke feeling groggy and decided to shoulder on. When news broke of the aborted double suicide attempt, the public felt the Madoffs were being manipulative in a ploy to garner sympathy. One victim stated that people who are smart enough to pull the wool over the eyes of millions were smart enough to know how many sleeping pills to swallow to get the job done. The couple became the primary punching bag of the country; there was no empathy for the fallen Caesar—or for Caesar's wife, who was not beyond suspicion.

With the carpet of her life pulled out from underneath her, Ruth became Mrs. Job, and she experienced the veracity of the adage, "Whom the Gods wish to punish, they first make happy." The initial kidney punch to her soul was the loss of all her gilded cages, seized as restitution to the victims who had been swindled in the largest financial scam ever perpetrated. New York had not experienced such a quantity of suspect wealth on the auction block since the Philippine government had auctioned off the contents of Imelda Marcos's Upper East Side townhouse.

When Ruth attempted to rent a modest home, her notoriety-by-association with her husband caused landlords to put out the *Not Welcome* mat. At age seventy-one, Ruth had to resort to couch-surfing, but almost the only offer of a place to hang her hat came from her sister Joan in Boca Raton. The sisterly solidarity was all the more remarkable as Bernie had lost Joan's life savings; in her seventies, she survived by driving airport taxis. As Florida was as rife as New York with victims, and even Ruth's gynecologist's mother had been bilked, she now went out incognito: gone were the Soft Baby Blonde highlights, and she used her maiden name. While the world had once been her oyster, after the scandal, Ruth received the Casey Anthony treatment. Moreover, the US Attorney's office put a moratorium on her spending, rejecting her *New York Times* subscription as too extravagant, along with TV service above basic cable. Although Ruth had escaped imprisonment, she lived in a stockade.

Worse than the loss of property and reputation was when her boys forced her into a Sophie's choice: choose between Bernie or her sons and grandchildren. Despite the ultimatum, Ruth was not willing to put asunder the marriage vows she had taken in the Laurelton Jewish Center. Conjugal fidelity, normally considered an admirable quality, only made her a further target of poisoned darts. A newspaper referred to her as Ruth-less, and a barrage of bloggers wrote, "Burn the witch!" A much better publicity ploy would have been to claim she had been as duped, and therefore as victimized, as everyone else. Putting the priorities of her heart above her head, she drove a 1996 Infiniti clunker to North Carolina to see Bernie, whose name had become synonymous with "greedy dirtbag," a.k.a. inmate number 61727-054. She said of these heart-wrenching encounters, "It was like having a husband who had died but you could still visit." However, since Bernie had been the pillar of her world since her early teens, she did what she had always done and stood by her man. Perhaps in a nod to "honor among thieves," Bernie steadfastly insisted on going down solo, placing blame only on his own shoulders.

Further condemnation fell on Ruth's former baby-blonde highlighted head when she fought to hold on to a chunk of her wealth; most people felt that instead of doing so, she should have been knee-deep in mea culpa, doing something like ladling soup for the lepers of Calcutta. She ended up cutting a deal with prosecutors to keep two and a half million dollars in exchange for surrendering a potential claim to eighty million dollars in assets. While it saved her from having to take a greeter job at Walmart, it was still a huge blow for a woman who had enjoyed a laissez-faire lifestyle with her American Express gold card. She tried to justify her payoff by presenting herself as a '50s housewife who had left the family finances to her husband. She stated, "The man who committed this horrible fraud is not the man whom I have known all these years." The public's response echoed the name of the confiscated Madoff yacht—*Bull.* Comedian Andy Borowitz parodied her words, "This is not the man I owned nine homes with. When you spend hundreds of millions of dollars with someone, you think you know him… I guess I was wrong."

Although Ruth had paid dearly for her years of living the uber dolce vita, her past sorrows were only a bare beginning compared to what loomed before her. She was in Boca Raton when she received a phone call that Mark had hung himself with his dog Grouper's leash in his six-million-dollar Soho home while his young son slept in the adjoining room. Ruth let out a primal scream. The salt she had poured over her uneaten food was now poured on her own wounds. In the Old Testament, the relationship between Naomi and her daughter-in-law Ruth was forged in steel; not so with the modern mother-in-law and daughter-in-law. When Ruth flew to New York, the widow barred her from the funeral service.

However, it was not the loss of her fortune, the public condemnation, or the suicide of her firstborn that led to her decision for the eggs to be sans the bacon (in light of what had transpired, Ruth was surely the eggs). In 2009, Sheryl Weinstein, a former executive of Hadassah, a Jewish charity that had been the victim of the Madoff swindle, published a kiss-and-tell book that disclosed she and Bernie had shared more than a kiss. Bernie refuted the accusation, but Sheryl had revealed information that only the wife of a monogamous man ought to know—that he wore boxers with buttons.

Shakespeare's Hamlet observed, "When troubles come, they come not in single spies / But in battalions." After Mark's suicide and her final break with Bernie, Ruth reconnected with Andrew. The reunion coincided with a resurgence of her son's cancer, which had been in remission for years. He attributed his illness to his father having ruined their lives. He called the Ponzi scheme a "father-son betrayal of biblical proportions"—one which had killed his brother quickly and was killing him slowly. What was left of Ruth's world shattered with his death. Bernie had destroyed many families but none worse than his own. When the robber baron suffered a heart attack behind bars, the *New York Post* wrote, "Apparently, Bernie Madoff does have a heart."

If the Ponzi scheme had been one of biblical proportions, so had Ruth's punishment; she had lost her husband, sons, social standing, and fortune. Ruth, the modern Icarus, had flown too near the sun, and her fall from grace was as dizzying as her rise.

The question remains if Ruth really was a member of the clueless wife's club. On the one hand, she may have been like another bottle blonde—the fictional Carmela Soprano—who had looked away from her husband's machinations. If that is the case, then her suffering is the gods dishing out her just deserts. On the other hand, if she really was kept in the dark, then she is a woman who was more sinned against than sinning. In either contingency, money, the biblical root of all evil, is the thread that runs through The Book of Ruth.

Chapter 19

The Comedy Is Over
(1948)

The Italian opera *Pagliacci* revolves around Canio, a clown;
what gives the lie to his smile is his tears over his wife's adultery.
Insane with jealousy, he murders both his faithless partner and
her lover. Life imitated art in an Italian soap opera involving a
crime of fashion.

The House of Gucci and its interlocking G insignia conjure
visions of luxury goods that carry heavyweight status and a hefty
price tag. From this legendary retailer came a handbag included
in New York's Museum of Modern Art and a best-selling floral
scarf inspired by Grace Kelly. Guccio Gucci, who had worked in
Paris and London as a bellboy at the Savoy Hotel, was inspired
by the high-quality luggage of its upper-class clientele, and when
he returned to Florence, he established a leather goods shop in
1921 along with his seamstress wife, Aida. The mom-and-pop
business became an international success, and by the 1930s,
it boasted branches in the world's most exclusive zip codes.
Despite the snooty attitude of its sales force, which caused *New
York* magazine to dub its Fifth Avenue outlet "the rudest store in
town," the rich queued for its posh products. In this manner, they
followed in the footsteps of Audrey Hepburn, Ingrid Bergman,
Elizabeth Taylor, Jacqueline Kennedy, and Sophia Loren. At his
1956 marriage to Grace Kelly, Prince Rainier gifted Gucci scarves
to his female guests; Frank Sinatra ordered dozens of Gucci
moccasins, and the interior of Cadillacs bore Gucci décor.

With Guccio's passing, his heirs began a descent into self-
destructive dysfunction. Their Cain and Abel antics provided the
stuff of tabloids' dreams as they resorted to boardroom brawls
where executives tossed thousand-dollar handbags at each other.
On a symbolic level, the double G insignia represented greed and
grief. Into this Mediterranean blood feud arrived a woman who

would leave her own mark of intrigue on this clan that made the Borgias look like the Waltons.

Patrizia Martinelli hailed from Milan, the daughter of a laundress mother, Silvana, and a truck driver father. With her mother's remarriage to Fernando Reggiani, a transport magnate, Patrizia was able to indulge in floor-length white mink coats. The Reggiani wealth allowed Patrizia to move amongst the upper crust, and she struck marital gold at a 1970 gala when she met Maurizio Gucci, who could offer endless *lire* and Gucci goods. He was drawn to the raven-haired beauty with violet eyes whose curves did wonders for her body-hugging red dress. Maurizio's relatives wondered what he saw in her after she took off her false eyelashes and stepped down from her towering high heels. His father, Rodolfo, labeled her a gold-digger who had been born into the lower class. (The Gucci clan had assiduously whitewashed their patriarch's own humble roots by mythologizing the dynasty's founder into a royally appointed saddle maker from Tuscany's nobility.) Rodolfo even went so far as to ask the Archbishop of Milan to intervene and to make his son come to his senses. Although Maurizio had always been under the thumb of his domineering father, he married the woman he lovingly called his "pocket-sized Venus."

Despite Maurizio's family's disapproval of his choice of a wife and the differences in their upbringings, the marriage was a happy one and produced two adored daughters, Alessandra and Allegra. The Guccis became the first couple of Milan, and Patrizia played the role of celebrity wife to the hilt, decked out in Valentino, Chanel, and Gucci. Signora Gucci became one of the most extravagant members of the Italian jet set as her husband lavished on her everything that a materialistic woman could crave: wealth, status, and one of the classiest and most recognizable names in fashion. Their over-the-top homes in Milan, Manhattan, and St. Moritz sported suede and leather walls, leopard throws, and penthouses with some of the world's most magnificent views. They purchased a 230-foot yacht, the *Creole*, the former owner of which had been the Greek shipping tycoon, Stavros Niarchos. The Guccis, hoping to rid the ship of the bad aura from Niarchos's two wives, who had each committed suicide, summoned a psychic to perform an exorcism.

Early adopters of celebrity coupledom, a chauffeur carried them around Manhattan in a Mercedes that sported a license plate that bore their combined names: Mauizia. They hung out with Jackie Onassis and the Kennedy brood whenever they were all in town. Patrizia famously summed up her lavish luxury lifestyle with this nugget of wisdom: "I would rather cry in a Rolls than be happy on a bicycle." The television shows *Dallas* and *Dynasty* did not even approach the extravagance of the high-flying Tuscans.

When Rodolfo died, his will bequeathed Maurizio 50 percent of his fashion empire, but this amount was not enough for the Italian Lady Macbeth. She wanted her husband to be the head honcho of the House of Gucci and to secure the dynasty for their daughters. In a Night of the Long Knives, Maurizio succeeded in ousting his cousins, as well as driving out the company's chairman, Aldo Gucci, without even giving him a chance to clear out his desk. Patrizia—twelve shades of Kris Jenner—not content with being the power behind the throne, raising her children, and managing her mega-homes and the *Creole*, designed a signature line of gold jewelry for Gucci that featured chunky pieces imprinted with a crocodile-skin pattern that proved a major flop. A far more worrisome problem was that Maurizio had grown weary of his wife, who manipulated him in the same fashion as had his controlling father. Tom Forden, a creative director for

Gucci, stated, "As a young man, he looked to Patrizia to support him and give him the strength to stand up to his own father, but as he gained power, he felt oppressed by her criticism." Soon there were reported sightings of the Gucci heir parading a string of mistresses about in New York, Milan, Rome, and St. Moritz. In 1985, he packed his bag, informing his wife he was going on a business trip; he then sent over his family doctor—armed with a bottle of valium—to inform her Maurizio would not be returning. The effect of this pronouncement was similar to the one Mount Vesuvius had on Pompeii. No doubt, in lieu of Maurizio's head, she banged her own on the conveniently leather-covered walls. At least she did not do to the doctor messenger what Cleopatra did to those who brought her bad news. The expression of Patrizia's fury was to come at a later date.

What further enraged her was that Maurizio proved unequal to holding onto the reins of his fashion house. In one emasculating comment on "Mau," as she called her spouse, she pronounced, "He is a seat cushion that takes the shape of the last person to sit on it." The heir to the House of Gucci had his back against his leather-covered wall; he had borrowed heavily to secure control of his company, as well as to finance his own lavish lifestyle, and his personal debt was as formidable as the mountains of his beloved St. Moritz. Patrizia had once remarked that the Guccis had followed the pattern of many family dynasties: the first generation builds, the second consolidates, and the third destroys. The Italian family would have done well to have heeded the words of the American founding father Benjamin Franklin: "A house divided against itself cannot stand." With a heavy heart, Maurizio sold his birthright—for far more than a "mess of pottage"—to the tune of one hundred seventy million dollars to Investcorp, a Bahrain-based investment company. For the first time since its founding, no Gucci was at the helm of the company that bore its name.

Maurizio offered Patrizia a one-hundred-thousand-dollar monthly allowance; she scoffed at the offer, which she referred to as "a plate of lentils." To escape the paparazzi, who were having a feeding frenzy with the high-profile divorce, she took her two daughters to their home in St. Moritz. One shudders to think how she reacted when she found Maurizio had changed the locks, preferring to keep it as a love nest for his new blond girlfriend, Paola Franchi, an interior designer. Maurizio had hired a "Magia Bianca" white witch to cleanse the mansion of his ex-wife's evil spirits. Patrizia devoted herself to a smear campaign of her ex and voiced an endless litany of complaints about the paltry divorce settlement. She lamented on an Italian chat show, "How am I supposed to live, with only three trillion lire in the bank, a house in Rome, and one in New York? I do have two daughters to take care of, you know." Life took a further downward spiral when Patrizia developed a brain tumor. She later stated, "When I went into the operating room, I said, 'I must survive, because, Maurizio, I will make you pay for all the bad.' "

For years Patrizia fermented in her bitterness, made even more acidic by the fact she never fell out of love, declaring, "Maurizio was my husband. I was and will always be in love with him." She would have remained a showy and pathetic member of the first wife's club except for the fact that a well-dressed hit man shot four bullets into Maurizio. The polizia were at a loss as to the identity of the perpetrator, as there were many suspects: his relatives, the mafia, who were angered at his newly acquired Swiss casino, and his embittered spouse. His body was barely cold when the widow moved into her former husband's Milan home along with her two teenage daughters. She stated, "He may have died, but I have just begun to live."

A break in the case came when the police, acting on a tip, questioned Ivano Savioni, a porter at a sleazy hotel, who said he had been contacted by Guiseppina Auriemma, Patrizia's personal psychic, to hire hit man Benedetto Ceraulo and getaway driver Orazio Cicala, who was deeply indebted to loan sharks, to murder Maurizio. Once Auriemma was in custody, she claimed Signora Gucci had given her a note in an attempt to buy silence, telling her, "Leave me out of it, and I'll shower you with gold." Aware money would be useless in prison, Auriemma promptly made a full confession. Later Patrizia said of her former clairvoyant, "Never let even a friendly wolf into the chicken coop. Sooner or later, it will get hungry." Two years after the murder, Patrizia entered a police car; aware of the photo op that the occasion presented, she wore a heady array of jewelry with a floor-length mink coat and clutched a Gucci handbag. She had proved the veracity of the Oscar Wilde quotation, "Each man kills the thing he loves."

The trial of the strange bedfellows—psychic, doorman, hit man, and society woman—electrified Italy, and the press dubbed her *Vedova Nera*: the Black Widow. The scandal became the ultimate real-life soap opera as it showcased the country's favorite interests: sex, money, vendetta, designer footwear, and astrology. Moreover, the setting was elegant Milan, not mob-infested Naples. One piece of evidence against Patrizia was a single word entry in her diary the night of Maurizio's murder: "Paradeisos"—the Greek word for Paradise. After her sentence of twenty-nine years, amidst the tears of her mother and daughters, Signora Gucci stated, "Truth is the daughter of time." Upon her conviction, Gucci's flagship store in Florence displayed silver handcuffs.

After fourteen years in prison in San Vittore, where Patrizia once attempted suicide, she became eligible for day release on the condition she obtain a job. Her response to the sweat-of-the-brow offer was she had never worked a day in her life and preferred to stay in her cell to water her plants, await Friday nights when her mother brought her meatloaf, and look after Bambi, her pet ferret. Patrizia was devastated when Bambi met his demise due to an inmate accidentally sitting on him. Lady Gucci eventually had a change of heart and took a part-time position at the Milan fashion house Bozart; afterward, she strolled through the fashion district with a blue and yellow macaw perched on her shoulder. Despite having orchestrated her husband's murder, the court ruled she was entitled to nine hundred thousand pounds a year from his estate. With back payments from her years in prison, trustees of the estate forked over more than sixteen million pounds, thereby disproving the adage that crime doesn't pay.

The crying clown Canio delivers the last line in *Pagliacci*, one that can serve as the curtain call for the Guccis: "The comedy is over."

Chapter 20

My Gold (1950)

The world's greatest tragic heroines sprang from the ancient Greeks, who squeezed every nuance of pain from the dark forces that knit their destinies. Medea, the archetypal woman scorned, wreaked vengeance on Jason by serving him a stew—with its chief ingredient their two sons. In her footsteps walked an heiress relentlessly pursued by the Furies.

The oxymoron "poor little rich girl" existed prior to Christina Onassis, but she proved to be its ill-starred embodiment. She was born in New York City, the only daughter of two Greek shipping dynasties: her father was Aristotle Socrates Onassis, and her mother was Athina Livanos. Her elder brother, Alexander, was the heir apparent, and Christina's role was to partake of pampered privilege and to propagate the dynasty.

From her earliest days, Christina was at the eye of the media storm; the public never grew jaded with news of the girl on whom the cornucopia had been upended. She first saw her family's floating Xanadu at age three when her father pointed to the yacht whose prow bore her name. While Shirley Temple sang "The Good Ship Lollipop," Christina had her own six-million-dollar version. The mural on her nursery wall came from the brush of *Madeline* artist Ludwig Bemelmans; her dolls wore handmade clothes from the House of Dior. On the bulkheads hung a Gauguin, a Pissarro, and two El Grecos. The barstools in the luxury liner were fashioned from the foreskins of whales, leading to Onassis's favorite bon mot, "You are sitting on the largest penis in the world." Little Christina was the owner of a purebred Mongolian horse, a gift from the King of Saudi Arabia. Other Onassis pleasure domes were located in Paris, London, New York, the Riviera; however, the one nearest and dearest to his heart, his fiefdom on the private island of Skorpios, was situated on the Ionian Sea. The constant stream of guests on the *Christina O* were the names of legend: Winston Churchill praised her youthful drawings; Greta Garbo and Gregory Peck fussed over her. Aristotle showered presents on his daughter and cooked her Greek dishes, though she favored her American nanny's cheeseburgers.

Though Christina was an adorable toddler, as she matured, her features favored her father, and she fell short of her mother Athina and her Aunt Eugenia's Grace Kelly beauty. Plump and shy, she also suffered as a silent witness to her parents' stormy marriage and their frequent absences as Aristotle pursued additional millions and Athina frequented jet set soirees. During Christina's long and lonely times without her parents, the palatial houses never equated to homes.

The first dramatis persona in Christina's tragedy was opera great Maria Callas, a guest on a Mediterranean cruise that also included Sir Winston and Lady Clementine Churchill. The diva and the tycoon developed a powerful attraction that no camouflage could cover. They danced the night away on the yacht's swimming pool, the décor of which displayed a mosaic of the Minotaur; it had the capacity to transform into a makeshift ballroom. Athina smoldered at her husband's public philandering; however, Aristotle—with his fortune and hubris at their height—was indifferent to her fury. When the *Christina O* docked at Monte Carlo, Maria and her husband departed for Italy with Onassis in hot pursuit. Athina'd had enough and, with children in tow, abandoned the ship. Christina recalled, "That night was confused—Daddy wasn't there. I imagined that I was losing something important. I didn't know what. Mother only said we had to leave, and she was sure we were not coming back." The heiress hated the other woman, who she blamed for her parents' divorce; whenever she visited her father, Aristotle made sure his mistress was out of sight, though her shadow was ever present.

The affair between the diva and the billionaire continued until Onassis set his sights on the world's most famous widow: former First Lady Jacqueline Kennedy. As Princess Grace and Prince Rainier had done a decade before, the Greek tycoon and the American celebrity held their wedding reception aboard the *Christina O*. Aristotle celebrated the acquisition of his ultimate trophy wife, while Jacqueline celebrated the acquisition of her trophy ring. Onassis's son and daughter wept—and not from tears of joy. Alexander said of his new stepmother, "It's a perfect match. My father loves names and Jackie loves money." The international press went into overdrive and dubbed the new Mrs. Onassis Jackie O; Christina employed a less charitable epithet.

Aristotle had planned to give his daughter twenty-one ships as a coming-of-age present; however, in retaliation against his marriage to the woman to whom she referred as "my father's unfortunate obsession," Christina took her own trip down the aisle in a three-minute Las Vegas civil ceremony. The groom, Joe Bolker, was a divorced realtor twenty-seven years her senior, and a father of four with a penchant for heiresses. Aristotle reacted with a Zeus-like fury and threatened to cut her off from her birthday present of a trust fund of seventy-five million dollars. Part of her father's anger stemmed from Bolker's Judaism; he feared his son-in-law's religion would alienate his Arab connection which was instrumental to his shipping empire. Distraught at the fatherly fury, Christina checked into a hospital, reputedly as a result of a suicide attempt. After a grueling nine months, the Bolkers divorced. Joe later said of his short-lived nuptial, "Listen, when a billion dollars leans on you, you can feel it." Aristotle rewarded his prodigal daughter with a whirlwind trip around the world.

Christina was thrilled to be reconciled with her father, but soon Hamlet's admonition came to call: "When sorrows come / They come not in single spies but in battalions." The first of these was when her Aunt Eugenia, who was married to Ari's archrival Stavros Niarchos, committed suicide. Three years later, twenty-four-year-old Alexander, whom their father referred to as his alpha and omega, died from injuries sustained in a plane crash. The crushing blow transformed the dashing Aristotle into an old man, and in their shared grief, father and daughter drew closer. Christina, still reeling from her losses, soon had to deal with another: her mother, who had married her brother-in-law, took an overdose of sleeping pills. When Christina arrived to pay her final respects to her mother, she found Niarchos dining with eighteen guests at a table adorned with candles, silver, and wine while Athina's body lay in the next room. The callousness of it shook Christina to the core. Mere months later, with the Fates weaving destinies overtime, Aristotle became ill. Christina lamented, "Happiness is not based on money. And the best proof of this is our family." At his funeral, Jackie showed up with Ted Kennedy who infuriated a grief-stricken Christina by talking about Jackie's share of the estate. Her stepdaughter wrote out a check for twenty-six million dollars and later remarked, "The joke is, I would have given her fifty times what I gave her for the pleasure of never having to see her again."

Perhaps as a posthumous apology to her father, four months after his passing, she wed the man whom Aristotle had wanted as a son-in-law, Greek shipping heir Alexander Andreadis. The union, undertaken for dynastic purposes, soon foundered on the rocky cliffs of the Aegean. On Skorpios, Alexander injured his leg in a motorcycle accident. His wife signed his cast, "Bon voyage, Alexandros, better luck next time." She then boarded her private jet for her luxurious apartment overlooking the harbor of Monte Carlo.

After the demise of her family and both her marriages, Christina once again found herself alone—and solitude had always proven an Orwellian Room 101 for her. As an antidote to depression, she medicated her pain with junk food and ballooned to two hundred pounds. Her private humiliation was fueled with public pillorying: gossip columnists referred to her as "Thunder thighs" and "the Greek Tanker." In the belief that diet Coke helped curtail cravings, since her beverage of choice was only available in the United States, she dispatched her private jet to America once a month for a fresh supply at a cost of thirty thousand dollars per trip for fuel, pilots' salaries, and beverage.

Obese and despairing, Christina desperately sought companionship, and, as with everything else, it was something for which she was willing to pay. In case friends might be elsewhere when needed, she put them on her payroll—at a rate of thirty thousand dollars a month—with the stipulation that they come when called. And when she played hostess, they were compelled to abide by her unique house rules. No one was allowed to go to bed until she had worked off her own amphetamine-induced insomnia. In addition, there was to be no lovemaking under her roof: if she did not have something, no one else could either. Maids were instructed to check the bed sheets each morning for telltale signs of transgression; offenders were exiled.

Christina once stated, "My most fervent wish is that I shall meet a man who loves me for myself and not my money." Husband number three was a peculiar choice: Sergei Kauzov, a Moscow-based member of the Communist Party. Perhaps as the daughter of Midas, she was attracted to his gold teeth, though the allure of his glass eye remains enigmatic. For her part, Christina gave up her European homes, and on his end, he relinquished his cellist wife, Natasha, and their nine-year-old daughter. Alas, just as the Russian winter defeated Napoleon of France, it did likewise for the Greek heiress. Fourteen months later—with a ship as alimony—the marriage hit the rocks.

The fourth trip down the aisle was reportedly Christina's great love. In 1984, she married French businessman Thierry Roussel, whom the international press dubbed "The World's Most Successful Gigolo." To mark the occasion, she gifted him ten million dollars; on a less romantic note, he requested she drop fifteen kilos. What would have been far more jarring to the bride was that unbeknownst to Christina, he had been living with a Swedish beauty, Gaby Landhage, for a decade and was not about to let a foray into holy matrimony interfere with his relationship. The marriage brought Christina her crown jewel: her daughter, Athina Helene Roussel. What dampened the joys of motherhood was that five months later, Gaby gave birth to a son. Christina still remained committed to her vows until Gaby's second child arrived; Christina obtained a quickie divorce. Nevertheless, she still wanted another child, and Thierry complied by conveniently supplying her with a bank of his sperm. Christina expressed her gratitude with a $160,000 Ferrari Testarossa sports car and the promise of a ten-million-dollar bonus if she delivered another baby.

Christina was distraught at the failure of her marriage to her American, Greek, Russian, and French husbands and flew to Buenos Aires hoping to find the happiness that had always proved elusive. In the city whose name translates to "good air," she paid Luis Sosa Basualdo one thousand dollars a day for companionship and sex. He remarked she was "about as sexy as a walloping hippo."

In South America, the thirty-seven-year-old Christina seemed to have at last managed to find contentment. She had lost forty-five pounds at a Swiss clinic; she doted on her daughter and found another prospect for romance: Jorge Tchomlekdjoglou, an Argentine she hoped would become husband number five. But on the night of November 19, 1988, Christina took her nightly sleeping pill; the next morning, her maid Eleni discovered her lifeless body in a bathtub. The official cause of death was a heart attack brought on by years of binge eating, grueling diets, and heavy doses of amphetamines.

The heiress lay in a white satin-lined casket, and even in death, she was subject to the scrutiny she had always endured. Camera crews were allowed into the chapel, and the deceased, clad in a white tunic with her hands folded around a single red rose, became for the final time the object of the paparazzi's flashbulbs. Her final resting place was in the family crypt in Skorpios, where the heiress lies beside her father the modern Midas, whose term of affection for his daughter had been, "*Chryso mou*," or "my gold."

Chapter 21

Rosebud
(1954)

A variation on the 1950s catchphrase from *The Adventures of Superman* states, "Faster than a speeding bullet! More powerful than a locomotive! Able to leap tall buildings in a single bound! Is it a bird? Is it a plane? No—it's fake news." William Randolph Hearst was the master of tabloid journalism, but the life of his granddaughter rivaled even his most sensational headlines.

Patricia Campbell Hearst was born the third of five daughters in Hillsborough, California, one of America's priciest enclaves. Although the mansion was magnificent, it did not compare to her grandfather's castle in San Simeon—California's Versailles—perched atop La Cuesta Encanta, the Enchanted Hill. The heiress attended a series of Catholic schools and, to the dismay of her parents, their beautiful debutante daughter fell in love with her math tutor, Steven Weed. When he left for a graduate position in philosophy at the University of California (of which her mother was a regent), the two moved in together, and Patty enrolled at Berkeley as an art history major. She showed scant interest in the great causes of the day: America's involvement in Vietnam was creeping its way to an ignominious close, the Watergate scandal that brought Nixon to his knees was swirling through Washington, and the Black Panthers were flexing their muscles. Berkeley was a hotbed of student rebellion, but Patty, groomed for a life of luxury and leisure, remained aloof to the radicalism. Her apathy soon underwent a radical metamorphosis.

In February 1974, Steven opened the door to a young woman who said she had car problems and needed to use his phone. The next moment, two armed men forced their way in, blindfolded Patty, and repeatedly beat her fiancé with a wine bottle. The intruders forced the traumatized teen, clad in a blue housecoat, into the trunk of their car. When the news broke, the press gave it as much attention as they had the Lindbergh baby kidnapping.

The amalgam of money and mayhem proved to make for irresistible copy.

The Symbionese Liberation Army, contemporary Robin Hoods who had pledged to steal from the rich to give to the poor, was behind the abduction. The SLA took their name from "symbiosis;" their ideology derived from a mix of black power and Maoism. The disappearance of the Hearst heiress received round-the-clock coverage, but the network news, unsure how to handle a gang of terrorist hippies, made the SLA counterculture superstars by broadcasting their every rant about capitalist pigs and imperialist warmongers. To add to this bouillabaisse, the SLA used a communal toothbrush, practiced free love, and had as its anthem, "Death to the fascist insect that preys on the life of the people." Randolph Apperson Hearst, the billionaire editor of *The San Francisco Examiner*, the cornerstone of his famous father's newspaper, frantically waited to find out the amount of his daughter's ransom.

The kidnapping by the certifiable radicals was sensational enough, but what followed raised the bar on bizarre. The SLA released a tape to the media in which Patty claimed the people she was with were her comrades and fellow soldiers. The recording ended by calling her wealthy parents pigs. In early April, another tape bore the message, "I have been given a choice of being released or joining the forces of the Symbionese Liberation Army and fighting for my freedom and the freedom of all oppressed people. I have chosen to stay and fight." The heiress made a further announcement in which she relinquished her name; from then on, she took up the name Tania in honor of Tamara "Tania" Bunke, the martyred lover of Che Guevarra. The homegrown terrorists also sent a photograph of Hearst standing in front of a flag bearing the SLA's seven-headed cobra insignia.

In lieu of money, the Symbionese Liberation Army wanted to hold Hearst hostage and swap her for two jailed group members charged with murder—an idea then-Governor Ronald Reagan immediately rejected. They also instructed Patty's father to fund a multimillion-dollar food program for welfare recipients. Although the family complied, implementation proved to be a disaster. Hearst hired people to distribute cans and produce that they threw from moving trucks, resulting in rioting as people fought over the handouts. The media went into an even greater orgy in April when Tania got her gun and participated in an SLA robbery of Hibernia Bank—one owned by the father of her former friend. Patty appeared in the jerky frames of a surveillance video with a beret on her head and M1 carbine in hand, shouting demands at terrorized tellers. The photograph became one of the most iconic of the decade. The picture also made the formerly sympathetic media change its perspective, and the press thirsted for the rich kid's blood—as did the public. A month later, Tania sprayed a Los Angeles sporting goods store with automatic fire as her cohorts robbed the premises. Clues led the police to a house where the group's core members were hiding; after a two-hour siege, six terrorists were dead. Jubilant LAPD cops joked SLA stood for "So Long Assholes." For sixteen months, the remaining gang remained on the run, surviving by their wits and petty theft. The police finally arrested Patty in San Francisco after a tip-off. The nation watched with bated breath to see who would emerge from the fray: Patty the heiress or Tania the radical. The answer came when, before stepping into the police vehicle, the Hearst heiress gave a clenched-fist salute; in custody, she stated her occupation as an urban guerilla.

For the trial—as closely followed as Charles Manson's, which had captivated the country seven years earlier—the Hearst family hired F. Lee Bailey, future star attorney of O. J. Simpson's Dream

Team. He portrayed Patty as a victim rather than a victimizer, and prominent psychiatrists testified that Patty suffered from Stockholm syndrome. He related that when she had first arrived at an SLA safe house in Daly City, her captors had locked her in a closet for fifty-seven days and only released her to subject her to rape and indoctrination. The defendant swore she could no more have escaped her captors than a monkey could have escaped its organ grinder. In contrast, the prosecutor painted her as a rebel in search of a cause who had found it with the homegrown hippie terrorists. The country held its collective breath as the jury deliberated whether Hearst was a crime victim or an heiress turncoat.

A popular television series of the '70s was *Happy Days*, but its name did not presage Patty's fate. Mainstream America wanted her to pay, and she was more unpopular than the Zodiac Killer who was then on the loose. The jury took only one day to decide on a verdict of guilty, and the judge meted out a sentence of seven years. Her co-defense attorney later recalled, "She was a victim of a cruel kidnapping. She was a victim of the American people, who despised her because she represented the radical nature of young people at the time. She was the victim of the rich, who thought of her as impudent and disrespectful, and a victim of the left and the poor, who saw her as a spoiled little rich girl." The Hearst family was enraged at what they believed was a travesty of justice; her sisters referred to her imprisonment as a second kidnapping. Her supporters felt Patty—except for her name and fortune—had been a typical teenager who had endured five years of torment followed by a three-ring-circus trial. Like Paul Simon's Julio, Patty's image stared back from the cover of *Newsweek*; in her case, she appeared there several times.

At the medium-security prison in Pleasanton, California, the heir to a dinosaur-sized trust fund of twenty-five million dollars worked as a waitress for two cents an hour and, as she quipped, "The tips are lousy." One of her fellow inmates was Lynette "Squeaky" Fromme of Manson family infamy, though Hearst held a dubious position as the prison's most celebrated inmate. However, when Squeaky escaped and attempted to assassinate President Gerald Ford, she garnered top prison billing upon recapture. The saga of Patricia Campbell Hearst came to an official close when President Jimmy Carter curtailed her prison sentence after twenty-two months; later, President Bill Clinton granted her a full pardon. The two reprieves may have accrued from having a family who could pull powerful strings. The presence of more than a hundred reporters and photographers, armed military police, and a hovering helicopter that all gathered at her release testified interest in her had not waned.

Patricia Campbell Hearst has donned many guises: pampered daughter of privilege, Berkeley student, urban guerilla, Pleasanton prisoner; the common denominator amongst all these reincarnations was her ability to survive, a resilience of which Grandfather Hearst would have approved. And what helped her do so post-incarceration was the steadfast support of Bernard Shaw, a divorced former police officer. They had met in 1976 at San Francisco's Top of the Mark restaurant the day after Hearst left jail on $1.5 million bail. Shaw was one of twenty bodyguards hired by the Hearst family. After the United States Supreme Court refused to hear her appeal and she had returned to her cell, Shaw drove sixty miles from his home four times a week to visit. On Valentine's Day in 1978, they were married in a brief but well-publicized Episcopalian ceremony at a naval base in San Francisco Bay. Shaw had insisted that it take place in a military compound out of fear of kooks. Her parents predicted

such a short shelf life for the union that they merely gave a Sears
vacuum cleaner as a present. But the marriage proved happy,
and they had daughters, Gillian and Lydia Hearst-Shaw. Of
meeting the woman he called the love of his life, Bernard stated,
"I remember I thought she was awfully small. And I thought she
was cute. She had a real nice smile." He also proved to be her
protector, ensuring she wore a bulletproof vest when she walked
from prison a free woman, though forever a captive of infamy.
Shaw was the opposite of Weed, who, in a nod to his name,
had turned on his former girlfriend when the mega-sized shit
hit the fan.

With the passage of forty decades, Patricia Hearst-Shaw has
donned another face, that of society matron. The role was almost
permanently derailed—when she became the ultimate "girl
interrupted." Today, the East Coast heiress, with her carefully
coiffed and highlighted hair, bears little resemblance to the
willowy, black-bereted, gun-toting Tania. Her only foray into the
outrageous occurred at a Thierry Mugler fashion show in Paris
where she strode down the runway in giant shoes and performed
a striptease. Another sighting in the spotlight was when she
acted in the musical *Cry Baby* with Johnny Depp. Other than
that, the newspaper heiress has largely stayed out of sight,
describing herself as "just a boring old small-town mom," not
surprising for someone who had already garnered far more than
her fifteen minutes of notoriety. Few echoes of the past followed
her to Wilton, Connecticut, an old-moneyed town of large houses
where neighbors included Keith Richards of the Rolling Stones
and actor Paul Newman. The only nod to yesteryear is that the
home has a state-of-the-art alarm system and guard dogs. But
what permeates the security is the indelible shadow cast by the
SLA, which will never completely disappear, nor will questions
over whether Tania was in actuality Patty's violent alter ego or

merely a brainwashed pawn. In either contingency, it is safe to assume that the designer-dressed matron represents everything Tania hated.

Currently, she is a widow with adult daughters, whom it is safe to say she never admonished with the words, "When I was your age…" She breeds "Frenchies"—a more voguish version of the traditional English bulldog, a breed that she presented at the Westminster Kennel Club show at Madison Square Gardens. On that occasion, the verdict went her way when her puppy, Diva, took home a prize and offered the public a glimpse of what had happened to a post-urban-guerilla bank-robber heiress.

There are still no easy answers in the curious case as to how Hearst metamorphosed from carrying a carbine to holding a grooming brush, but as Patty knows, the past, like a bulldog's jaw, never lets go. The question of the truth as to her role in the Symbionese Liberation Army provides a link to her grandfather's celluloid alter ego, Charles Foster Kane, whose dying word lay behind his mystery and can represent his granddaughter's own: "Rosebud."

Chapter 22

The House of Hancock (1954)

The British Prime Minister Margaret Thatcher garnered the epithet "the Iron Lady" because of her tough as nails tactics when she ruled from her crow's nest at 10 Downing Street. In the Land Down Under reigns another Iron Lady, so called because of her aggressiveness and the source of her fortune, one as vast as her native outback.

Lang Hancock was a prospector in the Pilbara, a sweltering wilderness in northwest Australia. In 1952, he was flying in an Auster aircraft with his second wife, Hope. As he navigated through the narrow gorges through torrential rain, he noticed walls of rust-colored mountains, a hue derived from oxidized iron. The enterprising Lang saw the natural resource as a river of gold. The vision laid the foundation of a mining empire that transformed him into the Australian King Midas. His only child, Georgina Hope Hancock, was born into the lap of luxury in Perth. Lang had hoped for a boy, whom he had planned to name George after his father. Nevertheless, dad and daughter were, as the expression states, "thick as thieves," and he took her to meetings around the globe to the amusement of bankers and sheiks. The Hancocks lived in the Pilbara, and on Saturdays, the family flew six hundred miles to buy groceries. After Hope developed breast cancer, they relocated to Perth to be near a hospital.

From her early years, Lang groomed Gina, as she preferred to be called, as his heir apparent, and the proud papa referred to her as his "right-hand man." A typical parenting tidbit of his, one that revealed his economic bias, was, "The best way to help the poor is not to become one of them." Gina was so possessive of her papa that she was averse to her mother riding with them in the family Rolls Royce. When she boarded at St. Hilda's, a girls' school in Perth, Lang came to visit in his Rolls where they spent hours talking. A far cry from Jane Eyre at Lowood, when Gina obtained her driver's license, her doting dad had ten cars delivered to her school so she could select the make and model.

When the BCC made a film about Lang entitled, *Man of Iron,* the crew interviewed the twelve-year-old Lang Mini-Me, who stated, "I think my father is nearly perfect. I think he's quite handsome, except a bit fat." Similarly, when a reporter wrote an article on the captain of industry, his daughter revealed her chief passion was for all things mineral. Years later, when asked her definition of beauty, she replied, "An iron mine." Lang said his daughter was not as tough as he was; then he added, "far tougher by a long way."

Gina attended the University of Sydney, intending to major in economics, but her studies only lasted a year. She found lectures by a left-leaning professor anathema; as a teen, she was already a devout capitalist. She once shouted herself hoarse (while wearing a sizable string of pearls) with the cry, "Axe the tax!" On another occasion, she showed her empathy was not with the travails of the working class, declaring, "If you're jealous of those with more money, don't just sit there and complain; spend less time drinking, smoking, and socializing." She held up African miners who worked for less than two dollars an hour as a wishful example. Alexander Abad-Santos, a journalist for *The Atlantic,* said of her that she "is that perfect mix of Bond villain, Marie Antoinette, and Cruella de Vil." She had learned economics at the knee of an industrialist who made Ayn Rand look like a socialist. Alienated from her classmates and college life, she returned to Perth.

The rope binding father and daughter frayed when Gina uncharacteristically put her heart before her pocketbook. In her late teens, she fell in love with an Englishman from the working

class, Greg Hayward, who went by the surname Milton. Lang
felt Hayward was not worthy of his heiress daughter, but Gina
persisted in her relationship. Feeling she was making a mistake,
he was a no-show at the wedding and did not walk her down the
aisle of Sydney's St. Andrew's Cathedral. The union produced
children John and Bianca, but the marriage floundered. Post-
divorce, Greg moved into a small flat and took a job as a truck
driver hauling meat carcasses. When visiting his children, he did
so while sitting on a blanket in the garage of his wife's mansion.
Eventually, he lost contact with John and Bianca and did not see
them again for two decades.

At age twenty-eight, Gina tried her hand at matrimony once
more with fifty-seven-year-old American tax lawyer Frank
Rinehart. She described him as "the finest gentleman I have ever
known." Lang again withheld his blessing and absented himself
from his daughter's Las Vegas wedding. Father knew best in this
case. Frank's rap sheet showed he had falsified his tax returns;
this led to disbarment and resulted in a one-year suspended
jail term. His son from a former marriage admitted that when
Frank had met the heiress, he did not have a stable job and
"was looking for a secure port in a storm." The union resulted
in daughters Hope and Ginia; her son John claimed Frank was
brutal and that when angered, he had punched John in the face.
As an adult, to distance himself from his hated stepfather, John
changed his name from Rinehart to Hancock. After Frank's death
in 1998, Gina discovered he had a past to which she had never
been privy during pillow talk. As a Manhattan attorney in the
1960s, he had lived with Lorraine Boyce and her children in an
apartment on Fifth Avenue. On the weekends, he returned to his
official residence in Massachusetts, one he shared with his wife,
Elizabeth, and their three sons. Frank died intestate when Hope
and Ginia were toddlers, and Gina sought ownership of his New

York City apartment, deaf to the seventy-year-old Boyce's pleas that she had lived there for twenty-six years. In the words from *The Godfather*, "It was only business."

When Frank passed away, Gina, a single mother of four who was unable to simultaneously tend to her aging father, hired Rose Lacson, a thirty-four-year-old woman from the Philippines, to care for the seventy-three-year-old Lang. To his daughter's abject horror, the multimillionaire began a relationship with the help, and Gina tried her utmost to have the thorn-in-her-side Rose deported. She pointed out to her father that he was the butt of dirty old man jokes and that there was no fool like an old fool. The reproaches fell on deaf ears, and he retaliated in a letter, "If you won't consider my well-being, at least allow me to remember you as a neat, trim, capable and attractive young lady—rather than the slothful, vindictive, and devious baby elephant that you have become." The latter was a dig at Mrs. Rinehart's weight, which had ballooned over the years. He threw in an extra kidney punch when he added, "I am glad your mother cannot see you now." Even more unforgivable in Gina's eyes, two years later, he committed the cardinal sin of *marrying* Rose, an act that must have resulted in Gina's cry being heard round the Pilbara. Gina was a no-show at the wedding.

In the throes of his infatuation, Lang built his bride a white-pillared water-view mansion perched on the Swan River called Prix d'Amour, the Prize of Love, patterned after Tara in *Gone with the Wind*. For their honeymoon, the workaholic took time out for a round-the-world honeymoon in his Learjet. Gina referred to her stepmother as "that Filipina prostitute who snared a multimillionaire twice her age." Lang passed away in 1992, and Rose became Perth's Merry Widow. She became less merry when her despised stepdaughter initiated legal action and accused her of causing her husband's death to gain control over the Hancock fortune. A detractor referred to Gina as a "human bulldozer," ruthless when crossed. The case dragged on for ten years, and the Rinehart legal eagles leveled charges that spanned the spectrum of adultery, drug abuse, hit men, and black magic. In the end, the former maid cleaned up and walked away with millions of dollars. However, Gina retained sole control of Hancock Prospecting, which laid the foundation of making her the wealthiest woman in Australia.

The Iron Lady does not bend when crossed; rather, she goes into pit bull mode. This character trait manifested in 2012 when a dynastic soap opera played out on an outback stage. Lang Hancock had created the Hope Margaret Hancock Trust for his four grandchildren, which entitled them to ownership of a quarter of his empire that would provide them with five billion dollars. Gina, anxious to retain the sole power of the throne, informed her children the day before the transfer of shares was to take place that she was postponing it to 2068—a date when the kids would be senior citizens. After they countered that she was circumventing their birthright, she threatened them, "The clock is ticking. There is one hour to bankruptcy and financial ruin." Her three eldest children described her maneuver as "deceptive, hopelessly conflicted, and disgraceful." Ginia, the youngest, sided with her mother, and her reward was costly gifts, such as a Rolls and the promise that she was the heir apparent. After John, Hope, and Bianca launched a lawsuit to gain their inheritance, Gina saw herself as the Australian King Lear, burdened with thankless children whom she referred to as "slackers." Another reason behind her less than maternal action was she felt her spoiled offspring were not capable of running a business. This was the gospel according to Gina: "Whatever I do, the House of Hancock comes first. Nothing will stand in the way of that. Nothing." Gina certainly gives Mommy Dearest a run for her money. An iron mine is an apt metaphor for her steely personality.

Without a hint of irony, Gina Rinehart spoiled her children yet later lashed out at them for being spoiled. She claimed they had all enjoyed privileged upbringings of private schools and private jets, overseas travel, designer clothes, expensive jewelry, helicopter lessons, and multimillion-dollar homes with water views and swimming pools and therefore did not have the requisite self-reliance to head Australia's foremost fortune. John, who had spent his life preparing to head his grandfather's company, was less than pleased when his mother informed him he would take the reins of the business "over my dead body," and as a result, he did not invite her to his wedding. He was so incensed by his mother that he vented to a reporter that Gina had threatened to cancel his ransom insurance. He stated, "What more can I do than communicate to any kidnappers out there—if you think you are going to get any money out of my mother, good luck."

Hope married an American and moved to New York City. After the lawsuit, she sent her mother an avalanche of desperate emails after Gina cut the purse strings. In one, she complained she did not have enough money for a housekeeper, cook, and bodyguard: "Even my friends who have nothing compared to your wealth have more staff. I don't think you understand what it means that the whole world thinks you are going to be wealthier than Bill Gates—it means we all need bodyguards and very safe homes!" Ultimately, after splitting with her husband, when she was down to her last sixty thousand dollars, Hope reconciled with good ole mom. Bianca, whose appearance makes her the recipient of a genetic lottery as well as a financial one, harbors so much rancor for her mother that not only did she not extend an invitation to her Hawaii nuptials, "mum" was also not even made aware of the wedding. The bride also kept her two sisters off the guest list for failing to back her and John's lawsuit. A working title for a miniseries on Rinehart could be: Mother Monster Magnate.

The Australian press had their own American-style *Dallas* drama with which to titillate their readers when yet another salacious tidbit made an appearance. Hilda Kickett, an Aboriginal, claimed to be Lang's illegitimate daughter, a result of a liaison with his young cook. She grew up in a Perth orphanage, where Lang contributed to her upkeep by sending her ten pairs of shoes a year. Kickett did not seek money, just family acknowledgment, which Gina never gave. If that did not kick up enough dust, a former live-in security guard accused the heiress of sexual harassment and claimed she had become abusive when he spurned her advances. He told a magazine his former boss was "just incredibly lonely and isolated."

King Midas was ecstatic with his gift until he tragically turned his daughter into a pillar of gold—an ancient Greek myth that has symbolic overtones for the Australian iron miner's daughter. Although Gina can wax poetic on the intricacies of finance, she could learn a lesson from a man born in a Kentucky log cabin, namely, that "A house divided against itself cannot stand." Abraham Lincoln's quotation referred to a country locked in a bloody civil war, but it is equally apropos to the House of Hancock.

Chapter 23

The Alchemist (1962)

An ancient Roman saying admonishes, "Caesar's wife must
be beyond suspicion." A Bavarian billionairess lived by this
creed until a scandal erupted that transformed her into Bambi,
blinking in the glare of the international headlights.

The names Rothschild, Rockefeller, and Vanderbilt conjure
images of economic Everests; however, another financially
august name remained relatively unknown until its skeletons
emerged from the family closet. Susanne Hanna Ursula was
born in Bad Homburg, an exclusive suburb of Frankfurt, to
Herbert Quandt and his third wife, Johanna. Her father was
the mastermind who made BMW, Bavarian Motor Works, into
a luxury car colossus. Their stratospheric fortune allowed them
to live a life that entailed "the best of everything," yet it carried
a hefty price tag. In 1978, fourteen convicts on day release from
the local prison plotted to kidnap Johanna and Susanne to gain
a twelve-million-dollar ransom. The local police foiled the plan,
but the incident turned mother and daughter into recluses,
and their home became a fortified villa for Susanne and her
brother, Stefan.

When Herbert passed away in 1982, he left his heirs sitting
pretty: his wife, who had once been his secretary, became
Germany's wealthiest woman, financially ranking just behind
Queen Elizabeth II of Great Britain and Queen Beatrix of the
Netherlands. Wary of outsiders, the Quandts are steadfast in
their refusal to grant interviews or pose for photographers;
unwelcome visitors are discouraged by a constant security force.
Johanna, who passed away in 2015, had a desire for anonymity
that made her the German Greta Garbo and garnered her
the epithet "a nun in a golden convent;" she held an iron grip
on BMW. Stefan, possessor of good looks and a bottomless
pocket, made annual appearances on Germany's Most Eligible

Bachelor List until his marriage. As for Susanne, she chose
not to tread the path of heiresses behaving badly. Never a fan
of resting on designer laurels, she obtained business degrees
from universities in London and Lausanne and worked in an
entry-level position in order to learn the family business from
the bottom up. Eschewing deferential treatment or untoward
scrutiny, she went by the alias of Susanne Kent. At work, she met
Jan Klatten, an engineer, who did not discover the background of
his girlfriend until she was certain he was not eying her many-
digit bank account. The couple married and moved to Munich,
where Susanne became a soccer mom to three children while
continuing to serve on BMW's board of directors. Life was akin
to soaring along the Autobahn in a luxury BMW—until it hit a
speed bump.

In 2007, at the ultra-luxurious Lanserhjof spa, set high in the
Tyrol above Innsbruck, Austria, the attractive, forty-five-year-
old Susanne was enjoying the sunshine poolside, immersed in
Paulo Coelho's best-selling novel. An unassuming, bespectacled
man who bore a marked resemblance to Clark Kent introduced
himself as Helg Sgarbi. He nodded at her book, mentioned he,
like the author, was from Brazil, and said the novel was his bible
as it conveyed the spiritual message one must never abandon
one's dreams. By most standards, it was not the most engaging of
pickup lines coming from someone who could best be described
as nondescript, yet the pragmatic Klatten, possessor of an MBA,
on the board of directors of BMW, married matron, and mother
of three was taken in by the charm of the soft-spoken Sgarbi, who
could sweet-talk in six languages. As a woman who had spent
her life coached on the necessity for discretion, she should have
been suspicious; instead she was enraptured. Helg's allure might
have stemmed from the fact that, in Susanne's own words, "He
was a good listener." For the last days of her holiday, Klatten

and Sgarbi strolled through the spa's beautiful Alpine grounds, sipped tea, and talked. After decades of holding back, Susanne found herself opening up. She later recalled, "He seemed very sad. That stirred a feeling in me that we had something in common." (As to what reasons Frau Klatten had to be sad, in the words of Simon and Garfunkel, "The information is not available to the ordinary man.")

Before they parted, they exchanged mobile phone numbers, and hours after her return to Munich, he was sending her text messages and telephoning with declarations of love. Four weeks later, their relationship crossed the line into the horizontal plane when they rendezvoused at a hotel in the south of France, not far from one of Susanne's seven homes. The affair escalated, and, when Klatten returned to Munich, she started meeting her lover at a Holiday Inn in the low-rent Schwabing suburb, which she hoped was down-market enough for there to be no chance of bumping into anyone from her rarified inner circle. Susanne took the added precaution of going straight to his sixth-floor room via an elevator from the underground parking garage to avoid being seen in the lobby. Other romantic getaways took place in the romantic backdrop of Monte Carlo.

During one of these trysts, Sgarbi tearfully told Susanne he had been on a business trip in Miami where he had run over a mafia godfather's daughter, and that now the mob was demanding ten million dollars in compensation or he would be swimming with the fish. In response, the besotted billionairess met him in room number 629, and after they made love, she opened her suitcase and gave the money to the man who had stolen her heart, along with her common sense. She helped him carry the eighty-eight-pound luggage to his Audi, and he kissed her and told her he was leaving for America to pay off the don, although he did not explain how he was going to carry that staggering amount of currency on a commercial airline. Perhaps Frau Klatten only read the financial pages, because Sgarbi had obviously borrowed the scenario from a chapter from the dapper don, John Gotti. In 1980, Gotti's unfortunate neighbor had accidentally run over his twelve-year-old son, and the mobster had arranged for his neighbor's dismemberment.

Appetite grows with the eating, and Sgarbi's dream—à la Coelho's novel—was to supplant Jan Klatten and become a BMW billionaire. However, his charms proved finite, and Susanne made it manifestly clear a marital relationship was not in the cards. She had never meant her affair to be more than a fling: she would not consider dissolving her long-term marriage, upsetting her mother and three children, and having her divorce wind up as fodder for the press. His demand served as her wake-up call, and she bid him *auf wiedersehen.*

The Swiss gigolo had taken out preemptive insurance against the day his source of income might dry up: in room 630 at the Holiday Inn, his accomplice had filmed their trysts—capturing every nuance of pillow talk, every sexual position. Sgarbi showed her the thirty-eight-minute tape as well as pornographic photos and threatened to share them with her husband, the board of BMW, and the media unless she paid him $420 million. Klatten succeeded in haggling the sum down to a far smaller amount, but she was just staging a dog-and-pony show. She had informed her husband and the police about the blackmail and prior extortion. Klatten was well aware of the price of her disclosure: no one of her status could go to the authorities on the matter of a blackmailing Romeo and expect it to remain under wraps. In her only interview, she stated, "That was a moment of clarity; you are now a victim, and you must defend yourself." She arranged a rendezvous; as Sgarbi waited at the highway rest stop in Austria expecting to once more collect a suitcase filled with cash, armed members of Cobra, the Austrian commando team, dressed in balaclavas, took him into custody. Clark Kent had met his kryptonite. The tabloids had an orgy feasting on a scandal that oozed money, sex, and blackmail. The public thought the story could not get any juicier—until it did.

Sgarbi's accomplice, the man who took the videos, was a former secondhand car dealer, Ernano Barretta, who was the head of an obscure pseudo-Catholic sect situated in Abruzzo, Italy. Some of his more outlandish claims were that he walked on water and exhibited stigmata; in addition, he had thirty disciples who delivered their earnings to him and paid sexual tithes. The polizia arrested the Latin Rasputin and charged him with extortion. An interesting result of his incarceration was his admission that he was the master manipulator who controlled Sgarbi, a devotee of his cult. The shysters had buried their ill-gotten gains on the grounds of Barretta's home base, the Valle Grande Country House; some of it had been transformed into luxury cars, including a Ferrari, a Lamborghini, and a Rolls Royce Silver Shadow (no BMW). The appearance of this colorful dramatis persona added a further element of salacious drama. What with the Italian guru, the Swiss gigolo, and the German billionaire, the scenario resembled an American *Peyton Place*, and it took yet another bizarre twist.

During the investigation, the larcenous Lothario stated that his shakedown against Susanne was not borne from materialism but rather for retribution. Sgarbi claimed he was exacting vengeance for the crimes of Gunther Quandt (Klatten's great-grandfather), who had used his grandfather, a Polish Jew, as a slave laborer in Quandt's BMW factory that produced war materials for the

Third Reich. Thus, he was sleeping with the enemy as a means of gaining reparations sprinkled with vendetta. The explosive revelation turned a spotlight on the Quandt dynasty, perhaps exposing the real reason they chose to dwell in the shadows. Journalists dug for dirt, and they stumbled upon a mother lode: the blue-and-white Bavarian logo camouflaged a black swastika. The spotlight on the dynasty's fortune recalled the quotation from *The Godfather*, "Behind every great fortune there is a crime."

The unwelcome scrutiny centered on Gunther Quandt; after he and his first wife, Magda (mother of his son Harald), had obtained a divorce, she married Nazi propaganda maestro Joseph Goebbels (nicknamed the Poison Dwarf) in a ceremony where Hitler had served as the best man. Magda had six children with Goebbels, all of whose names began with the letter 'H' in honor of the Führer. Susanne's great-uncle Harald was the only child to survive, as Magda and Joseph had poisoned their children before committing suicide in the Berlin bunker. Gunther's professional life was equally unsavory; in 1937, Hitler bestowed on him the title Wehrwirtschaftsfüeher, an honor reserved for the elite businessmen who were beneficial to the Third Reich. His armaments factories were staffed with more than fifty thousand forced civilian laborers, prisoners of war, and concentration camp workers (the average death rate of the workers was eighty per month). To round off Susanne's annus horribilis, perhaps because of the scandal, a German documentary was made entitled *The Silence of the Quandts*, which further publicized the family's bloodstained past—and the fact they had never made financial restitution to their surviving victims or their descendants. The revolting revelation rivaled the darkest pages of the Grimm Brothers' fairy tales.

When the Greek Pandora opened her box, a host of evils were unleashed, yet hiding amongst the horrors was Hope. In the same fashion, when the German Susanne embarked on her affair, slimy revelations were uncovered—though there was an echo of redemption. In court, Sgarbi agreed to plead guilty, perchance in atonement, which saved his former fling from having to testify. Perhaps the confession stemmed from an emotional tie for his former lover, and the gigolo extraordinaire finally became the gentleman Klatten had once believed he was.

Gunther Quandt had used slave labor to line his pockets just as the gigolo had faked affection to get his hands on the BMW fortune. The transforming of base metal into gold is a nod to the seamy underbelly of money. The medieval chemistry is also a symbolic nod to the novel that brought together the Swiss opportunist and the Bavarian heiress: *The Alchemist*.

Chapter 24

The Death of the Hired Hand (1962)

In the Robert Frost poem "The Death of the Hired Hand," Silas returns to Mary and Warren's farm asking for a job. Infirm and incapable of working, Mary admonishes her husband by saying, "Be kind." In contrast, an heiress did not show a similar quality of mercy to her gaucho.

Sam Cummings, the founder of Interarms, became a billionaire by supplying weapons to the world's warmongers, dictators, revolutionaries, and heads of state. He took no sides in international conflicts and remarked, "We like to say whoever wins, we win." The unapologetic mercenary's empire garners one hundred million dollars annually.

The Philadelphia-born Cummings moved to the tax-free haven of Monte Carlo, where he lived with his Swiss-born wife, Irmgard Blaettler. In 1959, the couple welcomed twin daughters, Susan and Diana, pronounced in French "Suzahn" and "Deeahna." The family lived in a magnificent fourteen-room home in close proximity to the celebrated casino, a focal point of the principality for more than a century. The view from their fashionable address showcased the yachts of the Mediterranean and the mountains of Corsica, the birthplace of Napoleon. On this citadel above the sea, the twins spent their fairy-tale childhood; Grace Kelly was their local princess and her pink palace its scenic backdrop. However, wealth came with a cost: the Cummings' home was replete with armor-plated, double-locked doors.

The twins were bilingual, speaking English with their father and French with their mother; their unofficial third language was twin talk—the sisters conversed in a secret code known only to them. In the summer months, the Cummings family traded the French Riviera for the Swiss Alps, where they owned a sprawling chalet in the mountainside village of Villars. Susan's childhood

sadness stemmed from the fact her father spent months traveling
for business. Wherever there was political turmoil, he was there:
in Cuba for Fidel Castro, in Haiti for Papa Doc Duvalier, in the
Dominican Republic for Rafael Trujillo. Unlike Diana, Susan was
an introvert and found comfort in the four-footed: cats, dogs,
and horses.

Despite her European roots, Susan was drawn to America; she
enrolled in Mount Vernon College in Washington and graduated
with a BA in the arts and humanities. However, her interest lay
with animals; had wealth not robbed her of incentive, she would
probably have veered to a career as a veterinarian. In 1982, Sam
bought his daughters an eighteenth-century stone mansion,
Ashland Farm, a 339-acre estate located in Warrenton, Virginia.
Along with its hefty $2.9 million price tag came history: Union
troops had used it as a base in the Civil War. Diana ended up
living in one of the cottages on the expansive grounds while
Susan, along with two dozen cats, occupied the main home.
A room displayed Susan's gun collection, which ranged from
ancient muskets to shiny handguns. Susan's favorites were
her Walther pistols; her father owned its American franchise,
including James Bond's weapon of choice. Father and daughter
shared their love of weaponry; another commonality was
extreme stinginess. Despite his many-digit bank accounts, Sam
flew standby and stayed in hotels that offered bargain rates.
From his home in Monte Carlo, Sam stayed in contact with
friends through typed postcards on which he filled every space—
even if he had to resort to describing the weather—because he so
abhorred waste.

Warrenton is known as horse country—this was its chief draw
for Susan. Offices, motels, and taverns sport pictures of horses,
and the weekly newspaper, the *Fauquier Times-Democrat*, is

dedicated to all things equestrian. The town serves as a seat of genteel wealth; the local gentry are the Mellons, the DuPonts, the Hammer heirs (as in Arm and Hammer), and the Kennedys. Besides showcasing the usual trappings of money such as Rolexes, Chanel purses, and personal chefs, the pricey zip code provides an added luxury: polo, dubbed the sport of kings. Not surprisingly, one of Warrenton's chief imports is the Argentine polo player, a man who can do a lot for the sport's adherents, and for many of the local horsewomen; such a man can serve as arm candy with six-pack abs. The subculture of the obliging Latin polo player might have remained an obscure local custom but for a romance between one of these Latin Valentinos and a European heiress.

In the summer of 1995, Susan decided to try polo both as a recreational outlet and as a way to meet a man. Although she was an heiress with a slim figure and an attractive face, she had trouble socializing with the local gentry. This stemmed from a combination of her aloof personality, her French-Swiss accent, which contrasted with the local drawl, and her tomboy garb of pants and no makeup that jarringly contrasted with the image of the Southern belle. When Susan joined the Willow Run Polo School, one with a view of the Blue Ridge Mountains, she was flattered at the attention from its star sportsman, Roberto Villegas, whose trademark was a red helmet. The polo groupies who attended the matches dressed in miniskirts and high heels referred to him as "the prize." Although romances between the polo pros and wealthy horsewomen were commonplace, what raised eyebrows was when the affair between Susan and Roberto morphed into a romance.

The lovers proved an odd couple: Susan was a university-educated Monaco heiress, while Roberto had been born in

Argentina on a farm without plumbing, electricity, or telephone. Villegas, who had left school after the seventh grade and had been too poor to afford a car, had become proficient on horseback, a skill he used as a ticket to America. As a newly arrived immigrant, he spoke no English and had only one piece of luggage, as well as green-tinged teeth, a product of exposure to the chemicals in the drinking water of his impoverished village. A local dentist gifted him a set of pearly whites, and he was soon on the road to becoming the leading ladies' man of the horse set. Susan was thrilled; her habitual glum expression transformed into a smile. Many viewed their relationship as one of expediency: he gave sex, and she gave money. In truth, the Scrooge-like heiress was no Sugar Mama. In order to remain with Susan, Roberto had foregone relocating with his polo team for the winter season; this had entailed forfeiting his four thousand dollar a month salary and left him financially dependent on Susan.

On a September Sunday in 1997, a high-society crowd gathered on the grassy field of the Gone Away Farm to watch a charity match between the U. S. polo team and Argentina. Roberto was a no-show, and his many friends and fans were concerned; the event's post-game party was going to provide an opportunity for the erstwhile farm boy to mingle with the ambassador of Argentina, an occasion Roberto would not have willingly foregone. When the explanation for his absence became apparent, the news pushed coverage of horses from the front pages of the *Fauquier Times-Democrat*.

Responding to a 911 call placed by Susan Cummings, law enforcement descended on Ashland Farms. Finding the sisters speaking in either French or twin talk, the police silently followed the young women through the mansion, where they noticed the profusion of both cats and shelves filled with an array of weapons. In a small kitchen, originally built as a maid's quarters, Roberto Villegas lay on the floor with multiple bullet wounds to his neck and chest. Beside him was a pool of blood and a Walther pistol.

The startling event divided the horse country and brought the international press to the customarily serene setting. In a nod to the idea that there is no guiltier pleasure than learning of the sins of the rich, the media had a proverbial field day. *Time Magazine* covered the case under the headline, "Murder in Pololand;" *Inside Edition* ran it as well. A local woman said of the sea of reporters who had descended on the upscale community, "There wouldn't be all this fuss if her daddy didn't have all that money." The drama had all the salacious elements: money, mayhem, and murder, sprinkled with a dose of *Lady Chatterley's Lover*. To add to the bubbling bouillabaisse, Cummings hired celebrity attorney Blair Howard, who had successfully defended Lorena Bobbitt; she had famously pleaded self-defense after cutting off her husband's penis and driving away with the offending member.

Those who sided with Susan claimed Roberto had a violent temper and had been abusive to his former girlfriends. Her detractors claimed she was the classic woman scorned, as Roberto had been openly cheating on her, something the spoiled Susan could not tolerate. What the detectives focused on was whether the marks on her arm, uniform in length and superficial, had been self-inflicted to bolster her claim of self-defense.

The entire polo community packed St. Stevens Catholic Church in ritzy Middleburg for Roberto's funeral service. The founder of the Palm Beach Polo Club gave the official eulogy, in which he stated, "He loved the sport of polo and everybody loved him."

At a local funeral home, mourners filed silently past the open-casket viewing where his body lay, dressed in his riding clothes. At his feet rested crossed polo mallets next to a ball signed by his teammates; on his head was his red helmet.

After one night in the Warrenton jail, Susan retreated to her estate and cats after putting up the seventy-five-thousand-dollar bail. She stated that when the nightmare was over, she would forge a life away from the polo crowd who had turned on her. She envisioned her future, "In the middle of nowhere...with lots of wildlife. It's terrible that people hurt one another so much."

During jury deliberation, a gaunt Susan waited for the verdict that would determine if she would remain in her estate home or a prison cell. A sentence of first-degree murder would mean life imprisonment; for the charge of voluntary manslaughter, she faced up to thirty years. Her recently widowed mother flew in from Monaco and joined her sister; they were her staunchest supporters. At the trial, the majority of spectators were sympathetic to the murder victim; they did not buy Susan's story that she had fired in fear for her life.

The jury found the heiress guilty of voluntary manslaughter; since in the state of Virginia, the jury is also responsible for the penalty phase, they shockingly only sentenced her to sixty days imprisonment and a fine of two thousand five hundred dollars. At a news conference, Cummings smiled and said she felt very happy; her lawyer called the outcome "unbelievable." In contrast, one of the people who had followed the trial groused, "Normally there would be a much more serious price to pay. You could get five years in Virginia for killing a horse."

What further aroused the community's anger was the preferential treatment the heiress received in the local jail, where she only stayed for forty-five days due to good behavior. This period of confinement may not have proved difficult as officers had transferred all the other inmates to different facilities. The authorities explained the reason for the evacuation was because the rest of the prisoners were serving longer sentences for less serious crimes, and thus Susanne may not have been their favorite person. The only posthumous justice for Roberto was that Howard's attorney fees ran in the six-figure range, and the Villegas family won a wrongful death suit, both hard pills to swallow for the tightfisted heiress.

To distance herself from the furor over how many felt that she was getting away with murder, Susan retreated to Ashland Farms, hoping to put the past behind her. She repeatedly asked her attorney why people were being so mean. The answer might be found in the title of Robert Frost's poem. Unlike Mary, who had shown kindness to Silas, Susan had been responsible for the death of the hired hand.

Chapter 25

Protects What's Good (1964)

In 1944, Evelyn Waugh wrote to an old friend, "I am writing a very beautiful book, to bring tears, about very rich, beautiful, highborn people who live in palaces and have no troubles except what they make themselves, and those are mainly the demons, sex and drink." In his novel *Brideshead Revisited*, the chief victim of these self-appointed troubles, a British lord, serves as a parable of the tragedy of entitlement. If Waugh were alive, he could write its sequel. Its demon: drugs, its protagonist: an American heiress.

The origins of some of the world's great fortunes have curious stories; acts of serendipity, dumb luck, or the building of a better mousetrap. In the 1950s, the Swedish Ruben Andersson adopted the surname Rausing when fellow servicemen nicknamed him "Rausingen," the lad from Raus. His wife, Elisabeth, suggested he invent a lightweight alternative to milk bottles, and the result was Tetra Pak. If you are an average human, through the purchase of items such as juice, yogurt, and ice cream, you will consume twenty-three Tetra Paks annually. Commercial success arrived when his sons, Hans and Gad, turned it into an international behemoth. With immense wealth came the desire to shelter it from Sweden's prohibitive taxes, and Britain became home to the reclusive billionaire brothers. In 1993, they led *The Sunday Times* list as the country's wealthiest men—men whose fortune eclipsed the queen's. Hans sold his half of the business to his sibling for a multibillion-dollar sum that allowed his children Sigrid, Lisbet, and Hans Kristian a life of unfathomable leisure. In the vein of the American Kardashian girls, the Swedish Rausing sisters rose to the challenge, while Hans K (as he's known, to distinguish his name from that of his father) faltered. He had been emotionally impaired as a "trustafarian;" this was compounded by being the only son, scion, and namesake of his six foot eight inch papa, who towered over him physically and in business acumen. His sense of inadequacy led Hans to seek enlightenment in India, but what he found instead was a full-blown drug addiction. He returned from his mecca of hippy hedonism in Katmandu emaciated, his upper arms thinner than his wrists. The Rausings wondered why their prodigal son, despite the blazing Indian sun, was so pale. The answer lies in a mathematical equation: a predisposition for drugs + limitless cash = Mount Everest-sized trouble.

Eva Louise was the daughter of Nancy and Tom Kemeni, the latter of whom was a millionaire executive for the Pepsi Cola Corporation. The family's main residence was in the resort town of Hilton Head, South Carolina, and other homes were in Barbados and London. The Kemenis, including daughter Be, moved often due to Tom's career, and Eva, who was born in Hong Kong, spent her childhood in Sydney, Milan, Rome, and London. As a teen, she majored in pharmacology at Occidental College, a private liberal arts school in Los Angeles. Her interest in pharmacology extended to illegal and prescription drugs. Prior to university, Eva had been a regular cannabis user; at Occidental (nicknamed Oxy), she flirted with harder drugs.

Bright and beautiful, Eva became a rehab veteran, attending as many as eleven; however, she always bolted before completion of treatment or relapsed upon release. Scott Alderman, a fellow detox alumnus, met her in 1986 when they were both patients at Gracie Square Psychiatric Hospital on the Upper East Side of Manhattan. (Thelonious Monk used to convalesce in the selfsame spot.) They bonded over commonalities: both were spoiled, Jewish, college dropouts and emotional and physical wrecks from the ravages of heroin. Scott was attracted to the warm, stick-thin blonde, who he recalled was "the royally fucked-up hippie chick of my dreams, like Edie Sedgwick." He said that although they had been using for the same amount of time, she had the countenance of someone who was coming off a twenty-year binge, even though she was only twenty-two. Post-discharge, they embarked on a five-day run; she was the first woman he had ever seen shoot up in her neck.

In the 1990s, rehab doubled as a matchmaker; at a high-end facility outside London, the troubled worlds of Eva Kemeny and Hans Kristian Rausing collided. For their 1992 wedding, the bride wore a headdress adorned with yellow flowers, and the Archbishop of Sweden presided over the ceremony. Hans, who had never had a serious job, still had unlimited income, and the Rausings embarked on a lifestyle of which even Jay Gatsby dared not dream. Home base was a wedding-white, six-story, fifty-room mansion in Chelsea, one of London's most desired zip codes (with price tags soaring north of one hundred million dollars). For a change of pace, they built a retreat in Barbados with twelve acres of beachfront and occupied a suite on the luxury cruise liner the *World*; its condo owners can visit, say, Copenhagen, Italy, and Athens, all without leaving their palatial floating apartments. *The Sunday Times* reported it "perpetually roams the seas like the Mary Celeste."

The couple, well-respected as philanthropists who gave to anti-drug charities, garnered glowing comments for their generosity from close acquaintance Prince Charles. The royal was on a first-name basis with the couple, and Eva often sat beside the heir to the throne at charitable events. Eva was co-patron with the Duchess of Cambridge of the drug charity Action on Addiction. The American beauty, elegantly attired, appeared on the social scene, a flamboyant partygoer who loved to dance—often on tables. Exuding warmth and humor, she put a human face on a fabulous family fortune.

The New Year's Eve welcoming in the millennium proved
portentous for both Eva and her sister. During a Barbados party,
Be met polo player Jack Kidd, great-grandson of press baron
Lord Beaverbrook. The millennium celebration augured even
more drama for the elder Kemeny sibling.

For a decade, Hans K. and Eva had lived in a protective bubble of
contentment with their four children, whom their mother called
her greatest achievement. Their charmed life burst on December
31, 1999, when Eva indulged in a glass of champagne, and like
her biblical namesake, proffered the same poison to her husband.
In a further Old Testament parallel, alcohol led to exile from
Eden. The small glass of bubbly to toast in a new century had
dire repercussions, along the vein of "one drink is too many, and
a thousand is not enough." After years of sobriety, liquor sent
them back on the dire road of addiction.

Encased in their cavernous home and disease, they became
hamsters running on a wheel of desperation; it mattered not
that their cage was a fifty-room mansion. Eva confided on her
Myspace account, "I fell back into the same hole as before."
When Alice fell down the rabbit hole, she had no idea where
she was going; however, Eva did, and yet she was powerless to
return. The Rausing family tried to rescue their black-sheep
couple and hired an eight-man unit of former SAS soldiers to
sabotage their efforts to buy drugs. At a reported cost of one
hundred thousand pounds per month, the team followed Eva,
hoping to scare off dealers. The tactic failed. Alderman wrote,
"If someone desperately wants to stay clean, she could be a
billionaire living in a shooting gallery and she won't use. And
if she wants to use, you can hire a SWAT team to stop her, and
it won't do any good." As they became increasingly unstable,
their children moved in with Hans' sister Sigrid, who obtained

custody; Hans and Eva accused her of stealing their children, and the loss fueled a further downward spiral. They began an odyssey to escape their demons, and the walls of the Barbados estate came to be more relied on to lock themselves in than to keep intruders out; the *World* became the *Flying Dutchman*—where the Rausings tried to outrun their demons. The press reveled in their seemingly globe-trotting ennui and wrote, "It takes billions to buy this much boredom."

Tom and Nancy must have been pleased their daughters had each landed a European billionaire; however, as Robert Frost presaged, "Nothing gold can stay." Be's marriage dissolved when she saw incriminating evidence on her husband's computer. Before she smashed the purveyor of infidelity and threw its remnants in the lake beside her home in Windsor, she sent out two hundred emails denouncing Jack as a cheating cad. She packed up their four children and returned to Hilton Head.

In 2008, when Eva and Hans attended a soiree at the American embassy, officials conducted a routine search and discovered crack cocaine and heroin in Eva's designer clutch; a police investigation of their mansion uncovered a further two-thousand-pound stash worth thousands of dollars. The incident turned what had been an open secret in their circle into a slow-motion car crash. Prince Charles rushed to their defense, successfully arguing for a second chance. The Rausings did not show up for court, and the prosecution, nudged by the powers that be, dropped the case. The police commissioner said of the preferential treatment, "It reminds me of the nineteenth-century legal comment, 'In England, justice is open to all—just like the Ritz.' " If the Rausings had been working-class blokes, they would have canceled their mail for the discernible future. However, the couple's entitlement worked against them: had they been incarcerated, they would have been forced into treatment. The scandal caused personal sorrow and public humiliation to the Kemeny and Rausing families but, in the words of Al Jolson, "You ain't heard nothin' yet."

In 2012, the police stopped Hans for erratic driving, and they understood the cause when they detected a still-warm glass crack pipe. In the trunk were bundles of letters addressed to his wife; his answers as to her whereabouts proved evasive. With their suspicions on high alert, they accompanied him to his mansion to see if there was a further cache of contraband. As they wandered throughout the fifty rooms, they may have marveled at the treasure trove of tapestries, paintings, and endless rooms.

Hans had instructed his three Filipino maids that the master bedroom was a no-entry zone and they no longer had to clean it or change the sheets. His explanation was Eva was ill and could not be disturbed; they assumed that was why Hans had started sleeping on a downstairs sofa. Eva's illness also explained why her Ferrari stood in the garage under layers of dust. When police entered the suite—cryptically sealed with duct tape— they discovered that, unlike in the rest of the pristine mansion, rubbish dominated, and the air was thick with flies. In a further nod to the bizarre, a tarpaulin, assorted items, and a fifty-inch flat-screen television covered the bed. The unfolding scenario was one for which no amount of academy training could have prepared the bobbies (British police). After they removed the items, a blonde head appeared; skeletal hands clutched a crack pipe.

The corpse—that had decomposed for two months—could only be identified by teeth, a fingerprint, and the serial number on a pacemaker. (Cocaine had weakened Eva's heart.) Hans had attempted to camouflage her passing by deodorizing the bed and piling it ever higher with miscellaneous items, an action prompted by either massive denial of his wife's demise or fear of going to the authorities. He explained the macabre event, "With the benefit of hindsight, I do not believe I acted rationally." Alexander Cameron, the Prime Minister's brother, represented Hans; the judge found him guilty of preventing lawful burial and pronounced a ten-month suspended jail term. Rausing's real sentence was self-purgatory, wondering what had happened to his privileged life. If the saga of Hans had appeared in one of fellow Swede Stieg Larsson's thrillers, it would have meshed in with the author's world of a modern Gothic entailing huge wealth, family fallout, vice, and death, all intertwined in a tragic and macabre tale.

The narrator of *Brideshead Revisited* opined, "My theme is memory, that winged host." For the heir, memory is a host that enslaves, much like the fortune that only purchased him a vault of anguish. In light of the saga of Hans and Eva, the motto of the Tetra Pak takes on an ironic overtone: *Protects what's good.*

Chapter 26

Googoosha
(1972)

Leo Tolstoy began his novel *Anna Karenina* with the words,
"Happy families are all alike; every unhappy family is unhappy in
its own way." The latter part of the quotation is exemplified by a
fractured First Family that provides a new dimension to the term
"dysfunctional." They also prove that at times the grander the
house, the greater the grief.

Once hailed as the legendary Silk Road, Uzbekistan's storied
wealth is long gone; electricity and gas are in short supply, but
the scarcest commodity is freedom. The czars ruthlessly ruled
until the fall of the Romanovs, and President Islam Karimov
instituted an authoritarian regime similar to that of North Korea.
As the self-proclaimed leader for life, he walked the footsteps
of despots who pilfer to deepen their pockets. Wealth was an
important perk of the position since Karimov had started life
in a Samarkand orphanage. With his second wife, Tatiana
Akbarovna, he had two daughters, Gulnara and Lola. The adored
children were not only endowed with great privilege, but they
were also blessed with beauty and brains. Karimov viewed
Gulnara, who favored him physically and in personality, as the
heiress apparent, and the coffers of Uzbekistan were her oyster.

Gulnara graduated from Tashkent State University, followed
by a course in jewelry design at the New York Fashion Institute
of Technology. The Renaissance woman garnered a black belt
in karate—and shopping—and obtained a master's degree
from Harvard. Never one to err on the side of all work and no
play, the eighteen-year-old became romantically involved with
Mansur Maqsudi, an American businessman of Afghan origin.
For an up-and-coming entrepreneur in 1991, the eighteen-year-
old Ms. Karimova was the most promising marital prospect in
Uzbekistan. Her father was the puppeteer of his nation, and six
foot tall Gulnara, who described herself as an "exotic Uzbekistan

beauty," could have served as a runway model. After the couple's wedding, Maqsudi derived his income as an Uzbek Coca-Cola executive; his father-in-law mandated that his soft drink was the only permissible one in his fiefdom.

Maqsudi and Gulnara had a daughter, Iman, and a son, Islam; the family divided their time between the United States and Tashkent. The marriage lost its luster after a decade, and Gulnara claimed her husband had tried to impose an oppressive Muslim way of life. She groused to *The Washington Post*, "I was not supposed to swim in the pool with my son because I was in a separate swimming suit [a bikini]." Maqsudi's version of the crumbling union's troubles was they were due to her wild living and out of control spending. The final straw came in 2001 when Gulnara took her children to an amusement park in New Jersey and discovered her husband had canceled their joint credit cards. In the ensuing battle royal, his wife's bodyguards pinned him against the wall while an enraged Gulnara snarled insults. The next morning, Maqsudi played with Iman and Islam, unaware it would be the last time. A few hours later, the missus called to inform him she was returning to Uzbekistan and dropped the tidbit he would never be allowed to ever speak with his children again if he sought custody. She left behind a note, "There's an interesting movie. I hope you'll get a chance to see it again," and she added the time, date, and channel on which it was to air. The film was 1989's *The War of the Roses*, about a contentious divorce that culminates with the couple's death.

Despite the shock of losing his family, Maqsudi's troubles were in their infancy. Divorce is never easy, but parting ways with the daughter of one of the world's most notorious dictators presents even greater than usual challenges. President Karimov's retaliation against his son-in-law was swift. He ordered the deportation of twenty-four of Maqsudi's relatives—who before the divorce had been treated like royalty—to neighboring Afghanistan, regardless of their nationalities, and three were imprisoned. Maqsudi's elderly parents were subjected to strip-searches before departure. Although the international custody case became a hotbed topic on Capitol Hill, few held hope there would be any concessions from the central Asian country where Karimov's will was gospel. Mr. Maqsudi sagely refused to speak to the media. Nevertheless, he fought for his children, and a New Jersey court ruled in his favor. When Gulnara refused to hand them over, the US issued an international arrest warrant. In the divorce from hell, allegations escalated: she claimed he illegally sold Saddam Hussein's oil, while he alleged she shipped Uzbek girls to Dubai to work in prostitution rings. Was the airing of dirty linen ever dirtier?

Back home, Gulnara desired to be more than just her father's daughter and stacked any number of hats onto her assisted blond hair. Indeed, she became like a Donatella Versace, Hillary Clinton, and Ivanka Trump rolled into one. Her father appointed her permanent ambassador to the United Nations, a position that carried with it the fringe benefit of diplomatic immunity. For her new role, she purchased a sixteen-million-dollar mansion in Switzerland and filled it with ancient treasures from her country's state museum, so her knickknacks would evince panache. Her fabulous wealth, estimated at $570 million, allowed her to enjoy a lifestyle of staggering opulence; her fortune was reported to have come from her presidency of Uzdunrobita, a national Uzbek mobile phone network, a gift from her father that made her the tenth richest woman in Switzerland. Gulnara became a robber baroness who seized her impoverished nation's companies on a whim, with her dad's power making her untouchable. In 2010, she had the negative distinction of being the single most-hated woman in Uzbekistan, which under Karimova, became known as "Corruptistan." As official duties were marginal, she morphed into a fascist fashionista, launched a clothing line—GULI—and planned a splashy showing for New York Fashion Week. Alas, even for designing daughters, some rain must fall. After human rights groups protested the show over slave labor in Uzbekistan—namely millions of children harvesting cotton with little or no remuneration—the plug was pulled. Perturbed at the glitch, she focused on her teenage fantasy of starring as a pop diva.

The Uzbekistan princess became a disco queen and recorded a number of videos that showcased her as an Arabian Nights fantasy bedecked in diamonds as big as the Kremlin, suggestively gyrating against the backdrop of the fading turquoise domes of ancient mosques. In another music video, "Dare How," she ran her hands over her body and crooned, "She looks fine, but she has a hundred things on her mind." Although she graced the cover of *Billboard* magazine—an honor for which she paid—and performed a rendition of "Besame Mucho" with Julio Iglesias, her pop videos barely registered on the cultural radar outside Uzbekistan. A claim made within the Uzbek firewalled Internet proclaiming her song had made it to number five on the American music charts did not bear too much scrutiny. In an Amazon review, a critic wrote, "Amazingly rhythmic sounds of torture. I never knew the sounds of children laboring in the hot sun for twelve hours a day could be so relaxing and Enya-esque."

In a nod to reinvention, Gulnara tried her bejeweled hand at philanthropy. She co-chaired the US Foundation for Aids Research, and a photograph showed her at its gala charity event at the Cannes Film Festival in the company of Bill Clinton, Sharon Stone, and Claudia Schiffer. One wonders if the irony of her participation in the event was lost on the glittering guests: homosexuality is illegal in Uzbekistan and is punishable by three years in prison. The nonprofit Human Rights Watch submitted a report about the Karimova regime to the UN Committee Against Torture that claimed his secret police had set a rolled-up newspaper on fire and used it on a victim's genitals during an interrogation. Another chilling fact is his country had been under United States sanctions since 2004 when it came to light that political prisoners had died after being immersed in scalding water; more graphically, they had been boiled alive. Doctors had sterilized women to control the impoverished rural population.

The unstoppable Gulnara was finally brought to a screeching halt; it was time for the Uzbek chicken to come home to roost. Prosecutors launched a criminal probe aimed at Zeromax, one of her many companies, claiming it was a vehicle for its owner to receive bribes from businesses wanting to enter the Uzbek market. The biggest payoff was $340 million, allegedly paid by the Swedish telecommunications company TeliaSonera. Swiss authorities stripped Gulnara of her diplomatic post and froze her $912 million in assets. Investigators also confiscated some of her safety deposit boxes, filled with jewelry and artworks valued in the millions. The sting created a domino effect, and her corporations in France, the Netherlands, Britain, Latvia, Ireland, Malta, Germany, Spain, Russia, Hong Kong, and the United Arab Emirates tottered. Other wrenching moments came with the seizure of her villas in Switzerland, London, and Saint-Tropez and her private jet in Malta. Craig Murray, the British ambassador to Uzbekistan, described the princess as "one hell of a package" who was "richer than Paris Hilton, undeniably smarter, and arguably sexier." He also added that she was a beautiful but deadly James Bond style villainess who was guilty of crimes far worse than theft: she had business rivals executed. A chip off the old block is the expression that comes to mind.

Little sis Lola Karimova-Tillyaeva, Uzbekistan's former ambassador to UNESCO, promptly distanced herself from the sibling scandal. No more a fan of slumming than her sister, she owns a forty-six-million-dollar mansion in Geneva as well as the fifty-eight-million-dollar Le Palais, a faux French chateau in Beverly Hills, which, among other niceties, sports a pond replete with swans built by the billionaire developer Mohammed Hadid. She denied reports her wealth was a result of being the dictator's daughter; she attributed it rather to her husband, Timur Tillyaev, being a very hard worker. Be that as it may, Tillyaev has a monopoly on all goods imported into Uzbekistan, so his own are exempt from inconvenient customs inspections. By all appearances, he seems the doting husband and father of three. His attentiveness may be because he is indeed uxorious, in remembrance of what happened to his brother-in-law and an awareness of daddy-in-law's penchant for boiling people alive. In a BBC interview, Lola claimed estrangement from Gulnara and said she had not spoken to Gulnara in twelve years—their only shared link was bad blood. Gulnara, a snarling Uzbek tigress, took to Twitter and accused Lola and her mother of practicing sorcery and of conspiring to poison her father against her. She stated, "Envy or jealousy always destroys unity, even inside one household." There was also a falling out between father and daughter, and the dictator reportedly beat up Gulnara in a 2013 spat. To add to her litany of woes, the beauty of which she often boasted began to desert her, and she resorted to increasing doses of Botox.

Then, in a deafening quiet, the ubiquitous Gulnara disappeared from the spotlight she had always coveted, her overused Twitter

eerily silent. As Mr. Karimova had expelled nearly all foreign
journalists, reporting on his country tended to be fragmentary.
Hence, what truly transpired in the murky Shakespearean-
drama-worthy world of Uzbekistan's ruling family is open to
conjecture. One school of thought is that Karimov, after failing
to cow his prodigal daughter into the submission evidenced
by the rest of his subjects, reached his breaking point. She had
proved too much of a liability due to her financial scandals, her
embarrassing Internet rants, and her pop videos that showcased
her sexual slithering, something that never set well with their
Islamic country. Another school of thought asserted Karimova,
elderly and in frail health, had been reduced to being a puppet
dictator and was no longer able to protect his daughter from the
legion of enemies she once stepped on with her stilettos.

In either contingency, Gulnara is in dire straits, unable to
communicate with her children. Islam flew to Tashkent to reason
with his grandparents, but armed guards barred entry. He
turned to the Western press, voicing concern over his mother's
safety—there are rumors she has been subjected to mercury
poisoning. Perhaps Tatiana and Lola do possess the power of
casting spells. The only Gulnara sighting has been a single,
smuggled-out photo that showed her with disheveled hair,
without makeup, sitting on an unmade bed. Rather than sipping
from a Baccarat crystal flute, she was drinking from a carton
of Nesquik. Her straitened circumstances were a far cry from
her former Twitter selfies, where she used to pose in fur and a
tiara. Yet it is still far better than incarceration in Uzbekistan's
prisons with their unique form of capital punishment, a startling
fall from grace for the erstwhile jet-setter. In a smuggled letter,
she wrote in a bizarre rant, "The blood of my wounds does not
clot anymore, it's everywhere. Its taste is of salt, and its smell is

sharp. Why? Why...?" Her cry of "why" shows tragedy has not delivered insight.

It is impossible to know which of the "hundred things on her mind" weighs heaviest on Gulnara; however, no doubt one of them is when she indulges in remembrance of things past. And one of these painful reveries must recall when she was the crown princess of her father's heart, and when he lavished on her a childhood term of endearment—the one she used as her pop princess persona—*Googoosha*.

Chapter 27

No More Tears (1979)

The familiar pharmaceutical behemoth with the red and white logo traditionally carries connotations of comfort: bandages for cuts, talcum for diaper rash, tear-less shampoo for toddlers. However, behind the product is a dynasty beset by the shadow of "the best of everything."

In 1887, Robert, James, and Edward, the three sons of a poor Pennsylvania farmer, founded Johnson & Johnson. The event that jump-started the family fortune was the Great War; the company produced plasters and gauze for soldiers fighting on the front. The public, desperate for tidbits about the ultrarich, were seldom disappointed when it came to the Johnson clan. They produced an endless stream of scandal: untimely deaths, drug abuse, sexcapades. For good measure, there were also allegations of murder, suicide, and incest. One antic that sparked a paparazzi feeding frenzy was when seventy-six-year-old Seward Johnson married his thirty-four-year-old Polish chambermaid, Barbara "Basia" Piasecka, who ended up becoming one of the world's wealthiest women—a true-life tale that offers hope for all middle-aged, Polish chambermaids.

The most heartbreaking chapter in the family history concerned the founder's great-great-granddaughter, Sale Trotter Case (Casey) Johnson, part of a generation of girls famous for behaving badly. She was the first of three daughters of Woody Johnson, who purchased the New York Jets for $635 million, and Nancy Sale Frey, a former model from St Louis. Casey was born in Florida and raised in Manhattan in a home situated on Fifth Avenue, replete with nannies, butlers, and a chef who prepared special dinners for the three little heiresses: Casey, Jamie, and Daisy.

While other young girls experienced the world of fashion through their Barbie dolls, Casey satisfied her cravings with the real thing: at ten, she had her first Chanel purse; at eleven, handmade snakeskin pumps; and at fifteen, a seventeen-thousand-dollar gold Cartier watch. Even though she did not possess a driver's license, the sixteen-year-old had her own car, and two years later flaunted breast implants.

Doctors diagnosed Casey with diabetes, and her increasingly erratic outbursts were attributed to the disease. However, a psychiatrist later explained she suffered from borderline personality disorder, a condition marked by violent mood swings. The heady mixture of physical and psychological afflictions, intermingled with extreme wealth, made for a curdled cocktail.

Casey attended Manhattan's exclusive Chapin School, and she later enrolled in Dwight High School, where she befriended fellow immediate gratification gal pal Paris Hilton. The hotel heiress never graduated from the school known to New York preppies as Dumb White Idiots Getting High Together, but brainy Casey did, and she moved on to Brown University. However, Providence proved too provincial for her, and more pertinently, the college would not allow her poodle, Zoe, to live in her dorm. Her dogs were her lifelong loves; however, like their owner, they were not bound by the laws of self-control. On occasion, her teacup pooch, who she carried everywhere, would relieve himself in her twelve-thousand-dollar Hermes Birkin purse. In 2005, she was staying at a luxurious suite at the Plaza Athénée in Manhattan when Turkus, her Chihuahua, developed the runs and randomly anointed the hotel. As usual, Daddy was there to clean up the mess to the tune of twenty thousand dollars.

Unable to bear being separated from her pet, the debutante abandoned academia in her freshman year and dabbled in the world of work as a beauty editor for the *Manhattan File*. She said of gainful employment that it was great to have someplace to be where you're needed—despite the measly paychecks. In addition, she made clear that she wanted to establish her own identity, "I'm Casey Johnson. I'm not 'the Johnson & Johnson Girl.' " The blonde beauty was a staple for the gossip columns, especially the *New York Post's Page Six*, where she was dubbed the "baby-oil heiress." When her magazine folded, and also as a way to distance herself from her parents' divorce in 2001, Casey moved to California, where she lived in a $3.2 million Beverly Hills estate. The home's décor was eclectic: Buddhas surrounded by incense candles, wall-to-wall tiger-print carpet, and the pièce de résistance—an Andy Warhol portrait of Marilyn Monroe. One room-sized closet would have made Imelda Marcos' eyes widen: it showcased more than a hundred pairs of Chanels, Manolo Blahniks, and Christian Louboutins. Scattered throughout the house were a plethora of pee pads, because, as Casey explained, her dogs had never really managed to be housebroken.

In Los Angeles, Casey hoped that the sun would cure her New York blues and the flashbulbs would concentrate on the celebrities rather than the debutantes. She had a harrowing run-in with a horde of paparazzi in Saint-Tropez when she and Paris were spotted as they returned to the yacht of Hilton's then-fiancé, Paris Latsis, after a shopping spree. When they spied the cameras, the young women started running with the photographers in hot pursuit. Casey claimed they were literally pushed into the ocean, with their shopping bags floating alongside. The trials and travails of Paris and Casey probably garnered little sympathy from anyone except for others in their rarified inner circle.

Casey suffered from idleness and its accompanying specter of boredom, and she claimed the biggest mistake of her life was turning down Paris' offer to co-star in her reality show *The*

Simple Life, which made Nicole Ritchie a star. Of her aimless existence, Casey stated, "It's so boring to do nothing. It's like, how many days a week can you actually go shopping?"

With a surfeit of financial worth, but a lack of its emotional equivalent, Casey visited an orphanage in Phnom Penh that had been established by her aunt, the possessor of jaw-dropping wealth. Elizabeth "Libet" Johnson had been married five times and was still in the throes of going through fifty-million-dollar homes and men like tissues—one of these was singer Michael Bolton. The Johnson women were accompanied by Casey's boyfriend, John Dee, former husband of actress Lara Flynn Boyle.

When the trio returned to the States, Casey had a suspicion of something "unkosher" between her boyfriend and her aunt. The leak came from *Page Six*, which offered excerpts of emails from Libet to Dee, penned in an intimate tone. Casey claimed she could have "taken the high road" and kept mum, but holding back was never her modus operandi. She publicly accused her aunt of seducing her boyfriend and sneered, "An old woman with a lot of money is a very powerful aphrodisiac." In an interview in *Vanity Fair*, Casey posed almost naked except for a flimsy scarf, seductively smoking a cigarette. The Johnson clan was mortified by the humiliation of this heiress-versus-heiress battle, and Woody severed all ties with his daughter, whom he considered a tabloid terrorist.

Alienated from her once doting dad and emotionally adrift, Casey desperately sought to fill the void. She adopted a blond baby from Kazakhstan and chose Nicky Hilton to be her godmother; her own was Diandra Douglas, ex-wife of actor Michael Douglas. In a questionable move, she named her daughter Ava-Monroe after Marilyn, the idol with whom she identified. She bought her lavish clothes—including a leopard baby bikini—but as with her dogs, failed to provide anything remotely resembling structure. Casey hoped her daughter would end her estrangement with her father and traveled east to introduce him to his first grandchild. When mother and daughter arrived at his Hampton estate, he was not home, and they received a far less than welcoming reception from his younger, future second wife, Suzanne Ircha. Words flew and Ircha dialed 911. The police arrived at the same time as Woody, who demanded that Casey get off his property, stay off, and never come back. Sale was embittered at her former husband's Pontius Pilate attitude, evinced by his washing his hands of his child. She stated, "Fathers are supposed to take a bullet for their kids, and he went the other way."

Sale was concerned with Casey's escalating use of pharmaceuticals—most of them not available from Johnson & Johnson. Already a veteran rehab dropout, Casey's behavior became even more bizarre. She changed her sexual preference from men to women, but those closest to her surmised her newfound lesbianism was an act of rebellion against Woody's abandonment. Moreover, her choice of lovers was a nod to the cliché of "looking for love in all the wrong places." The first was Courtenay Semel, daughter of former Yahoo CEO Terry Semel; during a spat, Courtenay beat Johnson up and set her hair on fire. After that breakup, the police arrested Casey for breaking into the home of her latest ex, English model Jasmine Lennard. They charged her with grand theft for stealing Jasmine's jewels and lingerie; as her calling card, Casey had left a used vibrator in Jasmine's bed. Casey remained in a Van Nuys jail till she posted twenty thousand dollars as bail. As the media went into overdrive, the Johnson family adopted a permanent defensive crouch and shuddered at the anxious thought, "What's she going to do next?"

In 2009, the best thing that could have happened to Ava-Monroe—but the worst that could have befallen Casey—occurred. Casey was set to enter the luxurious Cliffside Malibu clinic, and Sale arrived to take her three-year-old granddaughter back to New York. However, before this could take place, Casey threw her mother out of her house, luggage and all, and called the police, accusing her mother of trespassing and attempted kidnapping. A few months later, while Casey was hospitalized for diabetes, Sale took physical custody of Ava-Monroe "to keep her from harm's way," and then successfully petitioned to retain physical custody.

Casey, with her last vestige of responsibility and humanity gone, descended further into the abyss. Part of the spiral was her gal pal lover, reality star Tila Tequila, a companion as plastic as her lover's credit cards. When the couple announced their engagement, Tequila bragged, "My baby is a billionaire. She's the heiress of Johnson & Johnson. We are going to make love tonight for our honeymoon." In a rambling and racy web video, the couple, never averse to PDA, announced their engagement. Tequila, clad in lingerie, tweeted, "Tonight my beautiful girlfriend has just asked me to marry her. Bam! Check out this seventeen-carat ring from my baby." Casey, characteristically unable to distinguish the wheat from the chaff, planned to change her last name, and Ava-Monroe's, to Tequila's legal surname: Nguyen. Back east, the Johnson clan cringed. Even with the new name, the press would not hesitate to identify her by the family name of her birth.

Woody and Sale, at last on the same page in regard to their wild child, cut off access to her trust fund. Her mother felt that before Casey could rise, she would have to hit rock bottom. Casey holed up in an apartment, one without power, water, or gas as she could not pay the utility bills; creditors repossessed her Porsche. Her rental, whose gates bear the name Grumblenot, invited comparisons to Grey Gardens, the vermin-infested home of Jacqueline Kennedy's reclusive relatives, where the swimming pool provided a watery graveyard for rats. A distraught Casey took her insulin only sporadically, lived on junk food, and swigged NyQuil to seduce sleep. On December 29, 1999, the thirty-year-old tweeted at 1:12 a.m., "Sweet dreams everyone." In a nod to utter denial, she continued, "I'm getting a new car. Any ideas...? Can't be a two-seater 'cause we have a daughter..."

New Year's Eve, usually her most heady party night, was spent in solitude. On January 4, 2010, an unidentified visitor found Casey's lifeless body, and a hysterical 911 call reported Johnson was ice-cold, hands blue. Casey had died from a diabetic coma brought on by erratic insulin injections, compounded by her use of OxyContin, Ecstasy, and cocaine. Her death, undetected for several days, was the final curtain call for the girl born with the silver spoon who had lived a life part fairy tale, part dark morality tale. Her elevated birthright that she had described as "golden handcuffs" could not secure for her the comfort of the Johnson & Johnson baby shampoo tagline, "No more tears."

Chapter 28

Flowers in Their Attic (1997)

One rite of passage for teenage girls in the 1970s was V. C. Andrews' American Gothic novel. Her book recounted the waking nightmare of the fictional Dollanganger children, held hostage by their mother. They endured a childhood that ran the gamut from arsenic-laced donuts to brother-sister incest. However, the tale of an American heiress could give even Cathy Dollanganger a run for her money.

Doris Duke, daughter of the Daddy Warbucks cigarette tsar, in addition to inheriting a multimillion-dollar fortune, inherited her stepbrother's troubled son, Walker "Skipper" Inman, Jr. He wandered aimlessly around Aunt Duke's lavish fourteen-thousand-square-foot Hawaiian estate, shooting Christmas ornaments with a dart gun, setting random fires, and tossing ketchup-covered tampons into her pool. Doris sent him to a boarding school, and, at age twenty-one, Walker became the recipient of a $65 million fortune ($350 million in contemporary currency). Unfortunately, Walker's psychological IQ was not on par with his financial largesse, and his efforts at matrimony involved acrimony. Walker and his third wife, Daisha, set off on his eighty-foot yacht, *Devine Decadence*; their drug-fueled idyll ended in Panama, when he escorted her off their yacht, contacting her months later to mention he had remarried. A decade later, they met up in New Orleans; Daisha, working as a topless waitress, gave Walker another whirl at wedlock. The couple moved into Greenfield Plantation, Walker's inherited three-hundred-acre South Carolina property, replete with a camel named Sinbad and a lion cub. The groom wore a white tux with a red bow tie and a holstered ivory-handled pistol. After the exchange of vows, a caretaker reached into a box of white doves and tossed them skyward; unfortunately, they had perished, and their white corpses littered the ground. In the hope he would prove better with children than those with feathers, Daisha underwent in vitro fertilization. The couple christened their twins Walker Patterson and Georgia Noel Lahi after the twins' deceased paternal grandparents.

A year later the marriage broke down; Daisha claimed her husband beat her, and she fled with the children to her parents' home in Oregon. Under the guise of reconciliation, Walker invited her to join him in the Cayman Islands. Once there, he took off in a private plane for the States, with the seventeen-month-old toddlers in tow.

In the ensuing divorce—one that entailed a ten-year custody battle—the court-appointed legal representative deemed the father the more stable parent despite the kidnapping, the multiple marriages, and the drug and alcohol addiction. Through his high-priced attorneys, Walker allowed Daisha—whom he conditioned the twins to call "douchebag"—limited contact with her children. Her legal position was further hindered when she remarried, as her new husband was a registered sex offender who had pled guilty to molesting his stepdaughters. Inman, the anti-Atticus Finch, brainwashed the twins to believe that their mother was the enemy and that her drinking during pregnancy had left them imbeciles. Georgia later recounted, "He kept telling us that she didn't want to see us—that she was a drugged-out mess and drunk, that she fed us alcohol, put in our sippy cups."

From the outside looking in, it appeared Walker and Georgia had enviable lives. They snorkeled in Fiji, took fistfuls of diamonds to school for show-and-tell, and played with their pet camel and lion cub—at least until the latter met an unfortunate end when Walker fed it too many fast food burgers. While their peers attended summer camp, the twins traveled to Abu Dhabi, where their father bid millions at auctions or they sailed on the family yacht, *Devine Decadence*, which docked in New Zealand.

On the flip side, they spent their formative years inhaling their less than doting dad's freebase fumes, and he locked them into their bedrooms in their secluded Wyoming estate, dubbed Outlaw Acres, or at their ancestral South Carolina plantation. The mother-daughter separation was especially hard for Georgia, as she never even experienced the tenuous connection with her father that Walker established over a shared love of tear gas grenades, guns, and hookers. As a teen, she claimed Inman would pick her up by the ankle and drop her on her head because he wanted to make her stupid. The kids, ensnared in their palatial house of horrors, were deprived of friends; Georgia said she had no knowledge of games such as musical chairs. Understandably, parents were loath to bring their children to the mansion where its eccentric multimillionaire owner had a penchant for prurient magazines that left little to the imagination and for walking around his estate naked. Georgia stated, "The money didn't matter to me. If someone were to look at me and say 'wow,' I would say let's trade lives. I just wanted to be free. I was trapped because of it."

Walker repeatedly proved his kids were low on his hierarchy of priorities—when he had a hankering for Thai food, he disappeared for weeks to fly to Thailand for authentic cuisine. Although Walker and Georgia were in far more dire need of a Mary Poppins than the fictional Banks children, Inman, wrestling with his demons, haphazardly hired caregivers. The nannies, attracted by the generous salaries and international travel, nevertheless saw the downside of the silver lining job. Their shirtless employer displayed a back covered with an enormous tattoo of a nude woman in a sexual pose with an octopus, a visual inspired by Inman's fondness for "tentacle erotica." Guns, knives, and swords lay everywhere, and each available surface carried a souvenir cigarette burn.

Into this morass appeared the fifth Mrs. Inman, Daralee, who had met the heir while hitchhiking. The vehicle-deprived woman felt she had hit pay dirt when wooed by a man whose trust paid a $160,000 monthly allowance and who had inherited millions from a cigarette empire. She had a disconcerting habit of viciously picking at her skin and rarely surfaced before noon, something that gave the mansion's Hansel and Gretel a reprieve from their live-in wicked witch stepmother. Mrs. Inman had quite the rap sheet, including felony drug possession in Colorado and Utah. In 2007, a wasted Daralee drove her youthful charges to the school bus in demolition derby fashion; Georgia begged her to slow down. In response, stepmother dearest told her to, "Shut the fuck up! Did I ever get you into a motherfucking wreck?" The car careened into a tree, and when the police arrived, they discovered heroin and crystal meth. The kids prayed Daralee would end up behind bars, but although driving under the influence was a violation of her parole, she only received additional probation.

The poorest richest kids in the world were constantly on high alert for any of fifty shades of horror: when a skunk wandered into the mansion's Great Room, which was filled with family heirlooms—including a portrait of Doris Duke—Inman mowed the hapless animal down with a machine gun. The caregivers were in for a further jolt when they met their charges, who at night were locked in a room where food was strewn on the floor, and where a foul odor emanated from the corner where Walker and Georgia relieved themselves.

In addition to the weapons and tear gas grenades, a time bomb hovered in the mansion. Although Inman had control of his wealth, his personal demons had hold of his soul. He told the kids if they saw him overdose to splash cold water on his face.

On some occasions, he tempted the Grim Reaper to make a
house call: he warned his children if they heard a gunshot not
to intervene as he would probably be "kissing the luger"—his
euphemism for suicide. Inman self-medicated with an arsenal
of drugs that led to serious heart problems. In 2010, he passed
away in a Colorado hotel room. The kind of drug paraphernalia
strewn about the room made a forensic expert unnecessary.
Georgia, who had the antithesis of an Electra Complex, had
fantasized taking a gun to her father's head and little mourned
his passing.

Inman's death embroiled the twins in a legal morass, something
they had undergone on various occasions since they were
toddlers. In one corner were two of Walker's five wives, Daisha
and Daralee, battling for the right to raise the fourteen-year-old
twins. To the victor would belong the spoils: a trust fund worth
approximately sixty million dollars. The verdict decreed Georgia
and Walker were united with their mother. However, after years
of paternal negative reinforcement, when Daisha arrived, court
order in hand, Georgia threw rocks at her mother's windshield,
screaming, "Fuck you, Daisha!" When Daisha soldiered on, her
daughter kicked her hard in the shin. Fortunately, their mother
had enough maternal acumen to arrange for an ambulance to
the Wyoming Behavioral Institute, where the twins underwent
three months of treatment to help with their suicidal tendencies
and malnutrition. Jennifer Greenup, a therapist, claimed she
had never been privy to such psychological trauma. When they
returned home, Daisha wanted the kids to have something they
had never had—friends; she suggested they chum around with
Michael Jackson's brood. She thought they would have a lot in
common and perhaps felt the Neverland Ranch would be an
appropriate playground for her teens, who still believed in Santa
Claus. Daisha said of the proposed playdate, "Wouldn't that be

historic? The Jacksons and the Dukes, two of the most famous names, together?" When not at school, Georgia and Walker preferred to maintain their emotional firewall and holed up at their house, where Walker played *Grand Theft Auto*. Georgia admitted she was not ready for friends as she was ill-equipped for teenage drama.

Daisha took to heart her next legal battlefield: wresting her offspring's money from the grip of JP Morgan Chase and Citibank, who held the purse strings till the children turned twenty-one. The bank and Daisha locked horns when they deemed many of her requests too extravagant: $17,000 for a trip to Las Vegas (with $3,000 earmarked for limousines), a $4.2 million house on South Carolina's Isle of Palms, and a twenty-nine-million-dollar Utah ranch. They also balked at her demand for $50,000 for Christmas gifts (the bank deemed $5,000 an amount sufficient for Yuletide cheer), $6,000 for a Halloween party, and a hefty sum for an around the world trip. Her contention was she needed a $1,000 a month dining allowance because Georgia and Walker liked to eat out and were fond of Starbucks. Daisha balked at the monthly payout of $16,000 and argued it fell far short of the $180,000 their father had spent on their monthly care. The battle heated up when Daisha hired a SWAT team to stop the banks from serving her with legal papers demanding she account for her allocation of her children's money. The Inman family manages to make the Kardashian-Jenner clan look like a drama-free zone by comparison.

At age sixteen, the twins decided to air their very soiled linen in public and appeared on the Dr. Phil show. During the program, the twins reserved most of their wrath for their former caregivers, whom they described as Wisconsin versions of the Marquis de Sade. They claimed they had suffered endless abuse from those hired to protect them: they related that they had been burned with scalding water, forced to eat their own vomit and feces, starved, and thrown down stairs. Georgia added they involved the kids in rounds of Russian roulette for its entertainment value. Dr. Phil listened to the worse than Dickensian tales with eyes full of horror. As fantastical as their litany of abuse sounds, what matters is these incidents are real to the twins. Walker ended the interview by stating that the most important thing on his bucket list was vengeance against those who had made him and his sister suffer. He said, "I'm coming after the bastards. This is a battle cry. They're going down." Well aware of Walker's youthful training in blowing things up, their former caregivers, whether or not they were culpable of these real or imagined crimes, must have been strangers to tranquility. While Walker's rant was one borne of vindictiveness, his sister's was more heartfelt when she spoke of the wages of wealth, "People can look at this as a blessing all day long, but it's *blood* money. I never asked to be born into any of this. Sometimes I wish I was never born." Walker's mantra, words he had learned from his father, who had learned them from his Aunt Doris, who had learned them from her father, is, "You can't trust anyone."

At age eighteen, the twins filed a lawsuit against Citibank, in which they claimed the corporation was culpable for having distributed a trust fund that was earmarked for them when the bank knew their father was a junkie of diminished capacity. The ruling by a Manhattan judge was that although dad might have blown a fortune on heroin and on four wives, it was his money to squander.

In order to survive, Cathy and Chris Dollanganger turned their prison into an imaginary garden, a transformation the real-life twins were unable to accomplish. However, like their fictional counterparts, what helped Georgia and Walker endure was their love for one another—a fierce allegiance that comprises the flowers in their attic.

∼Epilogue∼

Epilogues, like all endings, are bittersweet. And, as last impressions—perhaps even more than first ones—are lasting, I will try my utmost to transfer my thoughts to words, a task that, as all writers know, is daunting.

Many criteria erect barriers between people: race, religion, and ethnicity make for the most prevalent of fences. However, socio-economic status is another great divide. Oftentimes, the denizens of the lower strata stereotypically view those from the upper echelons as stuck up, while the one percent view the poor as shiftless. However, a few lessons to be gleaned from *Women of Means* are that we all share more commonalities than differences, that heartache is universal, and that gold does not provide a shield against the slings and arrows of outrageous fortune. Delving into the lives of the heiresses shows that wealth, while providing protection against economic woes, delivers a different array of angst. Hence, when we look at those who live in McMansions, sail on white yachts on azure seas, and wear blinding bling, something to keep in mind is luxuries often serve to camouflage lives that may be rife with sorrow. Emotional baggage rides in the back seats of chauffeur-driven limousines in the same fashion as it does in a jalopy. Those who swim in the economic stratosphere do not have days filled only with champagne and caviar. The Greeks were astute with their concept of the Golden Mean: we do not want to be Mother Hubbards, but we should also not want to shoulder the Atlas-like burden that billions of dollars oftentimes bring.

Coinciding with the writing of the Epilogue is the news of the breakdown of the marriage of the founder of Amazon, Jeff Bezos, and his wife, Mackenzie, a split that came after twenty-five years of wedlock and four children. Their divorce exists at a level of wealth that is virtually unprecedented. The announcement illustrates that the pot of gold at the end of the rainbow is not always a key ingredient of happiness. Mackenzie, a Princeton grad and author, will undoubtedly not share in the unhappy fates of those profiled in *Women of Means*.

The following anecdotal dialogue between two twentieth-century literary greats punctures the illusion that money unlocks the door of contentment.

F. Scott Fitzgerald: "The rich are different from us."

Ernest Hemingway: "Yes. They have more money."

My hope for all of us is that this window into the biographies of the poor little rich girls makes us more content with our own lot.

Lucy Maud Montgomery's protagonist in *Ann of Green Gables* understood the deceptive nature of wealth, "Look at the sea, girls—all silver and shadow and vision of things not seen. We couldn't enjoy its loveliness any more if we had millions of dollars and ropes of diamonds."

∼Acknowledgments∼

The acknowledgment page is an avenue for reflection: the time to think back on my book's journey from a twinkle in my eye to the hands of my readers. An integral part of the metamorphosis is my literary agent, Roger Williams. His intelligence, dedication, and tenacity provide the cornerstone of the publication of *Women of Means*. I am endlessly grateful for the four books we have birthed together. Hopefully, other offspring await.

I am indebted to my editor, Brenda Knight, for the enthusiastic championing of my books. Her belief in me was the wind beneath my writing. Although our collaboration has not made me a woman of means, it has made me a woman of purpose, the best buoy to which to cling while struggling against the ceaseless waves of life. In a nod to a shared joke, Brenda has delivered a dose of jolly.

One of the unexpected consequences that came with publication was my entry into the village of fellow authors who have unstintingly offered endless encouragement, expertise, and friendship. You know who you are and what your solidarity has meant.

Writing is a time-consuming and solitary endeavor, and I appreciate my family's support of the time I spend with my significant other, my laptop. My most sincere mea culpa for meals ensconced in Styrofoam and for having local restaurants on speed dial. Alas, with a full-time job as a high school English teacher and a second as an author, time is the pearl without price.

There are so many best parts of writing: the creative process, the excitement of viewing the cover, the publication day. Another huge perk is interacting with readers. I would love to hear from you through email: wagmangeller@hotmail.com, my website marlenewagmangeller.com, or through Facebook. Reviews are positive feedback, and I would be most appreciative if you left one on Amazon or Goodreads.

I hope you partake of the joy in the reading, as I did in the writing, of *Women of Means*.

MARLENE WAGMAN-GELLER

San Diego, 2019

∼Richard Cory(1897)∼

By Edwin Arlington Robinson

Whenever Richard Cory went down town,
We people on the pavement looked at him:
He was a gentleman from sole to crown,
Clean favored, and imperially slim.

And he was always quietly arrayed,
And he was always human when he talked;
But still he fluttered pulses when he said,
"Good-morning," and he glittered when he walked.

And he was rich—yes, richer than a king—
And admirably schooled in every grace:
In fine, we thought that he was everything
To make us wish that we were in his place.

So on we worked, and waited for the light,
And went without the meat, and cursed the bread;
And Richard Cory, one calm summer night,
Went home and put a bullet through his head.

~Bibliography~

Almina Herbert, Countess of Carnarvon

Newman, Judith. "Remains of the Days—Three Books Explore the Reality behind the World of 'Downton Abbey'." *The New York Times*. February 3, 2012. https://www.nytimes.com/2012/02/05/books/review/three-books-explore-the-reality-behind-the-world-of-downton-abbey.html.

Seymour Miranda. "Lady Almina and the Real Downton Abbey by Fiona Carnarvon—Review." *The Guardian*. September 15, 2011. https://www.theguardian.com/books/2011/sep/15/lady-almina-downton-carnarvon-review.

Wilson, Christopher. "Dark Past of the Real Downton Abbey Duchess." *The Telegraph*. August 9, 2011. https://www.telegraph.co.uk/women/sex/8688994/Dark-past-of-the-real-Downton-Abbey-duchess.html.

Wilson, Christopher. "Downton's Greatest Secret: A Lonely Countess, an Illicit Love Affair with an Egyptian Prince...and an Earl Who Has No Right to His Title. The Extraordinary Claims about Real Life Lord." *Daily Mail*. October 21, 2011. http://www.dailymail.co.uk/femail/article-2051649/Downton-Abbey-A-lonely-countess-illicit-love-affair-Egyptian-prince.html.

Nancy Cunard

Chisholm, Anne. "Nancy Cunard: Queen of the Jazz Age." *The Guardian*. November 16, 2011. https://www.theguardian.com/fashion/2011/nov/16/nancy-cunard-gucci.

Kaplan, Carla. "The Lives of Others." *The Nation*. July 26, 2007. https://www.thenation.com/article/lives-others/.

Weber, Caroline. "The Rebel Heiress." *The New York Times*. April 1, 2007. https://www.nytimes.com/2007/04/01/books/review/weber.t.html.

Winton Evans, Katherine. "Hostages to Fortune: Heiresses Promiscuous and Proper. Nancy Cunard: A Biography. By Anne Chisholm." *The Washington Post*. July 15, 1979. https://www.washingtonpost.com/archive/entertainment/books/1979/07/15/hostages-to-fortune-heiresses-promiscuous-and-propernancy-cunard-a-biography-by-anne-chisholm-knopf-366-pp-15/83a92ffe-649b-4273-a0b3-cc7dd244e2ed/?utm_term=.ad61ab49fa6f.

Peggy Guggenheim

Miller, Lucasta. "The Goodtime Guggenheim." *The Guardian*. November 12, 2005. https://www.theguardian.com/books/2005/nov/12/highereducation.biography.

O'Sullivan, Michael. "Portrait of an Arts Patron in 'Peggy Guggenheim: Art Addict'." *The Guardian*. December 3, 2015. https://www.washingtonpost.com/goingoutguide/movies/portrait-of-an-arts-patron-in-peggy-guggenheim-art-addict/2015/12/03/1b7e9010-9918-11e5-b499-76cbec161973_story.html?utm_term=.84a21a3c2de5.

"The Priceless Peggy Guggenheim." *Independent*. October 21, 2009. https://www.independent.co.uk/arts-entertainment/art/features/the-priceless-peggy-guggenheim-1806124.html.

Yeazell, Ruth. "What Peggy Did." *The New Republic.* September 29, 2015. https://newrepublic.com/article/122968/artistic-outrageous-life-peggy-guggenheim.

Lady Edwina Mountbatten

Hallemann, Caroline. "Who Is Prince Philip's Uncle, Lord Mountbatten?" *Town & Country.* April 27, 2018. https://www.townandcountrymag.com/society/tradition/a14409174/lord-mountbatten-uncle-dickie-the-crown/.

Kirsch, Jonathan. "Curious Bedfellows." *Los Angeles Times.* December 14, 2007. http://www.latimes.com/la-bk-kirsch19aug19-story.html.

McLellan, Diana. "The Life and Loves of Lady Edwina Mountbatten." *The Washington Post.* September 1, 1991. https://www.washingtonpost.com/archive/entertainment/books/1991/09/01/the-life-and-loves-of-lady-edwina-mountbatten/a326825b-2d24-4e26-8b97-150e4240e8c8/?utm_term=.7eba1115d1c8.

Rennell, Tony. "My Mummy the Maneater: How the Wild Promiscuity of Edwina Mountbatten—Wife of Prince Charles' Mentor—Took a Heartbreaking Toll on Her Children." *Daily Mail.* November 30, 2012. UPDATED: December 1, 2012. http://www.dailymail.co.uk/news/article-2241195/How-wild-promiscuity-Edwina-Mountbatten--wife-Prince-Charles-mentor--took-heartbreaking-toll-children.html.

Brooke Astor

Berger, Marilyn. "Brooke Astor, 105, Aristocrat of the People, Dies." *New York Times*. August. 14, 2007. https://www. nytimes.com/2007/08/14/obituaries/14astor.html.

Browning, Dominique "Woman's Estate." *The New York Times*. January 2, 2009. https://www.nytimes. com/2009/01/04/books/review/Browning-t.html.

Reed, Christopher. "Brooke Astor." *The Guardian*. August 15, 2007 https://www.theguardian.com/news/2007/aug/16/ guardianobituaries.usa.

Schillinger, Liesl. "Astor's Place." *The New York Times*. June 17, 2007. https://www.nytimes.com/2007/06/17/books/ review/Schillinger-t.html.

Huguette Clark

Clark, Huguette. *The Telegraph*. May 25, 2011. https:// www.telegraph.co.uk/news/obituaries/finance- obituaries/8536420/Huguette-Clark.html.

Dedman, Bill and Paul Clark Newell Jr. "The extraordinary story of Huguette Clark and the $30m she left to her nurse." *The Guardian*. June 27, 2014. https://www. theguardian.com/lifeandstyle/2014/jun/27/huguette- clark-and-the-fortune-she-left-to-her-nurse.

Fox, Margalit. "Huguette Clark, Reclusive Heiress, Dies at 104." *The New York Times*. May 24, 2011. https://www. nytimes.com/2011/05/25/nyregion/huguette-clark- recluse-heiress-dies-at-104.html.

Gardner Jr., Ralph "The Life of a Recluse: Huguette Clark." *The Wall Street Journal*. June 9, 2014. https://

www.wsj.com/articles/the-life-of-a-recluse-huguette-clark-1402361656.

Schudel, Matt "Huguette Clark, copper heiress and recluse, dies at 104." *The Washington Post*. May 24, 2011. https://www.washingtonpost.com/local/obituaries/huguette-clark-copper-heiress-and-recluse-dies-at-104/2011/05/24/AFxfXrAH_story.html?utm_term=.9c974603ba39.

Barbara Hutton

Hailey, Jean R. "Heiress Barbara Hutton Dies at 66." *The Washington Post*. May 13, 1979. https://www.washingtonpost.com/archive/local/1979/05/13/heiress-barbara-hutton-dies-at-66/5ef69ce7-63ac-4f2d-bf89-62972348786d/?utm_term=.18adb9a4afa0.

Mansfield, Stephanie. "Inside the World's Richest Rivalry: Doris Duke and Barbara Hutton." *Town and Country Magazine*. April 26, 2017. https://www.townandcountrymag.com/society/money-and-power/a9540335/doris-duke-barbra-hutton-feud/.

Nemy, Enid. "Barbara Hutton Dies on Coast at 66." *The New York Times*. May 13, 1979. https://www.nytimes.com/1979/05/13/archives/barbara-hutton-dies-on-coast-at-66-seven-marriages-failed-barbara.html.

O'Connor, John J. "TV Review; 'Poor Little Rich Girl,' on Hutton." *The New York Times*. November 16, 1987. https://www.nytimes.com/1987/11/16/arts/tv-review-poor-little-rich-girl-on-hutton.html.

Wilson, Christopher. "The Heiress Who Blew the Woolworth's Billions on Vodka Breakfasts, Seven Husbands and Jewels Galore." *Daily Mail*. November 27, 2008. https://www.

dailymail.co.uk/femail/article-1090093/The-heiress-blew-Woolworths-billions-vodka-breakfasts-seven-husbands-jewels-galore.html.

Doris Duke

Collier, Peter. "Million Dollar Baby." *The Washington Post.* June 21, 1992. https://www.washingtonpost.com/archive/entertainment/books/1992/06/21/million-dollar-baby/b8c159b9-d9a9-4e9e-b28b-8021947eb9bc/?utm_term=.9d9b741a6e3c.

Hewitt, Bill "Where There's a Will." *People.* May 22, 1995. https://people.com/archive/where-theres-a-will-vol-43-no-20/.

Pace, Eric. "Doris Duke, 80, Heiress Whose Great Wealth Couldn't Buy Happiness, Is Dead." *The New York Times.* October 29, 1993. https://www.nytimes.com/1993/10/29/obituaries/doris-duke-80-heiress-whose-great-wealth-couldn-t-buy-happiness-is-dead.html.

Vickers, Hugo. "Obituary: Doris Duke." *Independent.* November 10, 1993. https://www.independent.co.uk/news/people/obituary-doris-duke-1503235.html.

Baroness Nica Rothschild

Cooke, Rachel. "Hannah Rothschild on Nica: 'I Saw a Woman Who Knew Where She Belonged'." *The Guardian.* April 21, 2012. https://www.theguardian.com/books/2012/apr/22/hannah-rothschild-nica-jazz-thelonious-monk-interview.

Davis, Clive. "The Baroness: The Search for Nica, the Rebellious Rothschild, By Hannah Rothschild."

Independent. May 19, 2012. https://www.independent.
co.uk/arts-entertainment/books/reviews/the-baroness-
the-search-for-nica-the-rebellious-rothschild-by-hannah-
rothschild-7763591.html.

Hudson, Christopher. "Sex and Drugs and All That Jazz:
How a Rebel Rothschild Baroness Fell for a Drug-
Fueled Music Genius." *Daily Mail*. May 17, 2012.
Updated: May 18, 2012. https://www.dailymail.co.uk/
home/books/article-2145859/Sex-drugs-JAZZ-How-
rebel-Rothschild-baroness-fell-drug-fuelled-music-
genius-THE-BARONESS-THE-SEARCH-FOR-NICA-
THE-REBELLIOUS-ROTHSCHILD-BY-HANNAH-
ROTHSCHILD.html.

Schillinger, Liesl. "On the Trail of the Bebop Baroness."
Newsweek. March 25, 2014. https://www.newsweek.com/
trail-bebop-baroness-62951.

Singer, Barry "The Baroness of Jazz." *The New York Times*.
October 17, 2008. https://www.nytimes.com/2008/10/19/
arts/music/19sing.html?mtrref=www.google.
h=2E8040D51E69F1D22542E67848F63403&gwt=pay.

Williams, Richard. "The Jazz Baroness and the Bebop
King." *The Guardian*. December 21, 2008. https://www.
theguardian.com/music/2008/dec/22/jazz.

Wilson, Frances. "The Baroness: The Search for Nica, the
Rebellious Rothschild by Hannah Rothschild: review." *The
Telegraph*. May 14, 2012. https://www.telegraph.co.uk/
culture/books/bookreviews/9257450/The-Baroness-The-
Search-for-Nica-the-Rebellious-Rothschild-by-Hannah-
Rothschild-review.html.

Leona Helmsley

Pilkington, Ed. "Farewell to the woman they called the Queen of Mean: Leona Helmsley dies at 87." *The Guardian*. August 20, 2007. https://www.theguardian.com/ business/2007/aug/21/usnews.

Toobin, Jeffrey. "Rich Bitch." *The New Yorker*. September 29, 2008. https://www.newyorker.com/ magazine/2008/09/29/rich-bitch.

Liliane Bettencourt

Horwell, Veronica. "Liliane Bettencourt Obituary." *The Guardian*. September 24, 2017. https://www.theguardian. com/world/2017/sep/24/liliane-bettencourt-obituary.

McDonough, Megan. "Liliane Bettencourt, L'Oréal Heiress and World's Richest Woman, Dies at 94." *The Washington Post*. September 21, 2017. https://www.washingtonpost. com/local/obituaries/liliane-bettencourt-billionaire-loreal-heiress-dies-at-94/2017/09/21/344028c2-9ef0-11e7-9083-fbfddf6804c2_story.html?utm_ term=.060a349016e9.

McFadden, Robert D. "Liliane Bettencourt, L'Oréal Heiress Vexed by Swindling Case, Is Dead at 94." *The New York Times*. September 21, 2017. https://www.nytimes. com/2017/09/21/world/europe/liliane-bettencourt-dead-loreal.html.

Sancton, Tom. "Never Envy the Richest Woman in the World." *Time*. September 5, 2017. http://time. com/4888142/never-envy-the-richest-woman-in-the-world/.

Weaver, Hilary. "Liliane Bettencourt, the World's Richest Woman, Dies at 94." *Vanity Fair*. September 21, 2017. https://www.vanityfair.com/style/2017/09/liliane-bettencourt-worlds-richest-woman-dies-at-94.

Barbara Baekeland

Allen, Jennifer. "After Mothjer Was Murdered." *The New York Times*. July 28, 1985. https://www.nytimes.com/1985/07/28/books/after-mothjer-was-murdcred.html.

Bradshaw, Peter. "Savage Grace." *The Guardian*. July 11, 2008. https://www.theguardian.com/culture/2008/jul/11/filmandmusic1.filmandmusic7.

Goleman, Daniel. "Books of the Times." *The New York Times*. July 10, 1985. https://www.nytimes.com/1985/07/10/books/books-of-the-times-109237.html.

Leafe, David. "Fatal Seduction: How a Society Millionairess Seduced Her Own Son to 'Cure' Him of Being Gay… and Paid with Her Life." *The Daily Mail*. June 27, 2008. https://www.dailymail.co.uk/femail/article-1030028/Fatal-Seduction-How-society-millionairess-seduced-son-cure-gay--paid-life.html.

Romney, Jonathan. "Savage Grace, 15." *Independent*. July 13, 2008. https://www.independent.co.uk/arts-entertainment/films/reviews/savage-grace-15-866231.html.

Schemering, Christopher. "The Fall of the House of Baekeland." *The Washington Post*. September 15, 1985. https://www.washingtonpost.com/archive/entertainment/books/1985/09/15/the-fall-of-the-

house-of-baekeland/41da760f-dba9-4ac8-bf81-
c2469642d657/?utm_term=.145c38fd4de1.

Gloria Vanderbilt

Higginbotham, Adam. "Last of the Big Spenders." *The
Telegraph*. November 23, 2004. https://www.telegraph.
co.uk/culture/3632253/Last-of-the-big-spenders.html.

Picardie, Justine. "Gloria Vanderbilt: Poor Little Rich Girl."
Telegraph Fashion. November 8, 2010. http://fashion.
telegraph.co.uk/news-features/TMG8102960/Gloria-
Vanderbilt-poor-little-rich-girl.html.

Sunny von Bülow

Foley, Stephen "After 27 Years in a Coma, Sunny Von Bülow
Dies." *Independent*. December 7, 2008. https://www.
independent.co.uk/news/world/americas/after-27-years-
in-a-coma-sunny-von-b-low-dies-1055818.html.

Nemy, Enid. "Sunny von Bülow, 76, Focus of Society Drama,
Dies." *The New York Times*. December 6, 2008. https://
www.nytimes.com/2008/12/07/nyregion/07vonbulow.
html?mtrref=www.google.com&gwh=6C
9EBA11D8CC71DD93D34185202E99BB&gwt=pay.

Sherwell, Philip. "Sunny Von Bülow: Socialite Who Took
the Secret of Her Coma to the Grave." *The Telegraph*.
December 6, 2008. https://www.telegraph.co.uk/news/
worldnews/northamerica/usa/3630080/Sunny-von-
Bulow-Socialite-who-took-the-secret-of-her-coma-to-the-
grave.html.

"Sunny Von Bülow: Heiress Whose Husband's Trial for Her
Attempted Murder Was Dramatized in the Film 'Reversal

of Fortune'." *Independent*. December 8, 2008. https://
www.independent.co.uk/news/obituaries/sunny-von-
b-low-heiress-whose-husbands-trial-for-her-attempted-
murder-was-dramatised-in-the-film-1056670.html.

Thorpe, Vanessa. "Sunny Von Bülow Dies after Years in
Coma." *The Guardian*. December 6, 2008. https://www.
theguardian.com/world/2008/dec/07/sunny-von-bulow-
usa.

Hélène Pastor

AFP and Miranda Aldersley. "Monaco Heiress Was Shot
Dead on the French Riviera by Bungling Hitmen Hired by
Son-In-Law Who Wanted Her £10 Billion Fortune, Court
Hears." *Daily Mail Online*. September 17, 2018. https://
www.dailymail.co.uk/news/article-6176181/Monaco-
heiress-killed-hitmen-hired-son-law-wanted-10bn-
fortune-court-hears.html.

Childs, Martin. "Hélène Pastor: Monaco's Richest Woman
Who Developed Her Family's Property Empire But Was
Shot Dead in an Ambush." *The Independent*. June 3, 2014.
https://www.independent.co.uk/incoming/h-l-ne-pastor-
monacos-richest-woman-who-developed-her-familys-
property-empire-but-was-shot-dead-in-9481151.html.

"Hélène Pastor—Obituary." *The Telegraph*. May 22, 2014.
https://www.telegraph.co.uk/news/obituaries/10849904/
Helene-Pastor-obituary.html.

Seal, Mark. "Murder Made in Monaco." *Vanity Fair*.
November 2014. https://www.vanityfair.com/
style/2014/11/helene-pastor-murder-monaco.

Farah Pahlavi

Branigin, William. "Empress Farah: Shah's 'Inspiration' in Final Days." *The Washington Post*. January 23, 1979. https://www.washingtonpost.com/archive/politics/1979/01/23/empress-farah-shahs-inspiration-in-final-days/b3ac8e17-c2b9-434d-a9d5-5753ea941b6e/?noredirect=on&utm_term=.1a1fdcde7dee.

"Homeward bound." *The Age*. February 9, 2005. https://www.theage.com.au/world/homeward-bound-20050209-gdziw2.html.

Hsu, Spencer S. "Reversal of Fortune." *The Washington Post*. July 22, 1996. https://www.washingtonpost.com/archive/lifestyle/1996/07/22/reversal-of-fortune/a6e145ed-b4b9-4aa2-86d9-985f2f21d109/?utm_term=.5ae52ca556d1.

Lone, Mahlia. "Memorable Romance: The Shah & I." *Good Times*. July 1, 2016. http://www.goodtimes.com.pk/memorable-romance-the-shah-i/.

Rodcliffe, Donnie. "Iran's Farah Diba, Empress on the Move." *The Washington Post*. July 13, 1977 https://www.washingtonpost.com/archive/lifestyle/1977/07/13/irans-farah-diba-empress-on-the-move/905dcdc1-ae75-4454-98fb-1d609aba4653/?utm_term=.43d077118811.

Sciolino, Elaine "The Last Empress." *The New York Times*. May 2, 2004. https://www.nytimes.com/2004/05/02/books/the-last-empress.html.

Jocelyn Wildenstein

Brinded, Lianna. "The Crazy Life of Billionaire Socialite Jocelyn Wildenstein." *Independent*. January 5, 2017.

https://www.independent.co.uk/news/people/crazy-life-billionaire-socialite-jocelyn-wildenstein-a7511736.html.

Heigl, Alex. "The Famous Life and Face of Jocelyn Wildenstein." *People*. December 09, 2016. https://people.com/crime/jocelyn-wildenstein-catwoman-what-to-know/.

Rush, George. "Jocelyne's Revenge." *Vanity Fair*. March 1998. https://www.vanityfair.com/news/1998/03/jocelyn-wildenstein-199803.

Ruth Madoff

Adams, Guy. "Ruth Madoff Reveals Suicide Pact after £40bn Fraud." *Independent*. October 28, 2011. https://www.independent.co.uk/news/world/americas/ruth-madoff-reveals-suicide-pact-after-16340bn-fraud-2376893.html.

"Have pity on Ruth Madoff." *Time Money*. November 14, 2009. http://time.com/money/2792812/have-pity-on-ruth-madoff/.

Hilzenrath, David S. "Book: Ruth Madoff Hurt More by Husband's Alleged Infidelity Than His Ponzi Scheme." *The Washington Post*. October 28, 2011. https://www.washingtonpost.com/business/economy/book-ruth-madoff-hurt-more-by-husbands-alleged-infidelity-than-his-ponzi-scheme/2011/10/28/gIQARSaYQM_story.html?utm_term=.3009272afd3b.

Kolhatkar, Sheelah. "Poor Ruth." *New York Magazine*. July 2, 2009. http://nymag.com/nymag/features/57772/index2.html.

Seal, Mark. "Ruth's World." *Vanity Fair*. September 2009. https://www.vanityfair.com/style/2009/09/ruth-madoff-profile.

Patrizia Gucci

Carlson, Adam and Steve Helling. "Decades After Hit Man Killed Gucci Mogul, the Ex-Wife Convicted of His Murder Speaks Out." *People*. July 13, 2018. https://people.com/crime/maurizio-gucci-death-ex-wife-patrizia-reggiani-speaks/.

Haworth, Abigail. "The Gucci Wife and the Hitman: Fashion's Darkest Tale." *The Guardian*. July 24, 2016. https://www.theguardian.com/fashion/2016/jul/24/the-gucci-wife-and-the-hitman-fashions-darkest-tale.

Squires, Nick. "Italy's 'Black Widow' Gucci Heiress Who Ordered Ex-Husband's Murder Entitled to Nearly £1 Million a Year from His Estate." *The Telegraph*. February 10, 2017. https://www.telegraph.co.uk/news/2017/02/10/italys-black-widow-entitled-nearly-1-million-year-despite-ordering/.

Christina Onassis

Green, Michelle. "Fate's Captive." *People*. December 05, 1988. https://people.com/archive/cover-story-fates-captive-vol-30-no-23/.

O'Malley, Kathy. 'Onassis', Tale Rich in Misery." *Chicago Tribune*. July 24, 1986. http://www.chicagotribune.com/news/ct-xpm-1986-07-24-8602230400-story.html.

Saxon, Wolfgang. "Christina Onassis, Shipping Magnate, Dies at 37." *The New York Times*. November 20, 1988. https://

www.nytimes.com/1988/11/20/obituaries/christina-onassis-shipping-magnate-dies-at-37.html.

Patty Hearst

Andrews, Travis M. "Fox Drops Patty Hearst Biopic after She Blasts the Jeffrey Toobin Book It Was Based On." *The Washington Post*. January 12, 2018. https://www.washingtonpost.com/news/morning-mix/wp/2018/01/12/fox-drops-patty-hearst-biopic-after-she-blasts-the-jeffrey-toobin-book-it-was-based-on/?noredirect=on&utm_term=.52678513da5f.

Brody, Richard "DVD of the Week: Patty Hearst." *The New Yorker*. Accessed August 13, 2018. https://www.newyorker.com/culture/richard-brody/dvd-of-the-week-patty-hearst.

Cooke, Rachel. "American Heiress: The Kidnapping, Crimes and Trial of Patty Hearst by Jeffrey Toobin—review." *The Guardian*. June 26, 2017. Last modified March 21, 2018. https://www.theguardian.com/books/2017/jun/26/american-heiress-kidnapping-crimes-trial-patty-hearst-jeffrey-toobin-review.

Liebman, Lisa. "There Are Still No Easy Answers in the Curious Case of Patty Hearst." *Vanity Fair*. February 9, 2018. https://www.vanityfair.com/hollywood/2018/02/patty-hearst-kidnapping-cnn-jeffrey-toobin.

Truesdell, Jeff. "Patty Hearst Turns from Heiress to Revolutionary and Then Back in New Archival Documentary." *People*. November 22, 2017. https://people.com/crime/patty-hearst-smithsonian-documentary-heiress/.

Gina Rinehart

Finnegan, William. "The Miner's Daughter." *The New Yorker*. March 25, 2013. https://www.newyorker.com/magazine/2013/03/25/the-miners-daughter.

Hume, Tim. "The Iron Ore Lady: Why the World's Richest Woman Is Mired in Controversy." *Independent*. June 16, 2012. https://www.independent.co.uk/news/people/profiles/the-iron-ore-lady-why-the-worlds-richest-woman-is-mired-in-controversy-7848535.html.

Leser, David. "Gina Rinehart, Australia's Billionaire 'Iron Lady'." *Newsweek*. February 13, 2012. https://www.newsweek.com/gina-rinehart-australias-billionaire-iron-lady-65689.

Rolfe, Brooke. "If Only It Was That Easy! Mining Billionaire Gina Rinehart Says Short Lunch Breaks and Late Nights in the Office Are a Must If You Want to Climb the Ladder at Work." *Daily Mail*. April 4, 2018. https://www.dailymail.co.uk/news/article-5579901/Mining-billionaire-Gina-Rinehart-reveals-one-thing-need-succeed-work.html.

Susanne Klatten

Popham, Peter. "The Gigolo, the German Heiress, and a £6m Revenge for Her Nazi Legacy." *Independent*. November 3, 2008. https://www.independent.co.uk/news/world/europe/the-gigolo-the-german-heiress-and-a-1636m-revenge-for-her-nazi-legacy-986855.html.

Squires, Nick. " 'Swiss Gigolo' Helg Sgarbi on Trial for Blackmailing BMW Heiress Susanne Klatten." *The Telegraph*. March 9, 2009. https://www.telegraph.co.uk/news/worldnews/europe/switzerland/4959590/Swiss-

gigolo-Helg-Sgarbi-on-trial-for-blackmailing-BMW-
heiress-Susanne-Klatten.html.

Wansell, Geoffrey. "How Could the World's Richest
Woman Betray Her Husband for This Weedy, Smirking
Gigolo—and Let Him Take Her for Millions?" *Daily Mail.*
October 21, 2009. https://www.dailymail.co.uk/femail/
article-1221593/How-COULD-worlds-richest-woman-
betray-husband-weedy-smirking-gigolo--let-millions.
html.

Susan Cummings

Dean, Eddie. "The Heiress and the Gaucho." *Washington
City Paper.* October 31, 1997. https://www.
washingtoncitypaper.com/news/article/13014204/the-
heiress-and-the-gaucho.

Marshall, Andrew. "Heiress Gets 60 Days' Jail for Killing
Lover." *Independent.* May 14, 1998. https://www.
independent.co.uk/news/heiress-gets-60-days-jail-for-
killing-lover-1159937.html.

O'Neill, Anne-Marie. "Death of the Hired Man." *People.*
October 13, 1997. https://people.com/archive/death-of-
the-hired-man-vol-48-no-15/.

Ordonez, Jennifer. "In Jail, Heiress Has Privileged Existence."
The Washington Post. May 21, 1998. https://www.
washingtonpost.com/wp-srv/local/longterm/library/polo/
polo.htm.

Eva Rausing

Bilefsky, Dan. "A Wealthy Family's Battle with Drugs Laid
Bare, but to What End?" *The New York Times.* August 11,

2017. https://www.nytimes.com/2017/08/11/books/a-wealthy-familys-battle-with-drugs-laid-bare-but-to-what-end.html.

Feigel, Lara. "Mayhem by Sigrid Rausing Review—Behind the Ghoulish Tabloid Headlines." *The Guardian*. September 7, 2017. https://www.theguardian.com/books/2017/sep/07/mayhem-by-sigrid-rausing-review.

Hamilton, Hamish. "A Gilded Family Torn Apart by Addiction...the Story of Drug Users Hans and Eva Rausing Is Recalled by Hans's Sister in This Brave Memoir." *Daily Mail*. September 2, 2017 https://www.dailymail.co.uk/home/event/article-4840260/Mayhem-review-Brave-ambivalent.html.

Holehouse, Matthew, Sam Marsden and Duncan Gardham. Eva Rausing's drug struggle: " 'I fell into the same hole as before.' " *The Telegraph*. July 11, 2012. https://www.telegraph.co.uk/news/uknews/crime/9392468/Eva-Rausings-drug-struggle-I-fell-into-the-same-hole-as-before.html.

Hourican, Emily. "A Life Packed with Tragedy and Drugs." *Independent*. March 17, 2014. https://www.independent.ie/lifestyle/a-life-packed-with-tragedy-and-drugs-30093886.html.

Lyall, Sarah. "Philanthropist Couple's Drug Downfall Ends in Death and Arrest." *The New York Times*. July 11, 2012. https://www.nytimes.com/2012/07/12/world/europe/british-tabloids-afire-with-death-of-heiress-eva-rausing.html.

Williams, David, Christian Gysin, Daniel Bates and Martin Robinson. "Exclusive: Family of Tragic Tetra Pak Wife Eva Rausing Reveal She Began Dabbling with 'Hard Drugs'

While at the Same College as Barack Obama as Husband Is Arrested for Murder." *Daily Mail*. July 12, 2012. UPDATED: December 14, 2012. https://www.dailymail. co.uk/news/article-2172818/Eva-Rausing-family-reveal-began-dabbling-hard-drugs-college-Barack-Obama. html.

Gulnara Karimov

Antelava, Natalia. "Tweets from Gulnara: The Dictator's Daughter." *The New Yorker*. December 21, 2012. https:// www.newyorker.com/news/news-desk/tweets-from-gulnara-the-dictators-daughter.

Kilner, James. "Uzbekistan Confirms It Holds Ex-President's Daughter in Custody." *The Telegraph*. July 28, 2017. https://www.telegraph.co.uk/news/2017/07/28/ uzbekistan-confirms-holds-ex-presidents-daughter-custody/.

Noack, Rick. "New Photos Show Uzbekistan's 'Jailed Princess' Allegedly Being Harassed by Guards." *The Washington Post*. September 16, 2014. https://www. washingtonpost.com/news/worldviews/wp/2014/09/16/ new-photos-show-uzbekistans-jailed-princess-allegedly-being-harassed-by-guards/?noredirect=on&utm_term=.01aa2d08ec41.

Nordland, Rod. "Where Is Googoosha, the Missing Uzbek First Daughter?" *The New York Times*. April 4, 2018. https://www.nytimes.com/2018/04/04/world/asia/ uzbekistan-islam-karimov-gulnara-karimova.html.

Reuters in Almaty. "Daughter of Former Uzbek Dictator Detained over Fraud Claims." *The Guardian*. July 28, 2017. https://www.theguardian.com/world/2017/jul/28/

gulnara-karomova-daughter-former-uzbek-dictator-held-fraud-claims.

Stewart, Will. "Glamorous Uzbek Princess Who Accrued a Vast Fortune under Her Father's Rule and Courted British Royalty and Celebrities Has Been Thrown into Jail over $2bn Corruption Allegations." July 28, 2017. https://www.dailymail.co.uk/news/article-4739088/Glamorous-Uzbek-princess-accused-2bn-corruption.html.

Walker, Shaun. "Dad's Accused of Boiling People Alive—but Googoosha (a.k.a. Gulnara Karimova) Just Wants to Be a Star." *Independent*. August 17, 2012. https://www.independent.co.uk/news/world/europe/dads-accused-of-boiling-people-alive-but-googoosha-aka-gulnara-karimova-just-wants-to-be-a-star-8054036.html.

Casey Johnson

Chang, Bee-Shyuan. "Trying to Outrun Wealth and Fame." *The New York Times*. October 12, 2011. https://www.nytimes.com/2011/10/13/fashion/trying-to-outrun-wealth-and-fame.html.

Fleeman, Mike. "Johnson & Johnson Heiress Casey Johnson Dies." *People*. January 04, 2010. https://people.com/celebrity/johnson-johnson-heiress-casey-johnson-dies/.

Gardner, David. "Catfight over Casey Johnson's Dogs as Distraught Tila Tequila Accuses Her Fiancée's Family of 'Planning to Bury Them with Casey'." *Daily Mail*. January 7, 2010. https://www.dailymail.co.uk/tvshowbiz/article-1241101/Tragic-heiress-Casey-Johnson-died-squalid-rat-invested-slum-water-electricity.html.

Post Staff Report. "The Real Story of Casey Johnson's Short Scandalous Life." *New York Post.* July 30, 2013. https://nypost.com/2013/07/30/the-real-story-of-casey-johnsons-short-scandalous-life/.

Georgia Inman

Erdely, Sabrina Rubin. "The Poorest Rich Kids in the World." *Rolling Stone.* August 12, 2013. https://www.rollingstone.com/culture/culture-news/the-poorest-rich-kids-in-the-world-80712/.

Foster, Peter. "Twin Heirs to Doris Duke Tobacco Fortune Claim Life of Abuse and Torture." *The Telegraph.* January 31, 2014. https://www.telegraph.co.uk/news/worldnews/northamerica/usa/10610689/Twin-heirs-to-Doris-Duke-tobacco-fortune-claim-life-of-abuse-and-torture.html.

Marsh, Julia and Lia Eustachewich. "Doris Duke Twins Lose Bid to Sue over 'Junkie' Dad Who Blew Their Billions." *New York Post.* November 29, 2016. https://nypost.com/2016/11/29/teen-tobacco-heirs-wont-be-getting-fortune-after-all/.

∼About the Author∼

Marlene Wagman-Geller received her Bachelor of Arts from York University and her teaching credentials from the University of Toronto and San Diego State University. Currently, she teaches high school English in National City, California, and shares her home with her husband, Joel, her daughter, Jordanna, her cat, Moe, and her puppy, Harley. Reviews of her books have appeared in *The New York Times* and dozens of other newspapers such as *The Washington Post, The Chicago Tribune,* and *The Huffington Post.*

Mango Publishing, established in 2014, publishes an eclectic list of books by diverse authors—both new and established voices—on topics ranging from business, personal growth, women's empowerment, LGBTQ studies, health, and spirituality to history, popular culture, time management, decluttering, lifestyle, mental wellness, aging, and sustainable living. We were recently named 2019's #1 fastest growing independent publisher by Publishers Weekly. Our success is driven by our main goal, which is to publish high quality books that will entertain readers as well as make a positive difference in their lives.

Our readers are our most important resource; we value your input, suggestions, and ideas. We'd love to hear from you—after all, we are publishing books for you!

Please stay in touch with us and follow us at:

Facebook: Mango Publishing

Twitter: @MangoPublishing

Instagram: @MangoPublishing

LinkedIn: Mango Publishing

Pinterest: Mango Publishing

Sign up for our newsletter at www.mango.bz and receive a free book!

Join us on Mango's journey to reinvent publishing, one book at a time.